What you **. . .**

~~conomy~~
In-depth research
Constant decision making
Ticker watching
Insiders' tips
Luck

What you *do* need . . .

THE BOOK

Here is the revolutionary investment method that overcomes the vagaries and risks of the market and individual judgment. Read the facts and figures inside. They will make you a believer—and quite possibly a millionaire.

HOW TO MAKE
$1,000,000
IN THE
STOCK MARKET
AUTOMATICALLY!

FOURTH REVISED EDITION

Robert Lichello

A SIGNET BOOK

SIGNET
Published by New American Library, a division of
Penguin Group (USA) Inc., 375 Hudson Street,
New York, New York 10014, USA
Penguin Group (Canada), 90 Eglinton Avenue East, Suite 700, Toronto,
Ontario M4P 2Y3, Canada (a division of Pearson Penguin Canada Inc.)
Penguin Books Ltd., 80 Strand, London WC2R 0RL, England
Penguin Ireland, 25 St. Stephen's Green, Dublin 2,
Ireland (a division of Penguin Books Ltd.)
Penguin Group (Australia), 250 Camberwell Road, Camberwell, Victoria 3124,
Australia (a division of Pearson Australia Group Pty. Ltd.)
Penguin Books India Pvt. Ltd., 11 Community Centre, Panchsheel Park,
New Delhi - 110 017, India
Penguin Group (NZ), cnr Airborne and Rosedale Roads, Albany,
Auckland 1310, New Zealand (a division of Pearson New Zealand Ltd.)
Penguin Books (South Africa) (Pty.) Ltd., 24 Sturdee Avenue,
Rosebank, Johannesburg 2196, South Africa

Penguin Books Ltd., Registered Offices:
80 Strand, London WC2R 0RL, England

Published by Signet, an imprint of New American Library,
a division of Penguin Group (USA) Inc.

First Printing, August 1977
First Printing (Fourth Revised Edition), December 2001
10 9 8 7 6 5 4 3

To the long-suffering investor,
who sorely *needs* a 21st-century
"Money Machine"

If hindrances obstruct thy way,
Thy magnanimity display,
And let thy strength be seen;
But Oh! if fortune fill thy sail
With more than a propitious gale,
Take half thy canvas in.

—Horace, *The Golden Mean*

Contents

Preface

History will record that AIM—Automatic Investment Management—was born on a battlefield . . . *after* the battle for investment survival was lost by millions of trusting investors in 1974, the worst financial disaster since the Great Depression of the thirties.

As a casualty of the war, I wandered through the smoke and wreckage of that battlefield and shuddered with horror at the enormity of the damage: damage to lives, to dreams, to plans, and worst of all, to faith itself.

Some of the more pitiful victims, like me, were those who had entrusted their entire financial future to mutual funds. Hardly greedy, we were so flushed with delight in those heady years prior to the day of reckoning that some of us even quit our jobs and dropped out, figuring that the huge capital gains distributions from our mutual funds would be more than sufficient to support us the rest of our lives! What? *Me* worry?

Oh, yes, we *did* worry. We *did* brood. We *did* despair as the market methodically and persistently siphoned off chunk after chunk of our precious nest egg until there was virtually nothing left of any consequence.

Some people say that everything happens for a reason. Is it presumptuous to believe that the financial debacles of the seventies *had* to happen for someone to invent a simple but effective formula to prevent a recurrence? I called the formula AIM—Automatic Investment Management.

AIM was what I call "investment jujitsu." In this

Asian form of combat, you use your opponent's own strength against him. If he pushes, you pull. The harder he pushes, the more off balance and vulnerable he is to a slight pull from you to send him sprawling. What a marvelous advantage that would be to the small (and weak) investor against the mighty stock market!

If it worked.

It did. And does.

Now, at the turn of the century, we meet again on the great battlefield (some warn) of the unavoidable *next* crisis. And from advance scouting reports, it could be a doozy. The doomsayers whisper Armageddon; the optimists suggest (a bit nervously) "correction."

As the year 2000 waned, history's longest bull market turned mean. Volatility reached epidemic proportions. The tech-heavy Nasdaq, which had logged its high only a few months earlier, nose-dived nearly 40 percent by the end of the year, leaving many stunned investors sitting on losses of *twice* that amount!

Now, more than at any other time in history, the ordinary investor needs help—and *fast!* Individuals in far greater numbers are required, without any training or expertise, to manage their own pension plans. Assets in 401(k) retirement plans, IRA's, Keoghs, and such are at historic highs. The scenario for disaster is set. The fuse is lit.

But *this* time, thanks to my continued work on the AIM formula, we're *ready!*

The first edition of this book, published in 1977, attracted worldwide attention. In succeeding years, at the request of many readers, I appended several new chapters (all included here) to answer the many questions raised by this phenomenal new method of investing. The response was more than gratifying. Each new edition won thousands of new converts and encouraged me to continue my quest for an even *better* AIM formula. But it was not until nearly a quarter of a century had passed that I finally grasped my elusive dream. This Fourth Revised Edition is the culmination of that quest! I am confident that it is one of the most rewarding books on investing ever published. Not just because I wrote it, but because it represents many, many grueling years of experimentation—during which the stock market suffered three of its most severe crises in history, and millions of investors learned, to their terrible dismay, the folly of conventional investment techniques. These methods did not and do not work on a risk-reward basis for the average investor: otherwise, bruised and battered victims wouldn't have given up and fled the stock market in those crisis years.

When I first wrote this book I was convinced that an absolutely new and radical approach to equity investment was necessary if the small investor—as well as the institutional investor—was ever to recover his confidence and his faith and realize that the stock market in the future *could be* the richest and most dependable source of profits in the entire investment sphere!

But for that to happen, a new investment method had to be found that would protect the investor's capital *and* offer him high performance potential! A method that would combine safety with high profit potential? Impossible! It can never be done!

But it has! And you're holding it in your hands right now!

This Fourth Revised Edition of my book contains the original AIM formula with which hundreds of thousands of my readers are already familiar. It also unveils my latest discovery, AIM-HI, which utilizes a slightly different but more explosive technology. While AIM-HI offers more potential for mouthwatering profits (at little or no additional risk) I would urge new readers to "begin at the beginning" and grasp the concept of the original AIM before attempting to put my AIM-HI (High Intensity) into practice. As you will soon discover, AIM-HI unleashes an astonishing amount of power in the AIM formula while maintaining our all-important safety restraints! Read it and reap! Veteran "AIMvestors" will also profit from the new material to be found throughout this edition of the book.

And if you're in a praying mood, say a little prayer for the *AIMless* investors as they stumble blindly into the perilous 21st century!

—Robert Lichello
New York, New York
January 12, 2001

Introduction

Most financial "breakthrough" books are obsolete by the time you read them. They are based on the first half of a familiar piece of wisdom: "Give a man food and you feed him for a day . . ." You may read these books with pleasure. You may even derive a bit of sustenance from their content. But on the following day, you will surely begin to starve.

The fault lies not with their authors but with the rigid economic, mathematical, and physical laws that govern us all. When too many of a ship's passengers attempt to flee in the same lifeboat, the lifeboat will sink. There is nothing wrong with the idea of a lifeboat. It works fine— until too many people attempt to clamber aboard.

Similarly, when a large number of people read the same how-to-make-money book and attempt to put its principles in action for themselves, the marketplace simply adjusts to narrow and, ultimately, close down an attractive profit opportunity that may have existed before. If there is money to be made by buying Item X, the people who already own a quantity of it will be the first to know. And they will demand higher and higher prices for it as all the new customers flood into the marketplace to make their purchases. When the fad dies—as all fads do—the original owners of Item X have made all the large profits. The newcomers now own all of Item X but there's nobody around to sell it to at anywhere near the prices they paid.

New investing techniques fail for the same reason. If everybody knows what everybody else is about to do, no advantage is gained by anybody doing it. No football team can possibly win if it alerts its opponents as to what play it is going to run on the next snap. It would then be a simple matter for the opposing team to adjust its defenses accordingly and *take advantage of the common knowledge.*

Knowledge derives its power from exclusivity. Once an author publishes a new technique that has enabled him to gain an advantage in the marketplace, the knowledge is no longer exclusive. The advantage evaporates. And the reader, who has been given food and has been "fed for a day," is soon hungry again.

The book you are about to read is based on the second half of the philosophy introduced earlier: "Teach a man how to grow food and he can feed himself for life." What makes this book totally different from any other book on investing you have ever read, and what prevents the knowledge it contains from ever being checkmated and rendered valueless by the marketplace, is the fact that it is firmly grounded in elementary mathematics. No one can deny the truth that one and one make two. Everyone in the world *knows* that one and one make two. Everyone *uses* that formula every day. But the fact that everyone knows and uses it does not and cannot change or affect in any way the mathematical certainty that one and one do make two. And yet, some people "feed themselves for life," indeed become quite wealthy calculating that one and one make two, while others, using the identical formula, never see their fortunes improve. The formula is there for all to see and for all to exploit. It has existed for thousands of years, and it offers the same exciting opportunities for wealth today as it always has.

This book, then, does not offer to feed you for a day. *However, it does offer to teach you how to feed yourself for life!* After you read it, after you have learned the simple but dynamic investment technique I call AIM—Automatic Investment Management—you will be able to earn profits from stocks or mutual funds with a degree of dependability, regularity, and *safety* never before possible with any other investment method.

You may call it "The Money Machine!" But whatever you do call it, here are some facts about AIM:

AIM does not require stock market expertise! Even if you have never bought a share of stock in your life, after you finish this book you will be able to outperform any run-of-the-mill stock market portfolio manager and perhaps most of the rest as well!

AIM does not require mathematical skill! No complicated formulas are involved.

AIM does not require time! It takes only 15 MINUTES A MONTH to perform all the functions necessary to achieve highly profitable results.

AIM does not require a large investment! Whether you have only a few hundred dollars to invest, or whether you have discretionary assets in the millions of dollars, AIM will manage your money with equal skill and efficiency.

AIM does not require effort! AIM itself does most of the work. It not only tells you *when* to buy or sell, it tells you *how much* to buy or sell! All you do is carry out its instructions.

AIM does not require additional investments! If a few hundred dollars is all you have to invest, AIM will work with that figure and, through an incredible technique of buying and selling at the right time, will multiply your investment many times over—forever, as long as you live—automatically.

AIM will accept additional investments in any amount at any time! Whenever you wish, you may add additional funds to your AIM program without disturbing its integrity in any way. AIM's self-adjusting mechanism will manage the new funds with the same intelligence it devotes to the old.

AIM will manage one stock for you—or a hundred! How many different stocks you want is up to you. A single AIM program will handle them all.

AIM is safe! Despite its awesome potential for multi-

plying your money, AIM is probably the safest investment method ever devised. It achieves this amazing
stability *by taking profits from the market as your stocks
rise and depositing them in your bank account.* When
stocks do fall, you may have profits comfortably tucked
away in your bank account that are *much larger than
your original investment*—funds that are *automatically*
held for the most lucrative buying opportunity and *automatically* used to *buy* at the very bottom of the market.
And these funds *automatically* earn bank interest while
they wait.

At this writing, many thousands of investors are using
AIM. All of us know, beyond the shadow of a doubt,
that AIM does everything I say it does. And when *millions* of investors begin to use it, as they will, it will do
exactly the same for them as it is doing for us! There is
nothing that any official of a stock exchange, or any
specialist on the floor of an exchange, or any stockbroker, or any other investor or combination of investors
can do to interfere with the full performance of Automatic Investment Management. The advantage of one
investor using AIM cannot cancel out the advantage of
any other investor using AIM. One and one still make
two. AIM is the premier investment technique of today; it
may be the premier investment technique of tomorrow.

Do not expect any stock tips in this book—there are
none. The search for the "right" stock or "right" mutual
fund leads straight to the poorhouse! And that's where
most traditional investors who have been brainwashed
into believing the "right" stock myth find themselves
today—literally or figuratively. There is no "right" stock.
Timing, not stock selection, is the key to success in the
stock market. And with Automatic Investment Management, timing is *automatic.* AIM, and AIM alone, makes
the decisions, no matter *what* stocks you hold in your
portfolio.

The average investor has only the most primitive concept of timing. The "Lump Sum" investor commits all
of his available funds to stocks that are his particular

favorites—and then sits back and waits for time to make him rich. He should live so long! And maybe if he does, it will. But millions of "Lump Summers" now know better. They find themselves sitting on unbearably heavy losses years—even decades—after making their single trusting commitment to the market. The reason: the stocks of hundreds of the biggest and most respected companies in America are now selling at a fraction of their former values.

The "Hit-or-Miss" investor buys stocks whenever he finds himself with excess funds on his hands, or whenever the mood strikes him, or whenever he comes across a stock tip, or whenever his emotions become inflamed by the general atmosphere of jubilant euphoria that periodically emanates from the financial community. He sells stock for the opposite reason—when the outlook for the market is grim, he takes his losses and runs. The "Hit-or-Miss" investor doesn't know where he's going, doesn't know where he's been, and is motivated only by a dim hope that if he keeps moving blindly around the arena, he'll stumble upon success. Only this never occurs because he never realizes he's a puppet and that unseen strings propel his enthusiasm and his disenchantment—his decisions, his stock selections, his every move. His timing is, in fact, controlled by others.

The "Careful Shopper" investor attempts to time his efforts to achieve above-average results in Wall Street. He has seen what happens to "Dollar Cost Averagers"—those who invest the same amount of money every month in order to buy more shares for their dollar when stocks decline. However, after years of buying higher and higher priced shares, a market collapse wipes out not only all profit but also much of the out-of-pocket investment as well. The "Careful Shopper" knows this! He is too smart to be caught in *that* trap. He makes his purchases only when stocks back off from their highs and appear to offer better value. That way he'll be able to buy more shares for his dollar.

Finally—usually after a stock market crash—the

"Careful Shopper" decides to add up his shares and divide them into his total investment to find out his average cost per share. The answer usually shocks him. For all his fancy footwork, for all his feinting and jabbing, for all his bobbing and weaving, his cost per share usually turns out to be higher than it would have been if he had used Dollar Cost Averaging. He had *thought* he was buying bargains. After all, when his stock had gone to $18 a share, he had ignored it until it settled back to $15. And when his stock reached $21, he certainly wouldn't buy at that price. No, he waited until it retreated a bit— to $16 a share. But now the stock is selling at $6 a share, and the "Careful Shopper," having lost most of his capital in a futile attempt to outwit the market, is beating his head against the door . . . of the poorhouse. The reason: you may have *thought* you were standing on a floor, but the fellow downstairs sees it as a ceiling! Yesterday's "low" can look impossibly high when you've tumbled down the stairs and are looking up.

Because there are no casualty statistics on the exact damage each of these types of investor has suffered in recent years, we have selected the best of the lot—the "Lump Summer"—to challenge AIM under a variety of circumstances in this book. Certainly the "Lump Summer," being fully invested at all times, has the best chance of all to make money in a rising market. The fact that he proves to be no match for AIM is exactly what we expected.

Now I challenge *you* to let AIM manage *your* investment program and prove to yourself that AIM can do a better job making money than you can. If you bet against it, you will lose. But all you will lose is your pride. You *will* be amazed when the profits start piling up like magic in your "Money Machine." And you will agree that the small amount of money you paid for this book was the greatest single investment you have ever made at any time in your life, bar none!

You are about to begin the greatest financial adventure of your life. I envy you the thrill of your first discovery. If you return rich from your voyage, as I believe you will, remember this: Among all the puffery and propaganda, among all the commercial hype, the flimflam, and the dressed-up dross that you slogged through in your daily life, you once came across a nugget of pure gold—Automatic Investment Management.

On *this* pull of the slot machine handle, you hit the jackpot!

The Treasure I Found
in a Barn

In the spring of 1958 I sat in the quietly elegant Bucks County, Pennsylvania, living room of one of the richest men I'd ever met. The words he'd just spoken to me had left me speechless.

"That's right," said Charles Darrow, "the Pennsylvania Railroad. I own it. And I'll sell it to you!"

"I'm not a financier," I replied finally. "And I certainly don't have that kind of money."

"How much do you have?"

I laughed a bit uneasily. "A hundred and three dollars."

"Would you be interested in buying it for that amount?"

"For a hundred and three dollars!" I said. "Why would you sell the Pennsylvania Railroad to me for a hundred and three dollars?"

"Because I have so much—and you have so little," he said. "What's the sport in acquiring everything so easily? There would be no more fun left in the game. . . . Now, do you or don't you want to buy it?"

I counted out my pitiful $103, and passed the bills over to him. In return, he handed me a certificate of ownership.

I was now the owner of the Pennsylvania Railroad!

I studied the certificate. "I feel," I said a trifle guiltily, "like a charity case, accepting something like this without having to earn it—or at least inheriting it. However, I must say I appreciate the gesture."

"I'm afraid your appreciation will have to be short-lived," Darrow said, a new cold tone in his voice.

I looked up. "What do you mean?"

"I mean you have just landed on Boardwalk, and that is going to cost you plenty." He grinned at me from across the Monopoly board.

"But I haven't any money left," I said.

Charles Darrow, the inventor of Monopoly, was jubilant. "Having something is one thing—keeping it is another," he said, and lifted the Pennsylvania Railroad deed from my hand.

I laughed. Win or lose, Monopoly was a fascinating game, and I could only marvel at the mind that had conceived it. Darrow had invented it back in the thirties, in the depths of the Depression, to amuse himself and his family because they hadn't the money to do much else. But he had plenty of money now, and the royalties from Parker Brothers, the manufacturer, still continued to pour in year after year, enabling the inventor and his family to live the kind of life other people only dream of.

"It's funny," he mused, "but I never could do it again. I've invented other games since then—a stock market game, for example—but every one of them flopped! I guess I could have saved myself considerable time and effort if I'd quit when I was ahead."

It was a philosophy I heard articulated again and again by the great and successful, and yet all of them shared an overriding compulsion for one more spin of the wheel—perhaps to prove to themselves that they could do it again. And *this* time, finally, to reach their *full* potential!

Obviously the "one more time" syndrome is part of the human condition. In the early seventies, staring in dismay at the tattered remains of a once comforting portfolio of stocks, I recalled the agonized reaction of another investor, quoted in the press, whose $35,000 portfolio was now worth something like $4,000. His shell-shocked epilogue rang down the curtain on a tragic era: "Four thousand dollars. What's four thousand dollars? Four thousand dollars is nothing, that's what it is."

One of my beloved mutual funds had tumbled from something like 13 to 5 and lay there showing no sign of life. "But it'll go back up again, won't it?" a fellow investor asked me, in a say-it-ain't-so plaint. Sorry that I couldn't give him better news, I told him, "It's a terminal case. Sell all and follow me."

My reasoning was that a mutual fund management so inept as to allow a demolition of its investors' assets on so gargantuan a scale would be dropping marbles all over the place for at least a decade—particularly since it was demonstrating no talent for getting itself together again. In December, 1978, each $5 that my friend banked from his mutual fund sale was worth about $8. The mutual fund wasn't selling for anywhere near that.

In the meantime, unemployed and freezing in an old farmhouse back in the hills I'd bought for $4,000, I was occupying myself with work on a formula that would prevent small investors from ever being savaged again. It was, admittedly, at once a foolish and presumptuous task: foolish because if it *could* be done, wouldn't it have been done a long, long time ago by a famed mathematician or perhaps a stock market wizard? And presumptuous because where did *I* get off tackling a project of this magnitude? Unemployment has a way of obliterating one's self-esteem. To bolster my faltering ego, I reminded myself of my undergraduate days, when I lived at Mrs. Hartley's rooming house in Morgantown, West Virgina.

If Mrs. Hartley's house is still there on Outlook Street, you would notice a length of string that emerges from the sunporch, travels a short distance to an outside doorway, then disappears inside. If you should enter this doorway, you would see that the string, passing through eyelets screwed into the wall, travels all the way upstairs, makes a sharp 90-degree turn to the right, and then traverses the short corridor to the bathroom. Its terminus: an eyelet screwed into the bathroom door.

Now, as anybody knows who has ever lived in a single-bath rooming house, when one uses the bathroom, one closes the door; and when one has departed, one leaves the door open so that others who wish to use the bathroom will know it is now vacant.

As an undergraduate, I lived in the converted sunporch of this house, and on many wintry mornings it was necessary for me to make several shivery probes outside, around, and up the stairs to see if the bathroom happened to be vacant before finally, fortuitously, finding it so. However, with the installation of the Lichello Early Warning System, a new day dawned. It was one small step for man, one giant leap for mankind. When the bathroom occupant, his labors completed, exited the bathroom and left the door open, a weight attached to the end of the string in my room sank and moved an indicator to the VACANT position. And when a new occupant entered the bathroom and closed the door, the weight was pulled to the upward position and the indicator pointed to OCCUPIED.

Crude as this system was, it worked—without torque modifiers, telluriums, rectifiers, reduction gears, electropneumatic systems, or even an equalizing valve on my interlock. It served its purpose so well that subsequent occupants of the converted sunporch continued to use it long after the university had transferred my grades to the Unemployment Office. To be honest, however, another system I'd rigged up to dash a glass of cold water in my face to wake me up in the morning was dismantled by the landlady, who was tired of having her pillows drenched.

So, you can see that I am something of a tinkerer—a tall, complicated, and disorganized individual enamored of small, compact, simple things—an admirer of *haiku* because, despite its deceptive simplicity, it's packed with work and it gets the job done. *Shibui*—the art that conceals art.

I also do not like to lose money, particularly in a mutual fund that tells me in its prospectus that it will not make the mistake many investors do of "overdiversifying" its investments—and then proceeds to stuff its portfolio with literally hundreds of securities; a mutual fund that says it won't take extraordinary risks by pursuing sensational gains—and then loads up on stock in soon-to-be-nationalized gold mines in unstable countries; a mutual fund whose "professional, full-time management" was apparently in the corner pub between 1968 and 1970 and didn't hear the sirens going off in Wall Street until they returned to their office and found that it had been converted into a savings bank in their absence.

Here's a quick trick that will save you money. Next time you get a mutual fund prospectus—any prospectus—fold down the upper right corner, then the upper left corner so the two flaps meet in front of you. Fold the entire prospectus lengthwise down the middle away from you. Hold it firmly on a desktop and pinch the long fold so that the left side and the right side splay out permanently like wings. Then sail it out of the nearest window.

The tinkerer in me predominated over the rational man, and for more than three long, discouraging years after the guillotine smash of 1970 I filled an entire room with literally thousands of pages of formulas in search of my elusive continuous investment plan that would surpass the universally accepted Dollar Cost Averaging in terms of safety and profit potential. All were failures. They reminded me of a drunk dancing the jig: I didn't know whether to applaud the performance or weep at the charade. But finally I struck gold.

The result was Synchrovest, and my book, *Superpower Investing*. I found myself being written up in such prestigious financial publications as *Business Week,* being interviewed on radio, and inundated with letters of gratitude from investors and stockbrokers all across the country. Critics used words like "power-packed, a gem, remarkable, a high-voltage blockbuster, the best new investment idea in a generation." It was a triumph for tinkerers everywhere.

Synchrovest filled a need, and will continue to do so for years to come. But the tinkerer in me was never satisfied. Was it possible, I wondered, to invent an Automatic Investment Management system to enable the investor with a lump sum of money, however small, to buy and sell—trade stocks as portfolio managers do—and multiply his portfolio many times over without putting any new money into it? *Could he use the market's own money, trading profits, to fatten his portfolio—automatically?* Could this system make the investor's buy and sell decisions *for* him, requiring nothing more from him than a few minutes of his time once a month or so? In short, was a legitimate Money Machine possible? A tinkerer's fantasy if there ever was one!

During the next two years, I occupied myself exclusively with this problem. There were many times when I despaired that mathematics, as such, was capable of doing what I wanted it to do. I wanted the figures themselves to *think* and *understand,* and I turned in frustration to such newer forms of relationship symbols as nonstandard numbering. It gave me a headache.

Back I went to mathematics, but all I had after two years was another roomful of charts. I needed another miracle, but none was forthcoming. Worse, my ancient barn was slowly crumbling, so I entered it to rescue anything of value before it collapsed completely. There, lying on the rotting floorboards, amid rusting chains and cannibalized push-type lawnmowers, was an old license plate. I picked it up. The date was 1926, the year of my birth. And the barely legible number was . . . 2X 1-50.

A chill ran up my spine. I returned to my office, sat down before my calculator, and began punching the keys. Because that license plate number had meant something to me! The faint numerals contained, I was absolutely certain, the linchpin of the elusive formula I had sought for so long!

To establish a test, I set up an imaginary situation in which, after a series of ups and downs, the market goes back to its starting point. The ordinary investor who bought $10,000 worth of stock at the outset is now worth $10,000. No loss and no gain.

But if the investor with $10,000 had used my Automatic Investment Management from the beginning he'd be worth . . .

And here my hand began to tremble so violently that I could barely punch the correct keys. Because I knew beforehand that my many years of work were about to come to an end, and that what I had discovered would revolutionize portfolio management: that it would make me and thousands of other investors who used it rich!

. . . *$1,173,555!* ONE MILLION ONE HUNDRED SEVENTY-THREE THOUSAND FIVE HUNDRED AND FIFTY-FIVE DOLLARS!

Equally stunning was the incredible safety factor built into the AIM system. At one point near the end of the program, when the ordinary investor's account showed a *loss* of 60 percent of his capital—$6,000—the investor using AIM was enjoying a mind-boggling *profit* of half a million dollars!

If numbers are the metaphysical counterpart of physical reality, on what physical basis could the extraordinary performance of AIM be judged? The champion runner who clips a couple of seconds off the four-minute mile is properly showered with accolades, because on the basis of physical evidence, the four-minute mile remains near the limits of present human capability. But what if a runner suddenly does it in *one* minute?

And if two investors with the same amount of money buy the same stocks and achieve results so totally dissimilar that they defy comparison, what then?

It's a whole new game, isn't it?

And guess who gets to deal!

TWO

The Money Managers: "Some of You Should Leave This Business"

The title and credits of Roberto Rossellini's 1947 film, *Germany Year Zero,* were superimposed, if memory serves, over a background of utter devastation. Rossellini's restless camera pans slowly but relentlessly past acres of bombed-out hulls of houses, past shells of factories and endless mountains of rubble. It is a lunar landscape of indescribable ruin where people once lived, worked, and played. Where a civilization had stood, the silent camera paints an interminable frieze of desolation.

This bleak image had parallels in the U.S. money community directly after the surgical strike of 1970 and the disaster of 1974, the most destructive one-two punch since the thirties, and the debacle in 1987.

The postmortems have been dutifully served up by the experts in their respective niches of the investment business, and no doubt more will follow. But the question that lingers, and will linger, is: "How come the experts went down the drain along with the amateurs?" Why did the people entrusted with the care and feeding of other people's money—the managers of pension funds, mutual funds, and university endowment funds—perform, on balance, as poorly as they did? It was to be expected that the small investors—those legendary losers often referred to in Wall Street with ill-concealed and unforgivable scorn as "odd lotters" because they tend to buy fewer than 100 shares at a clip—would lose their wash 'n wear shirts in a market reversal of this magni-

8

tude. But who would have predicted that the Sulka custom shirt crowd would also join the ranks of the defeated? Wasn't preservation of capital the first rule of money management, like the physician's motto *Primum non nocere,* "First of all, do no harm"?

Back in the sixties, when the performance derby was the hottest race in town and mutual fund portfolio managers were measuring one another's performance not on a normal five- or ten-year chart but on a *month-to-month* basis, a few sober voices were raised in the land—and were drowned out by the euphoric roar of the bettors. William McChesney Martin, head of the Federal Reserve, posted this extremely valid caveat:

"Increasingly, managers of mutual funds, and portfolio and pension fund administrators, are measuring their success in terms of relatively short-term market performance. In effect, they set a target on a growth stock, attain that target, unload, and then seek other opportunities. Given the large buying power of their institutions, there is an obvious risk that speculative in-and-out trading of this type may virtually corner the market in individual stocks. . . . However laudable the intent may be, it seems to me that practices of this nature contain poisonous qualities reminiscent in some respects of the old pool operations of the twenties."

And a salty New England investment counselor named David Babson, a pioneer in the field, warned against "a speculative orgy and a national crap game." But who was listening? Hadn't the University of Rochester—the University of *where*?—catapulted itself into the Big Time by becoming the fifth richest university in the nation, thanks to shrewd investment management? And hadn't Rochester and those other hot-handed universities merely been taking their cue from that famous statement by McGeorge Bundy, head of the Ford Foundation, which bestows all that lovely money on educational institutions:

"It is far from clear that trustees have reason to be proud of their performance in making money for their colleges. We recognize the risks of unconventional investing, but the true test of performance in the handling of money is the record of achievement, not the opinion of the respectable. We have the preliminary impression that over the long run, caution has cost our colleges and universities much more than imprudence or excessive risk-taking."

Many companies, too, sniffed that heady perfume and began to fund some or all of their pension plans by investing in stocks rather than insurance policies. And as the stocks rose in those magic days, the profits were not used, as one might expect, to increase pensions, but to cut back on the company's contribution to the plan. Everybody likes a bargain!

All this institutional money being dumped into the market helped fuel its spectacular rise. And even a university's portfolio, if it were well managed, could stand comparison with that of an aggressive mutual fund whose salesmen, latest quarterly report in hand, were out beating the bushes for customers and preaching the gospel of people's capitalism. Here's the portfolio performance record of the now-famous University of Rochester, for instance, as it would look if it were broken down into per share units, as a mutual fund:

Dec. 31, 1957: $1.64
Dec. 31, 1958: $1.89
Dec. 31, 1959: $2.13
Dec. 31, 1960: $2.23
Dec. 31, 1961: $2.44
Dec. 31, 1962: $2.26
Dec. 31, 1963: $2.70
Dec. 31, 1964: $3.17
Dec. 31, 1965: $4.13
Dec. 31, 1966: $4.06
Dec. 31, 1967: $4.95
Dec. 31, 1968: $4.78
Dec. 31, 1969: $4.95

When the end came in the early seventies, of course, most high-flying portfolios were bound up into bundles, weighed, and sold for scrap paper. A 50 percent drop in 1970 alone was not unusual, and then 1974 administered the *coup de grace.* You already know all about it.

Some of the better managed portfolios, though badly injured, hung onto the ropes until the bell saved them. The University of Rochester's half-billion-dollar portfolio went like this:

Dec. 31, 1970: $4.46
Dec. 31, 1971: $5.60
Dec. 31, 1972: $7.20
Dec. 31, 1973: $5.53
Dec. 31, 1974: $3.13

Rochester's investment philosophy, "You never sell the good ones," glowed like textbook truth so long as its portfolio performance radiated the yellow glow of gold. But Rochester's school colors include blue as well as yellow—blue as in 1974.

Many university endowment funds, company pension funds, and mutual funds performed a great deal worse than this (some without even the saving grace of having done well when doing well was being done by just about everybody) and, for obvious reasons, their overseers aren't all that disposed these days to dredge up the memory of those trying times. The hotshot gunslingers who were widely quoted in the sixties as saying that "there's too much risk in being out of the market, so we're fully invested" aren't around anymore. And, of course, some mutual funds that scintillated in the sixties no longer exist. But after the 1970 shellacking, some solid mutual funds that had taken the market's best shots and come through shaken but game did a bit of courageous public soul-searching in an attempt to understand why investors were no longer as eager to purchase shares as before.

James D. Fullerton, chairman of The Capital Group, Inc., told an audience: "In the speculative fever of 1967 and 1968, we fell into the trap of selling [the mutual fund] as a short-term, get-rich-quick scheme. When it failed to do the job for which it was never intended, many . . . investors and potential investors and financial observers lost confidence in it."

Curran W. Harvey, president of Rowe Price New Horizons Fund, Inc., a mutual fund that had been so attractive to investors that sales of its shares had to be stopped to prevent the fund's objectives from drowning in a flood of money that could not be judiciously invested, came to much the same conclusion: "The concept of performance was oversold. A reasonable period for judgment is five years. I think people bought mutual funds because of the record of 1967 and 1968. That's not a good reason. Just because a fund did well in a bull market doesn't necessarily mean it is well managed."

And, at an annual conference for money managers in New York City in 1971, the aforementioned David Babson, wielding a verbal whip, may not have driven the moneychangers from the temple, but he did have them wincing as he cracked it over their heads. Describing the boom/bust of 1967–70 as "the greatest period of skullduggery in American financial history," Babson blamed the pros, rather than amateur investors, for the rollercoaster ride. After reading a list of burned-out highflyers such as Four Seasons Nursing Centers, Lum's, and Performance Systems, which had decorated many a go-go portfolio, Babson commented: "Some of you should leave this business."

Computer Directions Advisors, Inc., of Silver Spring, Maryland, performed a similar exorcism on bank-pooled funds a couple of years later. The folks at CDA wanted to find out whether a guy throwing a dart at the financial page of a newspaper could do just as well as the banks with all their resources—at far less expense. After all, a lot of mutual fund managers had red faces in August of 1967 when Senator Thomas McIntyre of New Hampshire did just that in an attempt to prove that professional money management was so poor that the average bloke might just as well hurl darts at the stock listings. Senator

McIntyre went back ten years with the stocks he'd selected via the dartboard, invested a hypothetical $10,000 in them, and then brought the stock prices up to 1967. The Senator's results: $25,300, better performance than any mutual fund—even the most growth-oriented ones.

CDA ordered its computer to do the dartboard bit and come up with 100 random portfolios, each containing 25 stocks from the New York Stock Exchange. After that, said CDA, give us another 100 portfolios, but this time select your stocks from *both* the New York Stock Exchange and the American Stock Exchange. Oh, and don't forget to adjust for reinvestment of dividends. And when you're through, compare your performance with that of 100 bank-pooled funds, which include some of the major New York City banks. Also, compare your performance with Standard and Poor's 500 stock index.

The computer went into its routine and spat out the answers in percentage changes:

	1 yr. 1974	2 yrs. 1973–74	3 yrs. 1972–74	4 yrs. 1971–74	5 yrs. 1970–74
Average N.Y.S.E. random portfolio	—23	—40	—34	—24	—24
Average N.Y.S.E. & A.S.E. portfolio	—23	—45	—41	—32	—35
S&P 500 stock index	—27	—37	—26	—15	—11
100 bank-pooled funds	—26	—40	—31	—16	—19

We rounded off the figures, trading a smidgen of accuracy for a bit of punch. As can be seen, the banks managed to beat the Standard & Poor 500—a totally unmanaged group of securities—only in 1974, and then just by an eyelash. And as for proving their worth when matched against the computer's random selection process, well, you be the judge.

On balance, banks aren't as good at managing stock portfolios as mutual funds managers are, who, in turn, aren't a lot better at managing stock portfolios than *you* are. In the dozen years ending December 31, 1973, none of the major New York City banks for which figures were available could match the Standard & Poor index of 500 stocks in managing their pooled pension funds. The Standard & Poor 500 showed a 5.87 percent 12-year compound annual rate. Manufacturers Hanover came closest, with a gain of 5.11 percent per year. Two other banks checked in with annual gains of 4.82 percent and 3.65 percent respectively for their Employee Benefit Accounts.

In the seventies, pension funds represented the fastest-growing mountain of investment capital in the nation, so that the management of this awesome pile of money was of more than passing interest. As might be imagined, a number of companies had become disenchanted with the performance of their pension funds in recent years and were switching managements in the hope of doing better elsewhere. And when funds of this size are pulled out, the ground trembles. Some typical examples: Chase Manhattan lost a billion dollars in pension accounts once because of disappointing results, and fully half that amount was accounted for by only one account—Western Electric's $500 million. Bell Telephone's pension funds amount to more than $1 billion, and the company in 1974 shifted $265 million of it, mostly from Bankers Trust, to new managers because of poor performance.

All this nervous and disgruntled transmigration of assets probably has no more significance than a game of musical chairs for the simple reason that luck plays a major role in investment success. The money management whiz of today all too frequently wears the donkey's tail tomorrow, and the dull, unimaginative, plodding Milquetoast manager of yesterday suddenly appears as today's hero—usually because the market suddenly comes apart at the seams and catches Caspar with a bundle of cash he was too nervous to invest. Chase may lose a billion today in pension funds—and tomorrow pick up another account worth a billion, or maybe two, when the fed-up owner yanks it out of bank XYZ. That's the nature of the business. You are dealing with equity investments, which go up and down, and in some years they have mostly been going down. How can *any* investment manager look good in a rainstorm—unless he suddenly ducks into a doorway at the first sprinkle and waits for the downpour to stop. He'll stay dry, true, but when the rain stops he'll probably be late arriving at his destination.

In the meantime, the mountain of cash in private, non-insured pension funds is swelling at the rate of several billions a year. Because of the actuarial assumptions that confront most pension managers, they try for a portfolio growth rate of 5 percent or more per year. Since this is no longer as easy and automatic as it has been in the past, they are looking more and more into real estate enterprises as a means of securing a higher cash return. But each investment medium has its own problems, its own peculiar advantages and disadvantages, and illiquidity is the bugaboo of real estate investing. You can't pick up the phone and sell off a hotel or two just like that.

For better or worse, the stock market offers the best and the most practical mechanism for handling the investment needs of most people. Fortunately, in recent years, it has been "for better."

But is loss the fault of the stock market? Or is it the fault of primitive, outdated investment techniques that fail to avail themselves of the opportunities inherent in a rising *and* falling stock market? The T. Rowe Price Growth Stock Fund, the nation's largest no-load, had studied the wreckage of 1974 in retrospect. Can anything be learned from the experience? Can investment techniques be improved in order to soften the crunch the next time around? Chairman Charles W. Shaeffer believed so. "We have to learn how to be better sellers, not just good buyers," he told the annual shareholders meeting in April, 1975.

"When I look back over the forty years I have been in the investment business, I can think of many individuals and firms who were good buyers, but I can't think of any who were consistently good sellers. . . . When we get into periods of severe market declines, there are many people who reach the conclusion that the world is not going to end, and they start putting some of their money to work regardless of the surrounding pessimism. However, when one has to deal with the mass psychology that accompanies rampant bull markets, the result is that we all seem to succumb to the optimism and fail to do any meaningful selling."

Mr. Shaeffer's fund had one and a quarter billion dollars worth of assets. When he spoke, people paid attention.

Other money managers began to express the same sentiment—"We have to learn how to be better sellers." So did embittered stockholders who, in palmier times, would check from time to time on the progress of their garden and marvel at how large and ripe their vegetables were getting. Perhaps they would salivate and consider picking a tempting taste treat or two. No, they'd remind themselves, the vegetables will be larger and riper tomorrow—and then I'll *really* gorge myself! That night the frost came, and in the morning the garden was ruined.

John Ellis observed wisely in *Self-Reliant Investing* that "the investor who waits for his broker to tell him when to buy and sell almost certainly is programming himself for disappointment."

In light of the 1987 crash and recent events in the new millennium, the old axiom, "A bird in the hand is worth two in the bush," has taken on new importance.

One of the horrors financial gurus whisper of is outliving your capital, obviously believing "better dead than beg one's bread." An elderly lady, a lifelong resident of one of the finest hotels in Manhattan, solved that problem perfectly a few years back. The day her money ran out and she could no longer pay the rent, she quietly passed away. She could have anticipated the depletion of her capital and bought time by moving to less expensive quarters, but she apparently felt that life was not worth living elsewhere. And who can fault her for that?

Surely her example—although endowed with a touching old-world dignity—sent ripples of dismay throughout Boston, where dipping into one's capital is roughly equivalent to going on the dole. Yet, it is a new day we live in, and new days call for new thoughts. The future— is there really going to be one? In cold terms of life expectancy, the U.S. Public Health Service expects one, for they say the life expectancy of a 42-year-old is 32.5 years, of a 53-year-old is 23.3 years, of a 58-year-old is 19.5, of a 64-year-old 15.4, and of a 67-year-old, 13.5 years with a couple of years less for males and a couple more for females. So, if you believe, with the pessimists, that man has perhaps 15 years left, or if you share the optimist's claim of at least 30 years, or even if you are merely haunted by a shrinking and fugitive sense that something is happening so that life will never be quite the same again, the question may have entered your mind during a lull at the shop: "What the hell am I *doing?* What am I *planning* for?" By retirement time, the streams will all be polluted anyway, the air will be unbreathable, the food inedible, the crowds incredible, medical care unobtainable, and people unbelievable. So why not grab a slice of life before they up and eat it all?

Today, more than ever, and in more ways than one, it is beginning to make sense to "take some profits."

When the brass ring comes around again—and it will— grab it!

THREE

Stocks as an Inflation Hedge:
End of the Myth

Next to "Invest in America," Wall Street's most potent sales pitch has been that stocks are an "inflation hedge." Oft-cited in this context is the fact that since the end of World War II, the average issue on the New York Stock Exchange has outgained the Consumer Price Index by a wide margin. In 1971, for example, the score was: typical New York Stock Exchange issue, 417 percent; Consumer Price Index, 124 percent.

A broker will tell you, "See, even after adjusting for the rise in the cost of living, you still came out ahead close to three hundred percent. And that's just the record of an *average* stock. Now here's a list of stocks that we feel will outperform the averages in the inflationary years ahead. We particularly like the natural resources companies, because those minerals in the ground—that's real wealth. These companies should prove outstanding in an inflationary economy. We also think the companies with low labor costs are extremely interesting at this point, as well as companies that can raise their prices to balance off their increased costs. The paper companies? No, we're not recommending them at this time. Here, this 30-page report on the papers will explain our position. And here are a few folders that cover the paper industry, as well as an interim report on the papers that our firm has just put out explaining why we feel the market for their products has been thoroughly saturated. Certainly, take them with you. I'll throw in a few extra copies for your friends. My goodness, let me get you a bag for that."

Pardon me if I am somewhat skeptical. Between 1950 and 1974, I believe the score would really be something like: typical New York Stock Exchange issue, 271 percent; Consumer Price Index, 112 percent. No, ma'am, not quite as good as before. But a $10,000 investment in the Big Board stocks in 1950 would be worth $37,000 at the end of the period, not counting dividends. That same $10,000 in a savings account would be worth only $25,700. Not much, eh? Don't forget, banks were paying only 2 to 3 percent interest back in the year 1950.

Between 1946 and 1948? Well, let's see, consumer prices did shoot up rather alarmingly during those years—33 percent, as a matter of fact. Stock prices? They declined in each of those years. The question? Let's see if I understand the question. If you had bought stock in 1946, how long was it before you broke even? Why, you would have broken even in 1950. Pardon? Yes, I thought we were talking about dollars. If you mean how long was it before you regained the purchasing power of the dollars you started with, after adjusting for inflation, that would be 1954.

Are you familiar with this interesting study, by the way? It was done first in 1965, when these two University of Chicago economists discovered that the odds are something like 3 to 1—let's see, 78 out of 100 are the proper figures—that any stock you pick at random will not only prove profitable but will give you an average rate of return, including dividends, of 9 percent. Now they did the study again in 1973, and both figures remain the same, the odds and the rate of return.

Oh, you have a quote from Professor James Lorie, one of the authors of the study, and he says that 9 percent is not as rewarding as it used to be? Well, I—Say that again? Inflation averaged only 2 percent a year between 1926 and 1968, while back in the seventies we were experiencing double-digit inflation? But the good professor expected the rate of inflation to settle down to 6 per-

cent? I see. Well, in view of that, what does Professor
Lorie believe the return on common stocks *should* be,
on average? You did say 14 to 15 percent, didn't
you? . . .

Fade out.

Whether a party is a blast or a bore often depends on
when you get there. True, lots of investors had a ball
over the past decades, but most of today's investors did
not receive an invitation to the party (in the sense of
being lured to attend) until the celebrants had donned
funny little paper hats made of stock certificates reading
Four Seasons Nursing Homes, Commonwealth United,
Management Assistance, and Levin-Townsend, and were
running around in an alcoholic stupor setting fire to the
drapes. Somebody had already called the law, and no
sooner had most of today's investors arrived at the party
than they were collared, tossed into the paddy wagon
along with the others, and trundled off to the cooler.
The ones who had joined the party 25 years ago at least
had some fun, but most of us who came later did not.

To show you what I mean about timing, let's pretend
that it's 1960 again and You Are There. Using a base
of $10,000, make an equal dollar investment in all of
the New York Stock Exchange issues. Rebalance the
investment monthly to keep everybody honest. I'll put
my $10,000 in a Savings and Loan account. You flutter
the calendar leaves—and poof! here we are in 1972.
What do you have, assuming a reinvestment of all income? $35,920. Well, that sure beats my $17,112 in the
bank. Gosh, stocks sure *are* a great inflation hedge!
Okay, now rattle the calendar again. Here we are in
1974. Now how much do you have? $19,513. Look what
I have—$19,120!

Now watch me come out ahead—by moving the base
back one year to 1959.

No, when stocks collapse you don't hear much about
stocks being a hedge against inflation. Nobody likes to
be laughed at—not even a stockbroker.

FOUR

The Reliefer Who Made
a Fortune in the Stock Market

Many years ago, as a reporter, I was assigned to inter-
view a most unusual financial wizard, a 75-year-old re-
liefer who had parlayed nickels and dimes hoarded from
his $71.10-a-month welfare checks into $21,000 in the
stock market. (These amounts expressed in 2001 dollars
would be $392 in monthly checks parlayed into $115,700
in investments!) Unfortunately for him, Mr. S. had ne-
glected to inform the Welfare Department that he had
become financially self-sufficient and had not been entitled to receive any more monthly checks from them for
some time. Mr. S. found himself in trouble with the law.
The Welfare people wanted their money back.

I met him in a shabby, dark little room that smelled
of poverty. "Did you read the papers?" Mr. S. asked
gleefully. "I have never been so happy in my life. I am
glad it happened. When I had money, I told the people
every time I went to the bank that I wanted to die. Now
it is a new life!"

He picked up a newspaper and read slowly: "A
shabby bachelor with a sense of economy the government could use—"

His frail body straightened. His eyes misted. "They
say that about me! They say that if I would handle the
finances of the city, I could make them money and they
would not have to increase the taxes. You don't know
what it is for me to hear that from such big people!

"I did not know it was wrong to do what I did," he

said, sitting in a creaky chair by the window. "The Welfare has been so good to help me all these years, I wanted to pay them back. When I die, they would get the money anyway. I only hoped I could make my own way, that I would not have to take any more money from them. That is why I invested, because it was the only way I knew."

Then he went into his tiny kitchenette. From the little refrigerator he took a wine bottle containing two inches of wine. The faded label and the vapor-coating of the bottle indicated that the wine had been sparingly enjoyed. Mr. S. eagerly filled two glasses for us, then hurried into the kitchenette again and brought out bread and butter and a jar filled with broken pieces of graham crackers.

"Do you know how much cream it takes to make one pound of butter?" Mr. S. said as we ate. "You could not afford to buy so much cream, and yet a pound of butter costs little more today than thirty years ago. So, because of inflation, which reduces the value of money, a pound of butter costs really only fifteen cents or so. Milk is too expensive. The people who buy the milk subsidize the people who buy the butter. The poor always subsidize the rich. The poor buy margarine because they think they are saving money, but margarine does not contain the food values of butter. They save nothing."

Outside, the light was fading and the little room had grown darker. "I did not think I did wrong," Mr. S. said suddenly. "But I will be happy if they put me in jail, because that would be an experience, and I enjoy all experiences."

"Mr. S.," I said, remembering my assignment, "what is the mistake most investors make in the stock market?"

"The answer is ignorance. Buy only stocks in things which are necessary, and buy only the leaders: AT&T, General Motors, United States Steel, and so forth. They will always win in the end—and you will not go broke."

"How can you get rich by buying stocks like those?"

I asked in dismay. "Particularly if you don't have much money to begin with?"

"Do as I tell you. Yes, AT&T, yes, General Motors, yes, United States Steel. No, you do not run out this minute and invest all of your money in them. If you do that, the stocks will control *you*; you will not control the stocks. The stocks will go up, they will go down, or they will do neither. So, already you have only one chance out of three to make any profit. You are helpless. You say to them, 'Please have mercy on me, please make me rich.' Can you understand that if I did this, I could not make any money? Nobody could make any money if he did not have much money in the beginning. Even if I made a profit of 100 percent, what would I have? Ten dollars instead of five dollars? Fine, I have made five dollars. My life is over and I have made five dollars. Now I will tell you a parable: One farmer is rich, the other poor, but they both have the same harvest."

"I don't understand."

"It is not the size of the harvest," Mr. S. said, *"but the price you paid for the seed.* The poor farmer has the same harvest as the rich, but planted more seed!"

"Profit, then, being the difference between the seed and the harvest—"

"Yes. I would take down the charts from the walls that tell you the sales of the companies. They are the religion, but it's a false religion. Everybody says wonderful, the sales go up, this company will make more profit. Sales have no more to do with profit than how many letters the company writes every year. Profit is a return on investment. In life, too. This man is rich. He has many millions of dollars. He says how proud I am of what I have done. But he is not successful. He has paid too much for the *seed*. Perhaps he had much money to begin with. Perhaps he has lied, or stolen, or cheated the poor. These things are the cost of the seed.

"Over here, this poor man—he is not poor. He has little, but to begin with he had almost nothing. In his life, he has made more profit than the rich man. He is the successful man. In investing, too, a little seed can bring abundant harvest, if you are wise. Money is the seed, the stock is the soil. You do not plant in the fall, you do not harvest in the spring.''

"Does each stock have its own season?"

"Yes, and the stock market as well. If you plant in the proper season, and harvest in the proper season, then even a small amount of seed will bring many crops. This is a science. Investing is a science also."

My ears perked up. "You mean an art."

"No, no, a science, not an art."

"The experts say that investing is an art."

"They are wrong. It is a science, an exact science. When you do not understand what you are doing, you call it an art. Anyway, I have lost my appetite for making money. I have not invested for two years. I lost thirty thousand in the stock market crash in 1929, but that was before I knew."

"Knew what?"

"If I make a dollar, and you lose a dollar," said Mr. S., "how much are you behind?"

"A dollar?"

"Not a dollar. You are two dollars behind me. You must make first a dollar to break even with what you had before, and then another dollar to become even with me. So when you lose, you must now work twice as hard as me just to catch up. But I will not be standing still. Even if I have my money in the bank, I will not be standing still. Do you see? It is very difficult to make four dollars from two dollars, but much more difficult to make four dollars from one dollar, because you have lost one of the two dollars you had in the beginning."

Mr. S. paused. "I need nothing. I will die in a year. Already each day is a gift to me . . ."

The little room had grown so dark that I could not see Mr. S.'s face. I told him I had to return to the office. We stood up.

"They say they cannot understand the meaning of the pyramid—what it is trying to tell us," he said suddenly.

"There is no mystery. The pyramid speaks for itself. Is there anything stronger? The larger the base, the stronger it is. Nothing can destroy it—provided the ground itself is firm. And if you ask me which is the most important part of the pyramid, I could not answer. Every part is needed. If you do not have enough material, you can build a small pyramid first—like a child with blocks. Then, as you get more material, you make the pyramid higher, but larger, too, at the bottom. But first and always, a pyramid. Everybody asks when. When? But there is no when. When is here. Now. Everything is here, now. To lay the first stone, today you lay it."

He followed me to the door in the darkness. "Only two people have made my life sweeter. A doctor, a big man, who carried my suitcase out of the Old People's Home. And you, because you understand. Please come to see me again."

I promised myself I'd pay him another visit, but a reporter makes so many sincere promises to return to the chronic invalids in their hospitals, to the old and lonely who have their brief hour upon the stage and are heard of no more. And in the rush of the workaday world, the reporter keeps none of these promises.

Shortly afterward, Mr. S. pleaded guilty to a petty larceny charge, repaid $17,000 and costs to the Welfare Department, and was allowed to keep the remainder. He was not put in jail, much as he'd looked forward to it.

And then, within the year as he'd predicted, Mr. S. appeared on stage for his final bow. I am sure he would have loved his obituary—that anybody should take such notice of his passing! And I wish very, very much that I could go back to see him again. If only to tell him that at last I do understand.

FIVE

Automatic Investment Management: The Challenge

A number of summers ago, a band of oil-rich Arabs decided to make their move. They tossed suitcases full of currency into a fleet of Cadillacs, collected a gaggle of girls for good luck, and roared off toward the glittering gambling casinos of Western Europe.

Casino managers at Cannes, Deauville, and Monte Carlo popped fresh carnations into their lapels, donned their brightest "Hello, suckers" smiles, and ushered their honored guests inside for the sacred fleecing.

The Arabs smiled, too. And they kept smiling at the gaming tables all night long.

When they were quite through, the Arabs stuffed winnings reported at several millions of dollars into their suitcases, waved a fond farewell to the thin-lipped casino managers, and chuckled off to the Divonne-les-Bains casino near Geneva for another exhilarating romp with Lady Luck.

Did we say Lady Luck? We meant, rather, Sarasvati, Indian goddess of *knowledge,* or Atar, Persian god of *wisdom.* Or, for that matter, the ghost of Pythagoras, because the system the oil-rich Arabs employed to fleece the fleecers had nothing to do with luck and everything to do with science, and more specifically with mathematics, the Queen of the Sciences. The Arabs knew they'd win in the end. Every time they lost, they'd double their bet and play the same number again. Sooner or later, the law of averages would have to bail them out.

If an amateur used this system, true, he would *eventually* win—but when is eventually? The Arabs possessed seemingly unlimited wherewithal and, just as important, apparently were not restricted by a house limit on their bets which might have pulled the plug at a critical juncture on such a "double-up" system.

Remember the story of the youngster who applied for a job as delivery boy at his neighborhood grocery store for one month to earn some back-to-school spending money? He would work very cheaply, he told the owner: a penny the first day, two cents the second, four cents the third, and so forth, his insignificant salary being doubled every day. The owner, amused, agreed to the terms, even signing a contract to that effect. Long before the month was up, of course, the owner had gone bankrupt and the boy owned the store. Because in the third week, the sneaky little brat was earning thousands of dollars per day, and in the fourth week his salary had escalated into millions of dollars per day. His pay for his last day's work alone was a bristling $10,737,417!

In the sixties, we pondered the interesting implications of this phenomenon and developed a monthly investment system we called "Double Dollar Averaging," the publication of which created some discussion in Wall Street circles. It was a new twist on the old standby, Dollar Cost Averaging, which involves investing the same amount of money every month, a technique that often results in a lower cost per share over a period of time and thus a more favorable opportunity for eventual profits. With our "Double Dollar Averaging," the investor also invests the same amount of money every month, but on those months in which the price of his stock had declined 10 percent or more from its preceding price, he would invest twice as much as he invested last month. To accumulate reserve funds for the extra investments, we scaled down our standard monthly investment to 75 percent of the Dollar Cost Averager's. If he invested $100 a month, we invested $75. The trade-off seemed oftener to favor us than to penalize us.

"Double Dollar Averaging" was far less scary than the Arabs' gambling system because of its built-in safeguards. In roulette, you might lose a frightening number of times by playing the same number consistently. You might have to play that number a dozen times or more before it finally came up, and you would have to double your bet each time you lost. The Arabs, with their heavy resources, may not have suffered heart attacks as they stood at the tables, but they almost certainly twitched now and then with mild seizures as loss segued into loss and the suitcases grew lighter. We have already seen how the delivery boy, by a daily doubling of his tiny salary, became a millionaire before the month was out.

But with any stock, the price can't go lower than zero, and there are only so many times it can decline by 10 percent or more before it theoretically evaporates into nothingness. And, unlike games of chance, in which you've got *nothing* to show for losing, while the *price* of our stock market "chips" may decline, *we still have the same number of chips*. And these chips will almost certainly be worth something eventually. What's more, within the space of a single month, the stock may drop 20 percent or more, further reducing the number of times the investor would have to double his "bets."

Example
Double Dollar Averaging

MONTH	PRICE	INVESTMENT	SHARES BOUGHT
1	$13.98	$75	5.4
2	$12.64	$75	5.9
3	$12.41	$75	6.0
4	$12.02	$75	6.2
5	$8.51	$150	17.6
6	$6.32	$300	47.5
7	$5.46	$600	109.9
8	$5.35	$75	14.0
9	$5.57	$75	13.5

DOUBLE DOLLAR AVERAGING	LUMP-SUM INVESTING (MONTH 1)
INVESTMENT: $1,500	$1,500
SHARES BOUGHT: 226	107
LOSS MONTH 9 AT PRICE OF $6.48: $36 (2%)	$807 (54%)
PROFIT WHEN PRICE RETURNS TO ORIGINAL $13.98: $1,659	0
% PROFIT: 111%	0

Our Double Dollar Averaging proved to be not only safer than the old Dollar Cost Averaging, but potentially more profitable.

But there was a problem: What do you do if you're investing your little $75 a month and you accumulate many thousands of dollars of reserve money—and the market won't let you invest it? This could happen if your stock declined by *less* than 10 percent a month but nevertheless *kept* declining all the way to the bottom. On the other hand, your stock might decline 50 percent within the space of three months, giving you only three opportunities to double up. The first month you invest $150, the second month $300, and the third month $600. And when the dust settles and the market turns around and heads upward for another long bull market, you've still got thousands of dollars in reserve that you did not use, and you are likely to accumulate many thousands more before you get another opportunity to dip into the till again. In the meantime, your superiority over Dollar Cost Averaging could be fading because of your stinginess at the market's bottom.

To remedy this failing, it was necessary for us to dismantle the whole concept of Double Dollar Averaging and go back to the drawing board. It was not enough just to buy more shares than the Dollar Cost Averager on the way down. Doubling your monthly investment two or three times is fine if you have only a few hundred dollars in reserve. As a matter of fact, it would be perfect if you exhausted *all* your reserves at the very bottom of the market and purchased bucketfuls of cheap shares. But if your regular monthly investment is $75 or so, and you have piled up, say, $5,000 of reserve funds in the bank, your chances of spending all that money in a decline, however severe, are extremely remote.

That shortcoming was eventually overcome, mainly by introducing the element of percentage into our reckonings. If a *percentage* of the investor's reserves, rather than a formulated amount, is invested in a declining stock, the very size of the investor's reserves would dictate the investment for that particular month. If an investor has $1,000 in the bank, 10 percent of that is $100. If he has $5,000 in the bank, 10 percent of that is $500. Suddenly, the relationship makes sense. The more we have in the bank, the more we should invest in a falling market. No longer were we hamstrung by a rigid formula: Synchrovest, our exciting new investment method, was a clever investment adviser who not only knew when to buy and when to sell, but also how much reserve money we had in the bank! If Synchrovest suddenly advised us to invest 15 percent of our cash reserves, the actual amount of our investment on that particular month might be only $200. *Or it could be $20,000!* Synchrovest was saying: "You've got it. Invest it."

But, although Double Dollar Averaging and Synchrovest were, to my mind, significant improvements over Dollar Cost Averaging and, especially, Lump Sum investing with its terrifying feast-or-famine gamble, neither system could, in my opinion, usher in the Golden Age of Financial Security, although judging from the letters I'd received, Synchrovest seemed to be performing miracles for a number of investors. There may not have been anything better around, but I never stopped dreaming that there *could* be. For one thing, I continued to be disturbed over the risk element in investing. To a large extent, Double Dollar Averaging and Synchrovest reduced that risk—as it upped the possible rewards for the risk—but the guillotine blade was always out there, waiting. The old investment methods left much to be desired: Invest your $10,000 life savings in the market today and in a few months you could lose *half* that or more. This is a horrifying risk and, to our thinking, absolutely intolerable. If the potential rewards were, as a practical matter, many times $10,000, the risk might be justified. The bleak truth is, however, that the returns are for the most part quite small. You could, of course, break up your $10,000 life savings into small equal monthly investments and Dollar Cost Average—because that's supposed to be a safer way. And then, after years of buying higher and higher priced shares, the market will collapse and there you are with a loss of, yes, half or more. The stock market, like the service station attendant on the TV commercial who shows you what happens to your engine if you don't buy a certain automotive aid, says: "Pay me now or . . . pay me later."

Double Dollar Averaging and Synchrovest were at least partially successful attempts to protect the investor from being massacred in the marketplace. True enough, Synchrovest would sell out after a profit of 100 percent, put all the proceeds in the bank, and begin a new program for its master. At this point, with profits comfortably tucked away and held in reserve for attractive buying opportunities, it would be nearly impossible for the investor to suffer much of a loss of his original investment, no matter how steep the stock collapse. But what happens if the years go by and your stock or mutual fund not only does not double, but hangs around the same neighborhood, kicking at the curb? And *then* comes crashing down with all the other stocks? What happens to the money you faithfully invested over the years? You will lose part of it. Not nearly as much as other investors, probably, but it could still represent the kind of loss that no one can really afford, even psychologically, unless he is gainfully employed or has sufficient discretionary capital to shrug off paper losses.

Finally—and surely this is the aim of all investment— how much profit can we make, regardless of the investment technique we use? The old standbys, Lump Sum investing, Hit-or-Miss investing, and Dollar Cost Averaging probably lead to as much dollar loss as to gain, and even the winners are apt to be small winners. Large winners tend to be large investors. The rich they are different, even in the stock market.

Synchrovest attempted to give the small investor a shot at the pot of gold. Indeed, by taking the buy-and-sell decisions out of his hands and directing his every move, Synchrovest, with its logical system of checks and balances, could make him a fortune over a period of time. From a little, much.

But how *long* a period of time? we asked ourselves as we faithfully pursued our own Synchrovest program. How long were we really prepared to wait to double or triple our money? Suppose, after ten years of monthly investing, we manage to double our money. True, you can't do this in a bank—but what is our reward? Our reward is 100 percent profit. If we have invested $5,000, our reward is $5,000. And if we have invested $10,000, our reward is $10,000. Again, the size of the reward is directly related to the size of our investment. As those of you know who are familiar with Synchrovest, once you have doubled your money in a Synchrovest program, it is possible at that point to go on and make a very large amount of money in the years ahead.

But that first hurdle—the initial 100 percent rise—was an imposing one. Because it could take many years for a stock, or a portfolio of stocks, to double in value when new money is constantly being fed into it. For that matter, it could take several years just to increase by 50 percent.

Where did that leave the small investor? Not quite back in the same position in which he started. In the arena with the lions, yes, but mercifully equipped with helmet, breastplate, and shield—and a three-pronged fork with which to spear and snag a fleeing stock. From time to time he could even achieve spectacular results, especially during and immediately after a bone-crunching bust that had dyed-in-the-wool Lump Sum investors, Hit-or-Miss-ers, and Dollar Cost Averagers hysterically dumping their stocks. Still, the Synchrovest investor's eventual rewards depended not so much upon the strength of his faith as upon the size of his original investment, and many years of patience and fortitude were often required before returns of any decent size could be realized. Our conclusion was depressing, if not original: The poor ye will always have with you.

All these fears, remember, were colored by my own unemployment. Fans of Synchrovest might well insist that I have wildly underestimated the Synchrovest potential for the *average* employed investor.

What we now sought (aside from perfection itself) was first an investment method in which the extent of our possible loss could be predetermined. If we have $5,000 to invest, we know we cannot lose more than $5,000, regardless of what happens to the market. And perhaps we are prepared (as we should be) to lose some, most, or even all of that $5,000. We won't like it, surely, but it will not cripple us permanently. With continuous investment programs, there is no way we can fix the perimeter of our loss at the start. The market may begin to tumble in our first year, and we may lose a couple of hundred dollars. Hardly earthshaking. And, after all, we're investing for the *long* term, we tell ourselves. Or the market may collapse in our fifth year and peel a couple of thousand dollars from our portfolio. Now such a loss not only hurts badly—it could also arrive at a time in our lives in which we are not prepared to suffer a setback of that magnitude. Or the market goes to pieces in our tenth year or later and we suddenly find ourselves brutalized to the extent of $10,000! It is not necessary to describe the shock and disbelief of a small investor in the $100-a-month category who adds up the figures and stares at the wreckage of his future. He may be nearing retirement. He may be earning a smaller salary now and hanging onto his monthly investment program in the hope of at least a more comfortable future. His savings account may, in the meantime, have been riddled

by a variety of emergencies—and now his small investment program is a shambles too! Whatever his circumstances now, he could not possibly have predicted, in the
beginning, that he could one day lose $10,000 from sim-
ply investing $100 a month! The very hint of such a
possibility would send most of us fleeing in terror back
to U.S. Savings Bonds! Granted, much or all of that loss
might once have been profit; but investors have a way
of staking an emotional claim to profits—even if they
exist only on paper.

The personal agony of such losses in recent years has
not been adequately probed and publicized. The small
investor who suffered the most did not, as a rule, have
friends close to the media to whom he could communi-
cate his shock and despair over the fate of his savings.
And even if he had, how many financial horror stories
can any paper print without passing the threshold of
boredom? Eventually it becomes a matter of stacking
bodies like cordwood: the overall effect stuns and de-
presses, but it is not humanly possible to mourn each
victim individually.

Financial setbacks have never been pleasant in any
era, but the injunctions against losing voiced by Mr. S.,
the Welfare client, have, it seems to us, risen from speculative philosophy to scripture over the past few years. It
is later than we think. To lose 10 percent of our money
in a year in which the rate of inflation is 1 percent means
that we are down 11 percent for the year. To lose that
same 10 percent in a year when the rate of inflation is
12 percent means that we are down 22 percent. Although our portfolio has declined by the same 10 percent, our loss is now twice as severe! And now, if we
inject into our calculations the depressing fact that our
savings dollars are becoming harder and harder to set
aside, thanks to soaring taxes and an uncertain economy,
we begin to understand that we just don't have that
many dollars to invest anymore. And we begin to understand that we can no longer risk or endure stock market
losses with the same composure as before. We can no

longer *afford* to invest for the long term—another former heresy that's on its way to becoming legitimate. We can't afford the patience and we can't afford the risk. The unique situation that had existed in our economy and in our financial markets, particularly since World War II, has ended. And we've lost our faith in the ability of anyone, in or out of government, to solve the many problems that confront us.

What's left, it seems to us, is an investment climate so treacherous that all the old slogans have been rendered inoperable. Investing for income, investing for "appreciation," investing for growth, now echo like "Tippecanoe and Tyler too" and "23 skidoo." They have nothing to do with *today*. If you invest for income and lose a quarter of your principal, are you gaining income? If you invest for appreciation and lose a third of your principal, are you appreciating? If you invest for growth and lose half of your principal, are you growing? After ten years, you show a loss—are you *investing?*

Man has 206 bones in his body, but his designer saw fit to put half of them in very small parts of the body: his hands and feet. The message now seems obvious: "Grab the money and run!"

The problems encountered in this search for something better are, of course, telescoped in presentation here. An overview of the obstacles faced and the responses to them should satisfy all but the most fanatical student of mathematics and/or investing. What I sought was an investment method that would limit losses to the original value of the portfolio. That way, the investor could *know* the extent of the risk, and if the risk at any time appeared too high for him to sleep nights, he could "sell to the sleeping point." However, this should never really be necessary, since the money invested in the first place should be, first and foremost, funds he could afford to lose. Nevertheless, I wanted to *try* to incorporate into the system a ferocious palace guard of safety devices to defend even our original portfolio value from grievous injury.

What I wanted also was a system that maintained at
all times a sensitivity to market fluctuations, *a system
that took profits as soon as they appeared* rather than
waiting for the pot of gold at the end of the rainbow.
This much-advertised reward, like a mountain peak, is
always visible but seldom attained. And those who claim
it, like those standing atop a mountain peak, look back
and say yes, it's true, it really is here and this is the way
to get to it. But those who slog toward the peak never
seem to arrive. They *see* the peak—indeed it often appears so close they feel they could stretch out their
hands and touch it—but conquest continues to torment
them. This phenomenon is as frustrating to the mountain
climber as it is to the investor seeking his pot of gold—as
I can attest from personal participation in both activities.

The Automatic Investment Management system should
ignore the far-off pot of gold and instead pick up nuggets
of gold along the way. Capitalism, they say, is a case of
"jam tomorrow and never jam today." Well, after what
had been done to us in 1970 and 1974, we wanted our
jam *today*. And we wanted *more* jam tomorrow, and
more the day after that! Because you can't really get
rich in the stock market just by multiplying your own
money—unless you are very nearly rich to begin with.
You get rich by multiplying your money *and* the market's money. You buy two shares of a $5 stock for a
total of $10 and the stock doubles. You've got $20. Now,
instead of nodding in approval, relighting your pipe, and
resuming your rocking on the front porch, if you sold a
share and tucked that $10 in your shirt pocket, it
shouldn't matter to you in the slightest if the market
suddenly goes to hell and drags half of Wall Street with
it. *Because you can't lose a penny of your original investment.* It's safely buttoned up in your pocket! However,
you still own one share of stock—a freebie—and that
share of stock is worth something now and may be worth
a great deal more in the months to come. In effect, the
market is subsidizing your free ride.

Suppose the price of that stock is now $5, down from

its high of $10. It has lost 50 percent of its value. But since you have a $10 bill in your shirt pocket, your total worth is $15. You're still *ahead* 50 percent! Feeling magnanimous, you stop rocking long enough to take the $10 bill from your pocket and buy two more shares of the stock. You now own three shares of the stock, and lo and behold, it doubles in price. Your total worth is now $30. The stock has doubled in price, but you've tripled your original investment! Those are the bones of the Automatic Investment Management system. Fully fleshed, it would be a system that would keep our losses to a minimum, buy and sell stock for us at the proper times, and give us not just a shot at the pot of gold, but a reasonable expectation that *we would achieve it within a reasonable length of time*. Our Money Machine should demand minimal attention as well. Checking it once a month should be sufficient, allowing us to go about our own business without distraction.

It would also be a system that afforded the ordinary investor with only a few thousand dollars the opportunity to become a millionaire—an ambition so totally revolutionary that perhaps only a madman could entertain it without smiling.

Well, for better or worse, I was that madman. And after many years of exhausting work, I would gladly have conceded the fact had anybody been interested.

The problems were manifold. You have $10,000. How much stock should you buy right off, and how much money should you keep in reserve? Should one copy mutual funds and maintain a cash reserve somewhere between 5 and 10 percent? Have mutual funds been all that successful, and should anybody care one way or another *how* much cash they keep in reserve? How much profit should we have before selling off some stock, and how much loss before buying some more? Suppose at one point our stock is worth $10,000 and suddenly it is worth $5,000. Should we invest here, and if so, how much? How about investing $5,000? Fine, we put $5,000 into the market. Only one problem: we still have $30,000 cash in reserve because we were taking profits when the market was climbing. What are we going to do with that $30,000? The market is down 50 percent and isn't likely to go down any further; it will probably rebound here—and we're stuck with $30,000 in cash, which *should have been invested at the lows.* No good. Back to the drawing board. How about investing a *percentage* of our cash reserve? No good—it's too easy to exhaust all our cash reserves halfway down, and by the time the market hits bottom our pocketbook is empty. Back to the drawing board.

More problems: After a decline, after we have purchased lots and lots of cheap stock and our pocketbook is empty, at what point do we sell some stock to get some money to buy some more stock should the market turn around and fall again? How much should we sell? Also—and this was the most maddening perplexity—suppose we started off our program with $10,000 and now, thanks to profit-taking, we have a portfolio worth $15,000—$10,000 in stock and $5,000 in cash. Suddenly the market declines by 50 percent, and our stock is now worth only $5,000. Stocks are at the very bottom of a bear market—but we have no loss at all! We have $5,000 in stock and $5,000 in cash, a total of $10,000. With a market down by 50 percent, we should be in there buying like crazy—but how can we buy when our figures show that we have no loss? Why would we buy more stock when our portfolio shows no loss and no gain?

Start from scratch. How much to invest in stocks and how much to set aside in cash at the outset? Well, what are the odds of the market's going up and what are the odds of its going down? Fifty-fifty. The answer, therefore, is obvious. *We should put 50 percent of our money in stocks and keep 50 percent in reserve, because if the market is just as likely to rise as it is to fall, we will be able to take equal advantage of either move.*

Example: We put $5,000 in stock and keep $5,000 in cash. Our stocks could now theoretically go to zero in value, and we would simply transfer our $5,000 in cash to the stock market and buy loads of bargain-priced shares there at the bottom of the market. Then, when the market recovers, our large number of cheap shares would get us rich in a hurry! Very good. And look: The worst thing that could possibly happen to the stock market has happened. It has gone totally to powder, and our loss in this catastrophe of all financial catastrophes in history has been held to 50 percent! Less than that, actually, because we've earned interest on our cash reserves!

After a lot of coffee and cigarettes, I then came up with something I call Portfolio Control—a "governor" for our vehicle. It is the original value of our portfolio, and it determines whether we are losing or winning and advises appropriate action at all times. We start off with $5,000 in stock and $5,000 in cash. Total portfolio value: $10,000. Portfolio Control is therefore also $10,000. Sure, it makes sense to sell some stock when our total portfolio rises above our Portfolio Control, $10,000. But when we sell, we simply take the money out of the stock market and put it in the bank. Our total portfolio value does not change simply because we sold stock, exchanged some stock for money. Therefore, our Portfolio Control does not know whether we are heavy in stock at this time or heavy in cash. It is not only blind, it is also not very smart. If our Portfolio Control reads $10,000, and our portfolio value reads $15,000, we know we have a profit of $5,000 *but Portfolio Control does not know how much of our $15,000 is in stocks and how much in cash.*

At this point I made the decision to pack it all in. Including my labors on Synchrovest, I had devoted six years to research of this nature. Enough was enough!

And then I stumbled across the old license plate in the barn. Its number: 2X 1-50. The 1-50 caught my eye. Suppose we were to cut the Portfolio Control in half—divide it by 2—and used *that* figure to determine how much stock to buy and sell? After considerable lucubration, I determined that this same purpose could more simply be served by changing the very nature of the Portfolio Control. *Thereafter, the Portfolio Control consisted only of the original stock portion of our portfolio!*

Suddenly it was obvious that current was flowing through the circuits of the Money Machine. Something very exciting was happening!

Switch on again. We start off with a nest egg of $10,000. We put $5,000 in stock and keep $5,000 in reserve. The Portfolio Control now reads $5,000. If our stock increases in value, we sell off some and add the proceeds to our cash reserve. This transaction does not affect our Portfolio Control: it shows an investment of $5,000, and it insists that whenever our holdings rise in value above $5,000, we have a profit and should take it.

But suppose, instead, that our stocks fall to a value of $3,000, which represents a difference of $2,000 from our Portfolio Control of $5,000. We would then take $2,000 from our cash reserve and buy stock with it. Lights flash. We have $5,000 worth of stock again. Now, according to our Portfolio Control, we are even: $5,000 invested in stock, and stockholdings now worth $5,000. But we know this is not true. We actually have $7,000—not $5,000—invested, and we have a loss of $2,000. Attention must be paid to this loss. If not, and if the value of our stocks moves up to $6,000, we will find ourselves obeying Portfolio Control and selling off stocks at a loss, and that is no way to get rich.

All right, then, suppose we adjust our Portfolio Control whenever we buy more stock. Rerun: Our $5,000 stockholdings decline to $3,000. We take $2,000 out of our cash reserve and buy stock with it. Now our stockholdings are worth $5,000 again. At the same time, we *add* to our Portfolio Control the amount of our last investment—$2,000. Our Portfolio Control dials spin and stop at $7,000. Clever?

What's this? We have just invested $2,000 at the behest of our Automatic Investment Management, and now we find that while our stockholdings are worth $5,000 again, our Portfolio Control window is flashing a figure of $7,000. There's *still* a difference of $2,000 between Portfolio Control and the actual value of our stockholdings, despite the fact we've just invested $2,000. And if we go ahead and invest *another* $2,000, our stocks would be worth $7,000—and our Portfolio Control window would flash a figure of $9,000. We're *still* $2,000 awry! Obviously, we've stumbled into a hall of mirrors, clambered aboard a wheel within a wheel, and are hurtling toward infinity. Worse, although the stock market has stopped going down, we are soon forced to invest every cent of our cash reserve in a futile attempt to appease the voracious appetite of a Money Machine gone mad. Guess what happens now? The market collapses for real, and on the way down we don't have a single penny left in our cash reserve with which to scoop up those tempting, once-in-a-lifetime bargains. Again, this is no way to get rich.

Back to the drawing board. Those magic numerals, 1-50, got us over one hurdle. Can they do it again? Maybe they can. Maybe they are telling us to adjust our Portfolio Control figure whenever we buy more stock— because that, after all, is the most rational of moves— *but they are telling us to adjust it by 50 percent of the amount of our new investment.*

Switch on. Play back. Our $5,000 stockholdings declines to a value of $3,000. Our Portfolio Control window reads $5,000. We invest $2,000 to close the gap, and at the same time increase our Portfolio Control figure by *$1,000.* Our stock is now worth $5,000, while our Portfolio Control window reads $6,000. True, there is still a $1,000 difference, but it's only half as great a gap as before. And the following month, if the value of our stock remains the same, we would theoretically invest $1,000 as directed and increase our Portfolio Control by $500. The new figures now become $6,000 for the stock and $6,500 for our Portfolio Control. Are you picking up a pattern here? Your investments are being halved. Gears are meshing, switches are being thrown, and brakes are being energized in order to stop you from spending your money like a drunken sailor on a portfolio of stocks that has long ceased declining and does not demand an infusion of new capital.

In the preceding paragraph, you will find the word "theoretically," which may just be the most important word in this entire book.

To wit: It is possible to construct a *mathematically* perfect investment formula. We have done so—several times. And when we have applied this formula to a stock that soars up, plunges, and then recovers to its original price, we have discovered to our dismay that we have achieved a mathematically perfect profit of 10 percent or so. Better than nothing, true, but nothing to get excited about. The major flaw here is that our mathematically perfect formula sells stock *exactly* when it has a profit and buys stock *exactly* when it has a loss. It is a fussbudget, a nitpicker, a pinch-nosed government bureaucrat. Our $15 stock crashes to $4, and at the next price of $5, our mathematically perfect formula is in there yelling "Sell, sell!"

That, we repeat for the final time, is no way to get rich. What was needed here was the discipline of a Teuton, the cool of a riverboat gambler, the timing of a Rothschild, and the speculative instincts of a Baruch.

At this stage, being totally mad as I have already admitted, I had before me what I considered to be a viable creature with all organs, veins, and tissues intact and perfect—a financial Frankenstein lacking only the breath of life. And this, in my last moment of inspiration, I breathed into it. Call it soul, if you will, or call it SAFE—Stock Adjustment Factor Equalizer—it started the heartbeat of the Automatic Investment Management system and brought it to life. The Money Machine was now fully operational, and all systems were GO!

SAFE is nothing more than a figure representing 10 percent of our stockholdings, but it is also nothing short of miraculous. We use it as a filter, thus:

Once a month, we subtract our stockholdings from

our PORTFOLIO CONTROL. Or, if our stockholdings happen to be larger than our PORTFOLIO CONTROL, we subtract our PORTFOLIO CONTROL from our stockholdings. The larger number goes on top. The figure we derive is our BUY/SELL ADVICE. Before we act upon this figure, we pass it through our SAFE filter: we subtract our SAFE figure from it. The result is our MARKET ORDER. We obey *that* without question.

SAFE prevents us from selling or buying prematurely. It has two eyes, each with a visual field of 270 degrees, and is very, very bright. Watch, when the market makes a V and you're cash-shy because of the heavy buying you did on the leg down, how *coolly* SAFE feeds stock into the market. Its intention, you begin to realize, is not to nail down profits in a frenzy of greed, but to generate some cash in preparation for the next decline— when you'll be *needing* cash for another buying spree.

Automatic Investment Management was the unbelievably successful culmination of six draining years of work. It was exactly what I had sought and everything I wanted. I tested it in every conceivable kind of market— up, down, and sideways—and when I was through, I was so convinced that AIM—Automatic Investment Management—*would* lead us, with *safety,* to the Promised Land, that I immediately rushed out and placed all my own investment dollars into it.

You can't show any more faith than that!

SIX

Automatic Investment Management: The Reality

The preceding sketch of the thought processes as I wrestled with the problems of developing Automatic Investment Management can only hint at the frustrating labors and disappointments, and that's as it should be. Nothing is more self-serving and, in the final analysis, self-defeating, as inviting the customer backstage to observe the ropes, pulleys, klieg lights, mechanisms, cycloramas, wind machines—the whole glamorous *mise en scène* as viewed from its disillusioning cardboard rear. But a brief overview is necessary in this instance, when we are dealing with such a complex subject, to acquaint you—who may not be a stock market or mathematical expert—with the nature and dimensions of the problems to begin with, and the ways in which it was attacked. Such an introduction, we felt, might help ease the reader into a swifter and fuller comprehension of the final product—Automatic Investment Management. If you come to understand how the writer's mind works, and become familiar with his quirks, his logic, and his failings, understanding (if not appreciation) should follow.

Without our having to go into tedious detail concerning the engineering of your Money Machine, it will nevertheless become obvious to you as you use it that much more is going on inside it than meets the eye. It was not a flight of whimsy that prompted the earlier remark that we wanted the figures *themselves* to think and understand. Figures *can* understand—just as your little electronic calculator understands and obeys your directions, just as a computer understands what you want of it. Figures can also speak—"1,2,3,5." What did the figures say? They said 4, didn't you hear them? There is no 4 printed in that series of numbers—but the figures announced that a 4 is missing.

Sometimes it is not so simple to divine what the numbers are doing. Take your weight. Double it. Add 5. Multiply by 50. Add your age. Add 365. Subtract 615.

The answer reveals your weight. There are also a couple of digits left over. That's how old you are. Sorry about that.

The circuitry of our Money Machine may not concern you, but you must familiarize yourself with its controls in order to operate it. The first step in beginning your AIM program is to set up a permanent record sheet.

Column Number 1 on your record sheet is the STOCK VALUE column. Once every month (you may perform your investment chores once every *quarter* if you prefer, but for the purposes of this discussion, we assume a monthly routine) enter in this column the current value of your stockholdings. This figure will naturally change from month to month when you buy or sell stock, and it will fluctuate from month to month along with the rise and fall of the stocks you own.

Column Number 2 on your record sheet is the SAFE column (Stock Adjustment Factor Equalizer). *SAFE is a figure representing 10 percent of your STOCK VALUE*. It's easy to calculate. You can do it mentally by looking at the figure in your STOCK VALUE column and dropping the last digit. If the figure in your STOCK VALUE column reads $5,000, for example, you know your SAFE figure is 500. If STOCK VALUE reads $5,005, you would round off your SAFE figure to read 501.

Column Number 3 on your record sheet is the CASH column. Once every month on your regular day enter in this column the amount of cash you have on hand. This figure will decrease from month to month when you withdraw funds with which to buy stock. It will increase from month to month when you sell stock and deposit the proceeds of the sale in your bank account or Money Market Fund. It will also increase when interest is paid on your cash reserves and when you receive dividends from the stocks you own.

Column Number 4 on your record sheet is the all-important PORTFOLIO CONTROL column. It performs the same function in your Money Machine as another piece of advanced technology, the inertial guidance system, does in a nuclear-missile submarine. The atomic submarine must, as a rule, remain hidden beneath the ocean; and yet it is imperative that it be able to fix its exact position at all times. The missile it fires can be no more accurate than the error made in calculating its launch position. If circumstances permit, the sub can sneak up close to the surface at night, whisk up an antenna, and take a fix on a satellite; or sometimes it can check its position against charted features on the floor of the ocean. But most of the time it must rely on inertial guidance—ingenious self-contained arrangements of gyroscopes and small weights called accelerometers. The gyros hold the accelerometers in position, and as the sub slips through the water, the accelerometers register movement in every direction and feed appropriate signals into a computer, which translates them into speed, distance, and position. PORTFOLIO CONTROL constantly feels and measures the progress—or regress—of your stockholdings in terms of your investment in those stockholdings. When it determines that either a Buy or Sell target is looming into range, PORTFOLIO CONTROL automatically activates a Red Alert switch. This action does not, of itself, fire a missile; it merely permits a missile to be fired when the red button is pushed. And the order to fire does not emanate from PORTFOLIO CONTROL—it can come only from the Commander-in-Chief of Automatic Investment Management: SAFE. We will have more about SAFE later.

PORTFOLIO CONTROL also feeds speed, distance, and position signals to your next column.

Column Number 5 on your record sheet is the BUY (SELL) ADVICE column. It receives signals from PORTFOLIO CONTROL as target instructions and converts them into trajectories for the missile. The BUY (SELL) ADVICE column is the last stage before actual firing. The "Ready" command has been given. The "Set" command has been given. We await only the "Go!" signal.

This command to fire can come only from SAFE Headquarters, the Supreme Commander of our little operation here, and it follows last-second adjustments for speed, distance, and position.

Column Number 6 on your record sheet is the MARKET ORDER column—the firing line. It receives and acts upon orders from SAFE, and it obeys no one *but* SAFE. The MARKET ORDER column is nothing more than the actual order you give to your broker or mutual fund. If SAFE orders you to invest, say, $1,000, enter $1,000 in this column. If SAFE orders you to *sell* $1,000 worth of stock, enter ($1,000) in this column. It is simple to buy or sell *exactly* $1,000 worth of mutual funds. And many brokerage houses and banks offer programs that also enable you to buy or sell stocks in the *exact* amount you prefer. But such exactitude is not critical to the functioning of Automatic Investment Management. Fractional shares of stock do not affect your performance significantly.

Column Number 7, PORTFOLIO VALUE, is not strictly necessary, but we include it—as you may wish to do—merely to keep track of our progress. PORTFOLIO VALUE represents the combined total of our STOCK VALUE plus our CASH.

In just a moment, we are going to demonstrate, piece by piece, how AIM's various components operate. The briefing that follows will enable you to grasp the entire concept at a glance.

AIM requires only two simple steps for its operation. Once every month, determine your STOCK VALUE and write it on a piece of paper. Place the letter "S" in front of it to identify it as your STOCK VALUE:

S 5,464

Now look at your PORTFOLIO CONTROL. If it's *larger* than your STOCK VALUE, write it directly *above* the figure you have just written and place a "P" in front of it to identify it as PORTFOLIO CONTROL. If it's smaller, write it *below* the figure you have just written. The larger figure always goes on top.

Now simply subtract the bottom figure from the top:

$$\begin{array}{r} \text{P } 6,363 \\ -\text{S } 5,464 \\ \hline 899 \end{array}$$

AIM has just given you a "Purchase" advice for $899. *How do you know it's a "Purchase," not a "Sale"? Because of the letter "P" on the top line. It now stands for "Purchase." If the letter "S" were on top, AIM would be giving you a "Sale" advice. "P" for "Purchase," "S" for "Sale."*

Enter the $899 figure in your BUY(SELL) ADVICE column. (If it were a "Sale" advice, you would put the figure in parentheses to distinguish it from a "Purchase" advice.)

The second step, converting your BUY(SELL) ADVICE into a real MARKET ORDER, is equally simple. SAFE is boss here. *If SAFE is larger than your BUY (SELL) ADVICE, the answer is zero. You take no action whatsoever. Enter zero in your MARKET ORDER column and close your books until next month.*

If SAFE is *smaller,* simply subtract it from your BUY-(SELL) ADVICE.

$$P\ 6{,}363$$
$$\underline{-S\ 5{,}464}$$

$$899$$
$$\underline{-546}\quad\text{(SAFE)}$$
$$353$$

SAFE has given you a MARKET ORDER to purchase $353 worth of stock. Enter the figure in your
MARKET ORDER column, and actually purchase $353
worth of stock.

Obviously, if the letter "S" appeared in the top line
of your calculation, your final MARKET ORDER
would be to *sell* $353 worth of stock. You would then
enter ($353) in your MARKET ORDER column, and
then you would actually sell the stock.

These are the simple, easy-to-operate controls and
functions of your Money Machine. They need no oiling,
no maintenance, no batteries, and are virtually indestruc-
tible.

Unpack your new Money Machine and place it upon
a table. How much money would you like to entrust to
it? $10,000? Very good. Invest $5,000 in one or more
stocks or mutual funds and enter the $5,000 figure in
Column 1, the STOCK VALUE column. Next, deposit
$5,000 in a bank or a money fund (we'll discuss money
funds as an alternative to savings accounts later), and
enter the $5,000 figure in Column 3, the CASH column.
You now own stocks worth $5,000 and a cash balance
of $5,000. Compute 10 percent of your stock value—in
this case $500—and enter it in Column 2, the SAFE
column. In Column 4, PORTFOLIO CONTROL, enter
the figure $5,000, which is the amount you have invested
in stock at the beginning. That's all there is to it this
month. You're in business. Your record sheet should
look like this:

1 Stock Value	2 Safe	3 Cash	4 Portfolio Control	5 Buy(Sell) Advice	6 Market Order	7 Portfolio Value
$5,000	500	$5,000	$5,000	—	—	$10,000

The following month, determine the new value of your stockholdings. Let us assume it is now $5,500. Enter the $5,500 figure in Column 1, STOCK VALUE. Next, add the interest you have received on your savings account and the dividends you have received on your stocks to Column 3, CASH. Let us assume you have received $25 in interest and dividends for the month. Enter the $5,025 figure in Column 3, CASH. (As a practical matter, if you simply deposit your stock dividends in your cash account as received, the figure in Column 3, CASH, will always be identical to your bank account.)

Your record sheet should now look like this:

1 Stock Value	2 Safe	3 Cash	4 Portfolio Control	5 Buy(Sell) Advice	6 Market Order	7 Portfolio Value
$5,000	500	$5,000	$5,000	—	—	$10,000
$5,500	550	$5,025				$10,525

Remember the first step? On a separate piece of paper, write down your STOCK VALUE and identify it with the letter "S."

S 5,500

Now look at your PORTFOLIO CONTROL. It is obviously smaller than the figure you have just written down, so we place it *below* your STOCK VALUE figure, and we identify it with the letter "P." Then we subtract.

$$\begin{array}{r} S\ 5{,}500 \\ -P\ 5{,}000 \\ \hline 500 \end{array}$$

You know this is to be a "Sale" rather than a "Purchase" because the letter "S" appears in the dominant position on top, so you enter ($500) in Column 5, BUY (SELL) ADVICE. You have just been instructed by the people in BUY(SELL) ADVICE to sell $500 worth of stock. But you and I both know that only SAFE—Stock Adjustment Factor Equalizer—can give the final order. If the SAFE figure is *larger* than your BUY(SELL) ADVICE, consider your BUY(SELL) ADVICE overruled. And that is the case here. Your SAFE figure is $550, while your BUY(SELL) ADVICE is only $500. Enter the figure 0 in Column 6, MARKET ORDER. And since you have certainly not invested anything this time around, your PORTFOLIO CONTROL remains the same. Enter the same figure in PORTFOLIO CONTROL as already appears there in the line above.

1 Stock Value	2 Safe	3 Cash	4 Portfolio Control	5 Buy(Sell) Advice	6 Market Order	7 Portfolio Value
$5,000	500	$5,000	$5,000	—	—	$10,000
$5,500	550	$5,025	$5,000	($500)	0	$10,525

The following month, on your regular investment date, check your stockholdings in the newspaper and revalue your stock portfolio. We'll assume it's now worth $6,000, and that your bankbook now shows a balance of $5,050, thanks to interest. Enter the figures in the appropriate columns:

1 Stock Value	2 Safe	3 Cash	4 Portfolio Control	5 Buy(Sell) Advice	6 Market Order	7 Portfolio Value
$5,000	500	$5,000	$5,000	—	—	$10,000
$5,500	550	$5,025	$5,000	($500)	0	$10,525
$6,000	600	$5,050				$11,050

Write down your STOCK VALUE on a piece of paper:

S 6,000

And, since your PORTFOLIO CONTROL is still smaller than your STOCK VALUE, write your PORTFOLIO CONTROL *under* your STOCK VALUE figure and subtract:

$$\begin{array}{r} S\ 6,000 \\ -P\ 5,000 \\ \hline 1,000 \end{array}$$

You know this is a preliminary *sell* advice because of the predominance of the letter "S," so you enter ($1,000) in Column 5, BUY(SELL) ADVICE. Now you must check with SAFE for permission to proceed. SAFE at this point is 600, not nearly big enough to dominate the gang in BUY(SELL) ADVICE who have come up with that 1,000 figure. Proceed in good conscience by subtracting the SAFE figure, 600, from your BUY(SELL) ADVICE of 1,000:

$$\begin{array}{rl} S\ 6,000 & \\ -P\ 5,000 & \\ \hline 1,000 & \\ -600 & (SAFE) \\ \hline 400 & \end{array}$$

AIM has given you a direct order to sell $400 worth of stock. Enter ($400) in MARKET ORDER, Column 6, and then actually push the red button: Contact your broker or your mutual fund and sell $400 worth of stock. You haven't *bought* any stock, so your PORTFOLIO CONTROL, Column 4, remains the same.

1 Stock Value	2 Safe	3 Cash	4 Portfolio Control	5 Buy(Sell) Advice	6 Market Order	7 Portfolio Value
$5,000	500	$5,000	$5,000	—	—	$10,000
$5,500	550	$5,025	$5,000	($500)	0	$10,525
$6,000	600	$5,050	$5,000	($1,000)	($400)	$11,050

Next month, assuming that your stockholdings haven't moved in either direction and that you've earned another $25 in interest and dividends, your chart will look like this:

1 Stock Value	2 Safe	3 Cash	4 Portfolio Control	5 Buy(Sell) Advice	6 Market Order	7 Portfolio Value
$5,000	500	$5,000	$5,000	—	—	$10,000
$5,500	550	$5,025	$5,000	($500)	0	$10,525
$6,000	600	$5,050	$5,000	($1,000)	($400)	$11,050
$5,600	560	$5,475				$11,075

As you can see, your STOCK VALUE has been reduced by $400, the amount of your sale last month, and your CASH has increased by $400—the proceeds from that sale—plus the $25 in interest and dividends we assume you received during the month.

Once again you write your STOCK VALUE on a separate piece of paper:

S 5,600

And once again you look at your PORTFOLIO CONTROL. It is smaller than your STOCK VALUE, so you write it in a subservient position *under* your STOCK VALUE and then you subtract:

$$\begin{array}{r} S\ 5,600 \\ -P\ 5,000 \\ \hline 600 \end{array}$$

The answer is $600. You know it is a preliminary *sell* signal because the letter "S" in the top figure—"S" for *sell*—is in charge. Dutifully, you enter ($600) in your

BUY(SELL) ADVICE Column Number 5—and then call on SAFE for final instructions. The SAFE figure now stands at 560—not large enough to *completely* overwhelm the 600 figure. So you write it beneath the 600 figure and subtract:

$$
\begin{array}{r}
\text{S } 5,600 \\
-\text{P } 5,000 \\
\hline
600 \\
-560 \quad \text{(SAFE)} \\
\hline
40
\end{array}
$$

Although you now have a genuine MARKET ORDER to *sell* $40 worth of stock, you may, in good conscience, ignore any sell or purchase order under $100. SAFE provides a general amnesty for those of us who do not wish to participate in minor skirmishes. If this includes you, adjust your record sheet as follows:

1 Stock Value	2 Safe	3 Cash	4 Portfolio Control	5 Buy(Sell) Advice	6 Market Order	7 Portfolio Value
$5,000	500	$5,000	$5,000	—	—	$10,000
$5,500	550	$5,025	$5,000	($500)	0	$10,525
$6,000	600	$5,050	$5,000	($1,000)	($400)	$11,050
$5,600	560	$5,475	$5,000	($600)	0	$11,075

You're all set till next month. Your PORTFOLIO CONTROL, of course, remains the same. It is to be adjusted *only* when you make a purchase.

Next month—no more Mr. Nice Guy. The market skids downward and your stockholdings sink to a value of $4,400, while your CASH balance increases by $25, thanks to interest and dividends. You're delighted—or should be—that although the market has fallen 21 percent as measured by your stockholdings, your PORTFOLIO VALUE stands at $9,900 and shows a loss of only 1 percent! You enter the appropriate figures in Columns 1, 2, and 3:

1 Stock Value	2 Safe	3 Cash	4 Portfolio Control	5 Buy(Sell) Advice	6 Market Order	7 Portfolio Value
$5,000	500	$5,000	$5,000	—	—	$10,000
$5,500	550	$5,025	$5,000	($500)	0	$10,525
$6,000	600	$5,050	$5,000	($1,000)	($400)	$11,050
$5,600	560	$5,475	$5,000	($600)	0	$11,075
$4,400	440	$5,500				$9,900

I'm sure you know what to do by now. Write down your STOCK VALUE on a separate piece of paper:

$$S\ 4,400$$

Check your PORTFOLIO CONTROL. At 5,000, it is *higher* than your STOCK VALUE of 4,400—so write it *above* your STOCK VALUE and subtract:

$$\begin{array}{r} P\ 5,000 \\ -S\ 4,400 \\ \hline 600 \end{array}$$

Is that $600 a *sell* or a *purchase* advice? Correct. It is a *purchase* advice because the letter "P" in the superior position on top calls the shots. When you originally wrote that "P," it stood for PORTFOLIO CONTROL. Now, in this context, it has become magically transmogrified to stand for *purchase*.

Enter $600 in Column 5, BUY(SELL) ADVICE, and contact SAFE Headquarters. If SAFE is larger than 600 at this point, it would cancel out your BUY(SELL) ADVICE. But it is not larger. It is only 440. So you subtract it from the 600:

$$\begin{array}{r} P\ 5,000 \\ -S\ 4,400 \\ \hline 600 \\ -440 \quad \text{(SAFE)} \\ \hline 160 \end{array}$$

AIM has flashed a *purchase* signal. You enter $160 in Column 6, MARKET ORDER, and withdraw $160 from your CASH balance to buy $160 worth of stock.

Because you have now invested more money in the stock market, you must increase your PORTFOLIO CONTROL figure in Column 4 by one half the amount of your investment. In this case, you add $80—one half of $160—to PORTFOLIO CONTROL.

The following month, assuming that your stocks have neither risen nor fallen, and that you have earned another $25 in interest and dividends, your chart will look like this:

1 Stock Value	2 Safe	3 Cash	4 Portfolio Control	5 Buy(Sell) Advice	6 Market Order	7 Portfolio Value
$5,000	500	$5,000	$5,000	—	—	$10,000
$5,500	550	$5,025	$5,000	($500)	0	$10,525
$6,000	600	$5,050	$5,000	($1,000)	($400)	$11,050
$5,600	560	$5,475	$5,000	($600)	0	$11,075
$4,400	440	$5,500	$5,080	$600	$160	$9,900
$4,560	456	$5,365				$9,925

AIM has now opened the draft on your PORTFOLIO CONTROL to allow for hotter action—more aggressive downside investments should the decline continue—and yet the slide has not resumed. The market has not budged from the preceding month. That being the case, hasn't AIM been outmaneuvered by the market? With a larger and more demanding PORTFOLIO CONTROL, wouldn't the investor be compelled to make another investment to feed it, even though the market has not gone down? Let's see.

Write down your STOCK VALUE:

S 4,560

Check your PORTFOLIO CONTROL. At $5,080, it is *larger* than your STOCK VALUE, so place it *above* the STOCK VALUE and subtract:

$$
\begin{array}{r}
P\ 5,080 \\
-S\ 4,560 \\
\hline
520
\end{array}
$$

It's a *purchase* signal, so enter $520 in Column 5, BUY-(SELL) ADVICE. Contact SAFE for last-minute instructions.

SAFE now stands at 456, too puny to wipe out that 520 figure. Subtract SAFE, 456, from your *purchase* advice, 520.

$$
\begin{array}{r}
P\ 5,080 \\
-S\ 4,560 \\
\hline
520 \\
-456 \\
\hline
64
\end{array}
$$

You have a MARKET ORDER to purchase $64 worth of stock, but it's too small to fool with. AIM has slammed on the brakes and won't release them until the market moves in one direction or the other. True, your PORTFOLIO CONTROL is larger—but so is your STOCK VALUE, thanks to the purchase of stock. SAFE, too, is heftier, reflecting the increase in your stockholdings. And with a swollen STOCK VALUE and SAFE both ganging up on PORTFOLIO CONTROL to protect your CASH from being dumped haphazardly into the market, PORTFOLIO CONTROL is outranked. Checkmate.

Sometimes when a declining market suddenly shrieks to a stop, AIM will pump its brakes to avoid going into a spin. Instead of curtailing your investments entirely, it will call for sharply decreasing investments for a month or two—and then nothing—just to pick up a few cheap shares in case the market turns around and heads upward again.

Of all the features we incorporated into AIM, this automatic check was the hardest to design and is the one of which we are most proud. Not only does it act as watchdog over your cash reserves during hard times, but it doubles as Scrooge during the holidays of a heady boom, feeding less and less stock into the market as it barrels upward. "Cratchit," it says, depositing ever-diminishing shillings into your cash account, "you're not to get rich just yet, is that understood? True enough, you've passed through lean and parlous times and your cupboard is bare. I wish merely to replenish your store-house, to supply you with sufficient provender for the coming snows. And, heh heh, the snows always come, don't they?"

Like the gambler who recklessly wagers his total funds on a single spin of the wheel—and wins!—it is possible for the Lump Sum investor to outperform our Money Machine. But in order for him to do so, the stock or stocks he selects must not only rise perpetually—a most unlikely event—they must rise with a velocity sufficient to offset the growth of AIM's stockholdings *and* the growth of AIM's cash reserves. Because AIM's cash reserves are *always* earning 5 or 6 percent or more, regardless of what its stockholdings are doing. At a time when stocks are floating in a sea of lethargy and are, in addition, yielding only 1 or 2 percent, AIM's cash reserves continue to earn the higher bank (or money fund) rate. Further, if we are near the peak of the market, AIM will probably have the bulk of its assets in cash, rather than stocks, and will be earning much more in interest than the fully invested Lump Sum investor is earning in dividends. Why? Because stocks at their peak prices tend to yield less than savings accounts. Check the year 2000!

AIM will laugh at you if you compare its performance with that of the Lump Sum investor in a sideways market, because there is no way Lump Sum can win unless his stocks are yielding higher dividends than AIM is receiving in dividends and interest combined. AIM will also laugh at you if you match it against the Lump Sum investor in a falling market. With a portion of its assets in cash, it is not nearly as vulnerable to loss as the Lump

Summer—which might turn out to be the understatement of the year. This feature alone endears AIM to us—and we hope to you as well. Later, you will see charts that may seem almost beyond belief, showing AIM clutching fiercely to a substantial profit from the top of a bull market almost to the very bottom . . . while the Lump Summer, having lost *his* profits the moment the market returned to its starting point, watches his portfolio being shredded into confetti the rest of the way down. When the market recovers to the point at which he entered it, he has nothing at all to show for the experience, save an ulcer. He has merely broken even, while AIM's pockets are bulging with stock picked up for a song at the fire sale.

To prove the Money Machine's fantastic capabilities, it would be necessary, it seems to us, to run it "flat out" against the ordinary Lump Sum investor, using as its fuel as high an octane stock as would be likely. The extreme volatility of such a stock would push and pull the Money Machine into the wildest exertions, challenging its stamina and its intelligence, and straining its circuitry to the utmost. We would subject it to the most severe G forces and atmospheric changes it would ever be likely to encounter. If AIM could prove its mettle under such grueling circumstances, it would be logical to assume that it would serve us ably in calmer, but more typical, markets.

For the sake of simplicity, we will use a single hypothetical stock rather than a portfolio of such stocks. The distinction is purely imaginary, however. The fluctuations of the "stock" we will use can, if you like, be viewed as the fluctuations of a portfolio of stocks. There would be no difference in the results.

Our hypothetical stock table is a famous one that has often been used to demonstrate the merits of Dollar Cost Averaging and the pitfalls of Lump Sum investing: the investor who made a Lump Sum purchase at the beginning of the chart *never* enjoys a profit, while the Dollar Cost Averager always enters the profit column at the price of 8.

In the charts that follow, you will note that we have added two columns we have not previously introduced to you. These columns are headed SHARES BOT (SOLD) and SHARES OWNED. If you use AIM to acquire a single stock or a mutual fund, the addition of these two columns may prove convenient and timesaving for you, in that you can keep track of all transactions on your AIM record sheet alone. In our case, we have inserted them in order that you may see at a glance how many shares of the stock we have purchased or sold at any given time, as well as how many shares we now own. You will more easily be able to follow the functioning of our Money Machine in action.

For the purposes of this test, we have also affixed an INTEREST column to allow the reader to observe the interest dollars flowing dependably into our CASH balance month by month. While most banks do not pay interest monthly, money funds do. If it will put your mind at rest, you may assume that we are using a money fund to hold our CASH reserves (which we personally do in our own AIM program). In any event, there was never a point during the test program—despite the wild swings of the stock—at which AIM's CASH balance fell so low as to necessitate immediate use of unpaid interest on the account.

As for the rate of interest we earned on our CASH balance, we have assumed the then legal passbook rate offered by any savings bank on ordinary day-of-deposit-to-day-of-withdrawal accounts, 5¼ percent per annum. We have computed this as .0044 percent per month. This rate is below the 6 percent per annum rate presently available on 90-day money and the 6½ percent per annum rate offered on one-year accounts, but since a penalty is imposed on premature withdrawals from these accounts, the possible bookkeeping nightmare that might result from adjusting for penalties persuaded us to forgo the advantage of a higher rate.

As you'll soon discover, the interest rate—despite the many thousands of dollars it yielded us over the course of the test—was hardly important. We could just as well have gathered up all our interest dollars into bushel baskets and built a large bonfire with them for laughs while we enjoyed the *real* profits AIM generated for us. As a matter of fact, we are so sinfully flush that we have even ignored the thousands of dollars in dividends paid on the stock we own—much, much more than was earned by the Lump Sum investor, because we have so many more shares than he does. These dividends, incidentally, would easily pay for all our commission costs, with plenty left over. There will be other times, we're sure, when AIM will *need* those bonus dollars to help us achieve outstanding results compared with the Lump Summer, but this was not one of those times.

We have selected $10,000 as our investment for two reasons: first, because that figure is often used in making such comparisons; and second, because the amount is within the range of many working people today. Many of us may not have it just yet, but as the man said, "We could get that." Our point in creating AIM was to make it possible for the average thrifty working man or woman to get rich. Now, an investor with $100,000 or more certainly can get rich in time; he already has a leg up on it. But $100,000 is unquestionably beyond the range of most of us. Only 2.4 percent of adult Americans have a net worth exceeding $100,000, but 21.3 percent have a net worth of between $10,000 and $100,000. Another 13 percent of us are worth between $5,000 and $10,000, and it is our hope and our belief that AIM will give this last group as well at least a fighting chance at the jackpot: freedom from want and fear. Those are 1969 figures, by the way, and it is certain that the economic disasters of subsequent years have toppled many Americans out of the higher categories. Even in affluent 1988, the richest 10 percent of U.S. families owned 73 percent of the nation's wealth! Today, after three severe stock market debacles, an energy crisis, fulminating inflation, high unemployment figures, corporate and municipal bankruptcies, and a congeries of other economic tribulations, we may well be on our way to becoming a nation of paupers. If that is the case, AIM arrives on the scene not a moment too early.

Still, when all is said and done, are we really serious? Ten thousand dollars, after all, remains a relatively small amount of money to do the kind of job it would have to do to make us wealthy. Social Security filches many times $10,000 from our salaries over a lifetime in order to present us with a couple of $600 checks in our "harvest years" before we are carried offstage to make room for more Social Security *payers.* Ten thousand dollars is such a tiny seed.

But if one plants at the proper time, and harvests at the proper time, a bountiful reward can be ours.

In the test that follows, our hypothetical stock behaves this way every year:

January	$10
February	$ 8
March	$ 5
April	$ 4
May	$ 5
June	$ 8
July	$10
August	$ 8
September	$ 5
October	$ 4
November	$ 5
December	$ 8

The ordinary Lump Sum investor invests his $10,000 in the first January at the price of $10 a share, purchases 1,000 shares, and settles back to watch his money grow, just like the books say. Only at the end of the year, the ordinary investor has a $2,000 loss. The investor using AIM invests $5,000 in the first January at the price of $10 a share and purchases 500 shares. He puts the remaining $5,000 in a bank or money fund—and then switches on his Money Machine.

As the charts on pages 64–71 show, after only seven and a half years, our tiny seed of $10,000 has grown into the mind-blowing sum of one million one hundred seventy-three thousand five hundred and fifty-five dollars—and this in a stock (or portfolio of stocks) that closed at the same price at which it opened! The Lump Sum investor's $10,000 by comparison, has failed to take root. Truly, the Lump Summer—and this would include the majority of investors—has seen his seed fall upon stone.

The AIM investor has become rich. His cash interest alone, should he decide to sell all his stock at this point and deposit the proceeds in his bank account, would bring him about $65,000 a year—even at the rate of 5½ percent! He's set for life.

A legitimate criticism of our results might question the volatile behavior of our stock, or portfolio of stocks, and point out that most securities or portfolios of same do not swing in such wide directions. True enough. On the other hand, our minuscule investment (minuscule in the sense that we are asking it to perform a rather large miracle for us) of $10,000 was purely arbitrary. We could, instead, have invested $20,000, or $50,000, and applied this more reasonable investment to a stock that behaved in a less volatile and more typical manner. Would our results then have been more acceptable? Another very important point to bear in mind is that our stock vehicle did not behave in such a way as to afford AIM its maximum opportunities for trading success: the vehicle regularly dipped to a low of only $4, and AIM was not quite able to make its largest investments at this price. It had to make its major investments at $5 and make do with that opportunity. Denied a lower price than $4, which would have permitted it to make its most aggressive investments at the absolute low, AIM would have wished for at least a repetition of the $4 price so it could make another, although smaller, investment at

AUTOMATIC INVESTMENT MANAGEMENT

FIRST YEAR

$10,000 INVESTMENT

Stock Price	Stock Value	Safe	Cash	Shares Bot(Sold)	Shares Owned	Portfolio Control	Buy(Sell) Advice	Market Order	Interest	Portfolio Value
10	$ 5,000	500	$ 5,000	500	500	$ 5,000	$ —	$ —	$ 22	$ 10,000
8	$ 4,000	400	$ 5,022	75	575	$ 5,300	$ 1,000	$ 600	$ 19	$ 9,022
5	$ 2,875	288	$ 4,441	427	1,002	$ 6,369	$ 2,425	$ 2,137	$ 10	$ 7,316
4	$ 4,008	401	$ 2,314	490	1,492	$ 7,349	$ 2,361	$ 1,960	$ 2	$ 6,322
5	$ 7,460	746	$ 358	0	1,492	$ 7,349	$ 111	$ 0	$ 2	$ 7,816
8	$ 11,936	1194	$ 358	(424)	1,068	$ 7,349	($ 4,587)	$ 3,393	$ 17	$ 12,294
10	$ 10,680	1068	$ 3,768	(226)	842	$ 7,349	($ 3,331)	$ 2,263	$ 27	$ 14,448
8	$ 6,736	674	$ 6,058	0	842	$ 7,349	$ 613	$ 0	$ 27	$ 12,944
5	$ 4,210	421	$ 6,085	544	1,386	$ 8,708	$ 3,139	$ 2,718	$ 15	$ 10,295
4	$ 5,544	554	$ 3,382	653	2,039	$ 10,013	$ 3,164	$ 2,610	$ 3	$ 8,926
5	$ 10,195	1020	$ 775	0	2,039	$ 10,013	($ 182)	$ 0	$ 3	$ 10,970
8	$ 16,312	1631	$ 778	(584)	1,455	$ 10,013	($ 6,299)	($ 4,668)	$ 24	$ 17,090

AIM PROFIT: $7,090.   ORDINARY INVESTOR'S LOSS: ($2,000).

AUTOMATIC INVESTMENT MANAGEMENT

		SECOND YEAR			$10,000 INVESTMENT					
Stock Price	Stock Value	Safe	Cash	Shares Bot(Sold)	Shares Owned	Portfolio Control	Buy(Sell) Advice	Market Order	Interest	Portfolio Value
10	$ 14,550	1455	$ 5,470	(308)	1,147	$ 10,013	($ 4,537)	($ 3,082)	$ 38	$ 20,020
8	$ 9,176	918	$ 8,590	0	1,147	$ 10,013	$ 837	0	$ 38	$ 17,766
5	$ 5,735	574	$ 8,628	741	1,888	$ 11,865	$ 4,278	$ 3,704	$ 22	$ 14,363
4	$ 7,552	755	$ 4,946	890	2,778	$ 13,644	$ 4,313	$ 3,558	$ 6	$ 12,498
5	$ 13,890	1389	$ 1,394	0	2,778	$ 13,644	($ 246)	0	$ 6	$ 15,284
8	$ 22,224	2222	$ 1,400	(795)	1,983	$ 13,644	($ 8,580)	($ 6,358)	$ 34	$ 23,624
10	$ 19,830	1983	$ 7,792	(420)	1,563	$ 13,644	($ 6,186)	($ 4,203)	$ 53	$ 27,622
8	$ 12,504	1250	$ 12,048	0	1,563	$ 13,644	$ 1,140	0	$ 53	$ 24,552
5	$ 7,815	782	$ 12,101	1,009	2,572	$ 16,168	$ 5,829	$ 5,047	$ 31	$ 19,916
4	$ 10,288	1029	$ 7,085	1,213	3,785	$ 18,594	$ 5,880	$ 4,851	$ 10	$ 17,373
5	$ 18,925	1893	$ 2,244	0	3,785	$ 18,594	($ 332)	0	$ 10	$ 21,169
8	$ 30,280	3028	$ 2,254	(1,082)	2,703	$ 18,594	($ 11,686)	($ 8,658)	$ 48	$ 32,534

AIM PROFIT: $22,534.   ORDINARY INVESTOR'S LOSS: ($2,000).

AUTOMATIC INVESTMENT MANAGEMENT

THIRD YEAR **$10,000 INVESTMENT**

Stock Price	Stock Value	Safe	Cash.	Shares Bot(Sold)	Shares Owned	Portfolio Control	Buy(Sell) Advice	Market Order	Interest	Portfolio Value
10	$ 27,030	2703	$ 10,960	(573)	2,130	$ 18,594	($ 8,436)	($ 5,733)	$ 73	$ 37,990
8	$ 17,040	1704	$ 16,766	0	2,130	$ 18,594	$ 1,554	0	$ 74	$ 33,806
5	$ 10,650	1065	$ 16,840	1,376	3,506	$ 22,034	$ 7,944	$ 6,879	$ 44	$ 27,490
4	$ 14,024	1402	$ 10,005	1,652	5,158	$ 25,338	$ 8,010	$ 6,608	$ 15	$ 24,029
5	$ 25,790	2579	$ 3,412	0	5,158	$ 25,338	($ 452)	0	$ 15	$ 29,202
8	$ 41,264	4126	$ 3,427	(1,475)	3,683	$ 25,338	($ 15,926)	($ 11,800)	$ 67	$ 44,691
10	$ 36,830	3683	$ 15,294	(781)	2,902	$ 25,338	($ 11,492)	($ 7,809)	$ 102	$ 52,124
8	$ 23,216	2322	$ 23,205	0	2,902	$ 25,338	$ 2,122	0	$ 102	$ 46,421
5	$ 14,510	1451	$ 23,307	1,875	4,777	$ 30,027	$ 10,828	$ 9,377	$ 61	$ 37,817
4	$ 19,108	1911	$ 13,991	2,252	7,029	$ 34,531	$ 10,919	$ 9,008	$ 22	$ 33,099
5	$ 35,145	3515	$ 5,005	0	7,029	$ 34,531	($ 614)	0	$ 22	$ 40,150
8	$ 56,232	5623	$ 5,027	(2,010)	5,019	$ 34,531	($ 21,701)	($ 16,078)	$ 93	$ 61,259

AIM PROFIT: $51,259.   ORDINARY INVESTOR'S LOSS: ($2,000).

AUTOMATIC INVESTMENT MANAGEMENT

Stock Price	Stock Value	Safe	Cash	Shares Bot(Sold)	Shares Owned	Portfolio Control	Buy(Sell) Advice	Market Order	Interest	Portfolio Value
10	$ 50,190	5019	$ 21,198	(1,064)	3,955	$ 34,531	($ 15,659)	($ 10,640)	$ 140	$ 71,388
8	$ 31,640	3164	$ 31,978	0	3,955	$ 34,531	$ 2,891	0	$ 141	$ 63,618
5	$ 19,775	1978	$ 32,119	2,556	6,511	$ 40,920	$ 14,756	$ 12,778	$ 85	$ 51,894
4	$ 26,044	2604	$ 19,426	3,068	9,579	$ 47,056	$ 14,876	$ 12,272	$ 31	$ 45,470
5	$ 47,895	4790	$ 7,185	0	9,579	$ 47,056	($ 839)	0	$ 32	$ 55,080
8	$ 76,632	7663	$ 7,217	(2,739)	6,840	$ 47,056	($ 29,576)	$ 21,913	$ 128	$ 83,849
10	$ 68,400	6840	$ 29,258	(1,450)	5,390	$ 47,056	($ 21,344)	($ 14,504)	$ 193	$ 97,658
8	$ 43,120	4312	$ 43,955	0	5,390	$ 47,056	$ 3,936	0	$ 193	$ 87,075
5	$ 26,950	2695	$ 44,148	3,482	8,872	$ 55,762	$ 20,106	$ 17,411	$ 118	$ 71,098
4	$ 35,488	3549	$ 26,855	4,181	13,053	$ 64,125	$ 20,274	$ 16,725	$ 45	$ 62,343
5	$ 65,265	6527	$ 10,175	0	13,053	$ 64,125	($ 1,140)	0	$ 45	$ 75,440
8	$ 104,424	10442	$ 10,220	(3,732)	9,321	$ 64,125	($ 40,299)	($ 29,857)	$ 176	$ 114,644

AIM PROFIT: $104,644.   ORDINARY INVESTOR'S LOSS: ($2,000).

AUTOMATIC INVESTMENT MANAGEMENT

| $10,000 INVESTMENT

Stock Price	Stock Value	Safe	Cash	Shares Bot(Sold)	Shares Owned	Portfolio Control	Buy(Sell) Advice	Market Order	Interest	Portfolio Value
10	$ 93,210	9321	$ 40,253	(1,976)	7,345	$ 64,125	($ 29,085)	($ 19,764)	$ 264	$ 133,463
8	$ 58,760	5876	$ 60,281	0	7,345	$ 64,125	$ 5,365	0	$ 265	$ 119,041
5	$ 36,725	3673	$ 60,546	4,745	12,090	$ 75,989	$ 27,400	$ 23,727	$ 162	$ 97,271
4	$ 48,362	4836	$ 36,981	5,698	17,788	$ 87,385	$ 27,627	$ 22,791	$ 62	$ 85,343
5	$ 88,939	8894	$ 14,252	0	17,788	$ 87,385	($ 1,554)	0	$ 63	$ 103,191
8	$ 142,304	14230	$ 14,315	(5,086)	12,702	$ 87,385	$ 54,919	$ 40,689	$ 242	$ 156,619
10	$ 127,020	12702	$ 55,246	(2,693)	10,009	$ 87,385	$ 39,635	($ 26,933)	$ 362	$ 182,266
8	$ 80,072	8007	$ 82,541	0	10,009	$ 87,385	$ 7,313	0	$ 363	$ 162,613
8	$ 50,045	5005	$ 82,904	6,467	16,476	$ 103,553	$ 37,340	$ 32,335	$ 223	$ 132,949
4	$ 65,904	6590	$ 50,792	7,765	24,241	$ 119,083	$ 37,649	$ 31,059	$ 223	$ 116,696
5	$ 121,205	12121	$ 19,820	0	24,241	$ 119,083	($ 2,122)	0	$ 87	$ 141,025
8	$ 193,928	19393	$ 19,907	(6,932)	17,310	$ 119,083	($ 74,845)	($ 55,452)	$ 332	$ 213,835

AIM PROFIT: $203,835.   ORDINARY INVESTOR'S LOSS: ($2,000).

AUTOMATIC INVESTMENT MANAGEMENT

$10,000 Investment

Stock Price	Stock Value	Safe	Cash	Shares Bot(Sold)	Shares Owned	Portfolio Control	Buy(Sell) Advice	Market Order	Interest	Portfolio Value
10	$173,100	17310	$ 75,691	(3,671)	13,639	$119,083	($ 54,017)	($ 36,707)	$ 495	$ 248,791
8	$109,112	10911	$112,893	0	13,639	$119,083	$ 9,971	0	$ 497	$ 222,005
5	$ 68,195	6820	$113,390	8,814	22,453	$141,117	$ 50,888	$ 44,068	$ 305	$ 181,585
4	$ 89,812	8981	$ 69,627	10,581	33,034	$152,279	$ 51,305	$ 42,324	$ 120	$ 159,439
5	$165,170	16517	$ 27,423	0	33,034	$152,279	($ 2,891)	0	$ 121	$ 192,593
8	$264,272	26427	$ 27,544	(9,446)	23,588	$152,279	($101,993)	($ 75,566)	$ 454	$ 291,816
10	$235,880	23588	$103,564	(5,001)	18,587	$162,279	($ 73,601)	($ 50,013)	$ 676	$ 339,444
8	$148,696	14870	$154,253	0	18,587	$162,279	$ 13,583	0	$ 679	$ 302,949
5	$ 92,935	9294	$154,932	12,010	30,597	$192,304	$ 69,344	$ 60,050	$ 417	$ 247,867
4	$122,388	12239	$ 95,299	14,419	45,016	$221,143	$ 69,916	$ 57,677	$ 166	$ 217,687
5	$225,080	22508	$ 37,788	0	45,016	$221,143	($ 3,937)	0	$ 166	$ 262,868
8	$360,128	36013	$ 37,954	(12,872)	32,145	$221,143	($138,985)	($102,972)	$ 620	$ 398,082

AIM PROFIT: $388,082.   ORDINARY INVESTOR'S LOSS: ($2,000).

AUTOMATIC INVESTMENT MANAGEMENT

SEVENTH YEAR $10,000 INVESTMENT

Stock Price	Stock Value	Safe	Cash	Shares Bot(Sold)	Shares Owned	Portfolio Control	Buy/Sell Advice	Market Order	Interest	Portfolio Value
10	$321,450	32145	$141,546	(6,816)	25,329	$221,143	($100,307)	($68,162)	$923	$462,996
8	$202,632	20263	$210,631	0	25,329	$221,143	$18,511	0	$927	$413,263
5	$126,645	12665	$211,558	16,367	41,696	$262,060	$94,498	$81,833	$571	$338,203
4	$166,784	16678	$130,296	19,650	61,346	$301,359	$95,276	$78,598	$227	$297,080
5	$306,730	30673	$51,925	0	61,346	$301,359	($5,371)	0	$228	$358,655
8	$490,768	49077	$52,153	(17,542)	43,805	$301,359	($189,409)	($140,332)	$847	$542,921
10	$438,050	43805	$193,332	(9,289)	34,516	$301,359	($136,691)	($92,886)	$1259	$631,382
8	$276,128	27613	$287,477	0	34,516	$301,359	$25,231	0	$1265	$563,605
5	$172,580	17258	$288,742	22,304	56,820	$357,120	$128,779	$111,521	$780	$461,322
4	$227,280	22728	$178,001	26,778	83,598	$410,676	$129,840	$107,112	$312	$405,281
5	$417,990	41799	$71,201	0	83,598	$410,676	($7,314)	0	$313	$489,191
8	$688,784	68878	$71,514	(23,904)	59,694	$410,676	($258,108)	($191,230)	$1156	$760,298

AIM PROFIT: $730,298.   ORDINARY INVESTOR'S LOSS: ($2,000).

AUTOMATIC INVESTMENT MANAGEMENT

EIGHTH YEAR $10,000 INVESTMENT

Stock Price	Stock Value	Safe	Cash	Shares Bot(Sold)	Shares Owned	Portfolio Control	Buy(Sell) Advice	Market Order	Interest	Portfolio Value
10	$596,940	59694	$263,900	(12,657)	47,037	$410,676	($ 186,264)	($ 126,570)	$ 1718	$ 860,840
8	$376,296	37630	$392,188	0	47,037	$410,676	$ 34,380	0	$ 1726	$ 768,484
5	$235,185	23519	$393,914	30,394	77,431	$486,662	$ 175,491	$ 151,972	$ 1065	$ 629,099
4	$309,724	30972	$243,007	36,492	113,923	$559,645	$ 176,938	$ 145,966	$ 427	$ 552,731
5	$569,615	56962	$ 97,468	0	113,923	$559,645	($ 9,970)	0	$ 429	$ 667,083
8	$911,384	91138	$ 97,897	(32,575)	81,348	$559,645	($ 351,739)	($ 260,601)	$ 1577	$1,009,281
10	$813,480	81348	$360,075		81,348	$559,645				$1,173,555

FINAL AIM PROFIT: $1,163,555.   ORDINARY INVESTOR'S PROFIT: 0.

that level. Stocks aren't always moving up or down, AIM would chide us.

Or, lacking a repetition of the $4 price, AIM would have preferred that we reconstruct the chart to make $5 the low—and immediately repeat *that* price to enable it to pump its brakes and make an additional investment at $5. After all, AIM would argue, it would be more typical not only for $5 to represent the low, but for the low price to repeat at least once before the market decided to begin its upward climb. There's no pleasing everyone.

We might have used a less nervous stock and extended the time frame to ten years or more. Or we might have assumed a higher interest rate on our cash reserves: money funds could easily have done this for us. Either technique would have worked to our benefit and helped compensate for a more sluggish stock portfolio. The experienced investor, however, will recognize the test for what it is—not an exhibit of how simple it is to make a million with AIM, but proof that AIM *can* achieve super-spectacular results in situations where other investment approaches cannot even get off the ground, and proof that Automatic Investment Management functions well and dependably no matter how severely it is buffeted and torn by Wall Street turmoil. In the first year alone, at the first $4 price, the Lump Sum investor had lost $6,000, 60 percent of his capital, within four months. His $10,000 was now worth only $4,000. AIM held *its* loss to a slender $3,678—37 percent. Six months later, when the $4 price came around again, the Lump Sum investor was again down $6,000, or 60-percent loss. But the hustling AIM investor, anticipating the off-tackle play, made a quick adjustment and met the ball-carrier with a jarring tackle, yielding a loss of only $1,074—11 percent. And that was the last time, the very last time, that AIM was ever to show a loss. The Lump Sum investor was forced to continue his dreary round of 60-percent losses twice every year for the remainder of the game.

Yes, we know you still have many questions. Suppose the stock had gone up, instead of down? And had gone straight up? Wouldn't the Lump Sum investor have made his million, and wouldn't the AIM investor have had to settle for a paltry few hundred thousand dollars? That reminds us of the minister telling his parishioners, "Every member of this congregation is going to die someday, much as you hate to think about it, so it behooves you all to live your lives accordingly." During the course of the sermon, the minister noticed one man chuckling. Afterwards he took the man aside and asked the reason for his unseemly mirth, in view of the sober topic of the sermon. "The joke's on you, Reverend," the man laughed. "I'm not a member of this congregation."

AIM will laugh, too, if you assume such a performance of a stock. For in order for the Lump Sum investor to make his million dollars—just a million, not the larger sum that AIM earned—that $10 stock would have to soar to the astronomical price of $1,010 per share! Viewed another way, it's a $50 stock that must take an outer-space trip to a planet called $5,050-A-Share!

In this era of cheap psychedelia, only a complex mind could entertain a hallucination of such ethereal splendor. If you can do it, you have our sincerest compliments and admiration.

Let's do look at a stock that rises 50 percent first, then plummets to a price 50 percent below its original. This is not so far-fetched at all these days: in late 1974 we saw some stocks fall 20 percent and even 40 percent in a single session! For the fainthearted among us, though, we will assume that these are quarterly prices, and that we are receiving 6 percent per annum from our bank on our cash reserves, an effective rate obtainable in the mid-seventies on 90-day money.

Our hypothetical chart (page 75) is once again a well-known one that has been used in the past to illustrate the superiority of systematic investing over Lump Sum investing. Again AIM is matched against an ordinary Lump Sum investor who makes no profit whatever on his investment. If AIM could show a profit of only $1 at the conclusion of the program, how would we measure the margin of AIM's superiority over the Lump Sum investor? Has AIM done 100 percent better? A thousand percent better? Ten thousand percent? We will leave the reckoning to the metaphysicians. If you look at the chart, the plain fact is that AIM not only piled up an astonishing profit of $4,693—a 47 percent increase—in a stock now selling at its original price, but has gathered to its bosom 74 additional shares!

Yet the purpose of this chart is not to kick sand in the Lump Summer's face again, but to draw the reader's attention to the remarkable way in which AIM takes advantage of rising as well as falling prices, and how it protects its profits on the way down. Here is a stock that initially rose from $10 to $15 per share, an increase of 50 percent. At this level, the Lump Summer is gloating over a profit of $5,000. AIM, on the other hand, has a profit of only $2,722. The important thing here is that the Lump Summer's profit is reflected entirely in his stock, while AIM has been busily converting its profits into cash all along. When the price of the stock reached $15 per share, AIM had a cozy $6,722 in cash. After selling $400 more worth of stock at this price, AIM's CASH balance amounted to $7,122. In view of the strong rise the stock has already experienced, the wisdom of AIM's precaution is self-evident. An investor who is 100 percent invested after a 50-percent rise in the stock market probably short-sells U.S. savings bonds on the side. But our shrewd Money Machine has moved heavily to the cash side. It *knows* you aren't likely to get rich in a rising stock *per se*. It *knows* that you *can* get rich by buying and selling stocks—using the profits (other people's money) to energize your performance. And it therefore willingly surrenders a portion of the short-term profits available on the upside to the fully invested Lump Sum investor.

Now observe what happens when the stock slides back

AUTOMATIC INVESTMENT MANAGEMENT

$10,000 Investment

Stock Price	Stock Value	Safe	Cash	Shares Bot(Sold)	Shares Owned	Portfolio Control	Buy(Sell) Advice	Market Order	Interest	Portfolio Value
10	$ 5,000	500	$ 5,000		500	$ 5,000	—	—	$ 75	$ 10,000
11	$ 5,500	550	$ 5,075	0	500	$ 5,000	($ 500)	0	$ 76	$ 10,575
12	$ 6,000	600	$ 5,151	(33)	467	$ 5,000	($ 1,000)	($ 400)	$ 83	$ 11,151
13	$ 6,071	607	$ 5,634	(36)	431	$ 5,000	($ 1,071)	($ 464)	$ 91	$ 11,705
14	$ 6,038	604	$ 6,189	(31)	400	$ 5,000	($ 1,038)	($ 434)	$ 99	$ 12,227
15	$ 6,000	600	$ 6,722	(27)	373	$ 5,000	($ 1,000)	($ 400)	$ 107	$ 12,722
14	$ 5,222	522	$ 7,229	0	373	$ 5,000	($ 222)	0	$ 108	$ 12,451
13	$ 4,849	485	$ 7,337	0	373	$ 5,000	$ 151	0	$ 110	$ 12,186
12	$ 4,476	448	$ 7,447	0	373	$ 5,000	$ 524	0	$ 112	$ 11,923
11	$ 4,103	410	$ 7,559	44	417	$ 5,244	$ 897	$ 487	$ 106	$ 11,662
10	$ 4,170	417	$ 7,178	66	483	$ 5,573	$ 1,074	$ 657	$ 98	$ 11,348
9	$ 4,347	435	$ 6,619	88	571	$ 5,969	$ 1,226	$ 791	$ 87	$ 10,966
8	$ 4,568	457	$ 5,915	118	689	$ 6,441	$ 1,401	$ 944	$ 75	$ 10,483
7	$ 4,823	482	$ 5,046	162	851	$ 7,009	$ 1,618	$ 1,136	$ 59	$ 9,869
6	$ 5,106	511	$ 3,969	232	1,083	$ 7,705	$ 1,903	$ 1,392	$ 39	$ 9,075
5	$ 5,415	542	$ 2,616	350	1,433	$ 8,579	$ 2,290	$ 1,748	$ 13	$ 8,031
6	$ 8,598	860	$ 881	0	1,433	$ 8,579	$ 19	0	$ 13	$ 9,479
7	$ 10,031	1003	$ 894	(64)	1,369	$ 8,579	($ 1,452)	($ 449)	$ 20	$ 10,925
8	$ 10,952	1095	$ 1,363	(160)	1,209	$ 8,579	($ 2,373)	($ 1,278)	$ 40	$ 12,315
9	$ 10,881	1088	$ 2,681	(135)	1,074	$ 8,579	($ 2,302)	($ 1,214)	$ 58	$ 13,562
10	$ 10,740	1074	$ 3,953		1,074					$ 14,693

AIM INVESTOR		LUMP SUM INVESTOR	
TOTAL VALUE:	$14,693		$10,000
PROFIT:	$4,693		0
% PROFIT:	47%		0
SHARES:	1,074		1,000

down to $10. The ordinary investor, totally at the mercy of the market, has been relieved of every cent of his profits. This is where he came in.

AIM? AIM is over there biting the shekels to make sure they're genuine—*because it is still sitting on a profit of $1,348!*

Only at $7 a share, a price that is 53 percent below the peak price of $15, did AIM see its last dollar in profits evaporate. The Lump Summer, meanwhile, is staring bleakly at a portfolio that is beginning to look like a turkey after Thanksgiving dinner. He has already lost $3,000, or 30 percent.

Down goes the stock to a bottom of $5 a share, ripping another $2,000 drumstick off the Lump Sum investor and leaving him with only half of his original turkey.

AIM, making its very largest investment at the absolute low, quickly checks the damage done to its own portfolio after this horrendous 67-percent slide and finds that *it has lost less than 20 percent of its power!* It is listing slightly and the skipper calls for ballast. AIM promptly supplies the ballast, in the form of crates of extra stock it has purchased during the storm. Because now, when we need all the weight we can get, *AIM is 43 percent heavier than the Lump Summer!* It owns 433 more shares!

Eventually, the storm subsides and the stock recovers to the price of $7. AIM is below deck in the counting-house, totting up a profit of $925—9¼ percent.

That tiny, almost invisible speck aft on the horizon, bound for Breakeven Island with a cargo of outdated investment philosophies aboard and her navigator in irons, is the good ship Lump Summer, her Plimsoll mark still 30 percent below the surface . . . and her captain walking the plank.

At the base of your Money Machine you will see two golden drawers, both locked. Individual keys are supplied with each unit. The top drawer contains securities. When you buy or sell stock, you must, of course, unlock this drawer and deposit or remove stock certificates.

(Please forgive a weary inventor's flights of fancy. This is all imaginary, of course!)

The bottom drawer you will rarely use, if ever. It contains mutual fund capital gains distributions. There will be investors who will use AIM to acquire one or more mutual funds. When funds declare capital gains distributions—and these can be quite large in bull markets—AIM disgorges the money down a chute and it ends up in this drawer. If you need this money to live on, you may unlock the drawer and take it out provided you make a simple adjustment in AIM's mechanism. Please adjust your PORTFOLIO CONTROL as follows: Subtract from PORTFOLIO CONTROL the amount of money you have taken out.

If you do not need capital gains distributions to live on, kindly do not touch the drawer. AIM's self-regulating mechanism will automatically remove the money from the drawer and feed it back into the market. No adjustments whatever are necessary. (In other words, if you are having your capital gains reinvested, do nothing!)

On the right side of your Money Machine you will see a slot about three inches wide. Deposit in this slot any additional monies you may wish to add to your investment program from time to time—a Christmas bonus, an inheritance, "found" money of any kind for which you will have no foreseeable need. Simply feed the bills into the slot provided, give your Money Machine a friendly pat or two for good luck, and go about your business. AIM will make good use of the money, of that you can be sure. Before you do so, however, please alert AIM to what's going on. It hates surprises. First, invest half of your new money in the stock market and deposit the other half in your bank account or money fund. Increase your PORTFOLIO CONTROL by the amount of money you have just invested in stock.

These adjustments to PORTFOLIO CONTROL when adding or subtracting funds serve to alert SAFE that you have increased or decreased speed. SAFE will then automatically amend future orders to compensate for the difference. If you do not intend to deposit new money or accept mutual fund capital gains distributions in cash, these instructions may be conveniently ignored.

Here's how simple it is to add new money to your AIM program. The last line on your record sheet might look like this:

1 Stock Value	2 Safe	3 Cash	4 Portfolio Control	5 Buy(Sell) Advice	6 Market Order	7 Portfolio Value
$16,000	1600	$8,000	$16,000	0	0	$24,000

You receive a $3,000 bonus from your job and wish to add it to your AIM program. Put half of it, $1,500, into stocks. (There is no need to wait until your regular investment date to do this. Anytime is a good time.) Your new STOCK VALUE increases to $17,500.

1 Stock Value	2 Safe	3 Cash	4 Portfolio Control	5 Buy(Sell) Advice	6 Market Order	7 Portfolio Value
$16,000	1600	$8,000	$16,000	0	0	$24,000
$17,500	1750					

Put the other half of your bonus, $1,500, into your AIM cash account. Your CASH balance naturally increases to $9,500.

1 Stock Value	2 Safe	3 Cash	4 Portfolio Control	5 Buy(Sell) Advice	6 Market Order	7 Portfolio Value
$16,000	1600	$8,000	$16,000	0	0	$24,000
$17,500	1750	$9,500				$27,000

Finally, increase your PORTFOLIO CONTROL by the amount you have just invested in stock—in this case, $1,500. Your PORTFOLIO CONTROL will now jump from $16,000 to $17,500 to reflect the additional stock you bought:

1 Stock Value	2 Safe	3 Cash	4 Portfolio Control	5 Buy(Sell) Advice	6 Market Order	7 Portfolio Value
$16,000	1600	$8,000	$16,000	0	0	$24,000
$17,500	1750	$9,500	$17,500	(3,000 added)		$27,000

That's the way your record sheet will look.

You will note that although AIM grudgingly allowed you to invest half of your bonus immediately in stocks, AIM and AIM alone will decide when to invest the other half. And you can be very sure it will be the *right* time. This feature alone will keep the average investor from making a critical mistake with his sudden windfall by rushing out and investing *all* of it in stocks—at the very peak of the market!

Automatic Investment Management represents a radical departure from conventional investment techniques. Whereas previous ill-fated approaches have emphasized evaluation and selection of securities, with all the attendant mystique, we are concerned not so much with what to buy as how to buy and sell it. Of what use is a stock that appreciates 50 percent if we also own a stock that depreciates by the same amount? Do we cut our losses and let our profits run, as some would have us do? Or do we cut our profits and let our losses run, as others would have us do, while buying more of the losing stock? Or perhaps we should buy more of the rising stock, since that is doing so well for us. And, since we have no ready cash at the moment, how about selling our losing stock and using those proceeds for our purpose? But if we buy more of a rising stock at dearer prices, we will be raising our overall cost per share. And if the stock should start tumbling, we will own more shares and our loss will be ever so much greater. We are forever chasing our own tail, and our comical performance is applauded by the men who make those numbers dance.

"Buy the good stuff and put them away," most of

them advise us with a straight face. "Time. It takes time. Lock them up and forget them. Time is the whole thing."

Well, time is not the whole thing. One's *position* in time is the whole thing. The really big fortunes have already been made in "the good stuff"—by the folks who were in the right *position* in time, by the founders and relatives of founders and friends of the founders of our corporate giants today. An 18-year-old *might* do fairly well by buying "the good stuff" even now and locking it up for 40 or 50 years, but a 40-year-old or 50-year-old who buys the good stuff for the long pull will probably *not* do very well. He is at the wrong position in time, much like the drunk who called a tavern owner at his home at five in the morning and mumbled, "Time does your bar open?" The owner shouted, "Ten o'clock!" and slammed down the phone. An hour later the phone rang again. "Time does your bar open?" came the slurred voice. "I told you ten o'clock!" the tavern owner yelled. "Nobody gets in before ten!" "Don't wanna get in," the drunk muttered. "Wanna get out."

It's all a question of where you *are* in time.

AIM deals with numbers, whether those numbers are generated by IBM, General Motors, or the company that has sold a billion burgers coast to coast and used a whole pound of ground beef. AIM does not deal with human emotion. You cannot persuade it, con it, or give it any advice whatever. It and it alone will be the arbiter. It will call all the signals and run all the plays. It has no fear. The word "greed" does not compute. Many an impatient owner, driven to frantic nail-biting by AIM's large cash balance at what *seems* to be the very bottom of the market, will shake his Money Machine violently in an attempt to dislodge some of that lucre and funnel it into stocks before the market starts going back up. Such a move betrays pathetic but understandable ignorance of AIM's goals. In the first place, preservation of capital is AIM's primary responsibility; please do not ask AIM to violate that responsibility. And in the second place, AIM can do very well, amazingly well, by investing only a *little* at what now appear to be bargain prices—more "bang" for the buck! It might surprise you to discover how well it can do by nibbling a bit and browsing a lot while it moves from counter to counter and skeptically examines the various markdowns. The real bargains, AIM knows, are in the basement. *That's* where it hauls out its purse and begins gobbling. Now, the elevator isn't always on its way down to the basement, but sooner or later somebody will push the button and down it will go. At that time, AIM will jump aboard and you will be very happy you waited. And then you will understand what a supreme gift patience is.

We've programmed AIM to speak three words and three words only. It will speak them only when its owner, after all that has happened and still believing that he can do better on his own, picks it up, carries it down to the cellar, and stores it among his old income tax records, each showing unbelievable capital losses.

The three words are: "Lots of luck."

SEVEN

The Money Machine in Action

Earlier we noted that there is only one way in which the ordinary fully invested Lump Sum investor can outperform Automatic Investment Management, and that is by *somehow* selecting a stock or a portfolio of stocks that goes up and keeps going up without looking back—and does so with a velocity sufficient to offset the often superior interest AIM is earning on its CASH balance in the bank or in a money fund. Admittedly, this is a likelihood we would place roughly on a par with our setting aside another six years in which to labor full-time on yet another investment system. Not hardly. But there nevertheless have been exhilarating periods in financial history during which the market as a whole has moved relentlessly upward, dragging with it not only most of the dogs on the American Stock Exchange but the Over-the-Counter confederacy as well, which, as you know, consumes more Red Heart than the K-9 Corps. At such times are the go-go gurus born, stockbrokers are elevated to sainthood, and investment advisors lead their procession of followers skyward into clouds of glory. Even the amateur steps up to the plate, swings, and connects on the very first pitch!

Such heady times occasionally recur. Then suddenly, cynicism and disbelief come to dwell among us as house guests, and, well, they just feel *comfortable* here. They might just stay awhile. And yet, as Jules Simon observed so many years ago, "In reality, history is of no avail. Humanity is caught every day with traps that have served before." At this very moment, someone, somewhere, is developing an irresistible pitch that will relieve the *next* generation of *its* painfully acquired nest egg.

We look backward to illustrate the kind of feverish market we mean and superimpose over it the enviable record of a large speculative investment company, Rowe Price New Horizons Fund, the frisky sprinter out of the T. Rowe Price stables in Baltimore. In January of 1966, the month-end price per share of New Horizons was $4.64. (See charts on pages 88–97.) In succeeding months and years, New Horizons galloped up to $11.17 in November of 1968, skidded to $6.10 in the mud puddles of June, 1970, and then, under the whip, drove to an astonishing $15.36 at its peak in May of 1972. One or two mutual funds may have done even better in this giddy market, but alas, letters to them are now returned stamped ADDRESSEE UNKNOWN. *De mortuis nil nisi bonum.* New Horizons survived because it sniffed suspicious fumes and decided to pull over for a pit stop; its management voted to suspend sales to new shareholders in the best interest of existing shareholders. To have invested an avalanche of new money into stocks already near their exploding point would have proved disastrous—as it did to some other funds.

My favorite quarterly report from one go-go mutual fund that broke apart and sank was, if memory serves, its last. It appeared to have been spoken by Humphrey Bogart as Captain Queeg at his court-martial, and it went something like this: "As you can see, I have now taken over as portfolio manager of your fund. The former portfolio manager has been dismissed. He was a young fellow, and he came here with impeccable credentials, that's true. Marvelous background. And he did fine, fine, when the seas were calm and the sailing easy. Oh, yes, he did fine then. All those young fellows, wet behind the ears, don't even have their sea legs yet, they do fine when the sailing is easy. In a calm sea, everybody is a pilot. I tried to tell him, I tried many times to warn him. I said, 'Don't buy that junk. What you're buying is junk, *junk!*' But he wouldn't listen. Not him. He knew it all.

"And then, the seas grew angry. The waves crashed

around us. We were taking on water. We were up to
our scuppers. I—I grabbed the wheel, tried to take it
away from him. 'Don't you see where you're going?' I
shouted. I shouted at him, 'You're heading for the rocks.
Bring her around!' But he wouldn't listen. Not him. So
I said to him, 'Mister, I am relieving you from command
of this ship!' And I did. I took command. I brought her
under control. I hove to. Yes, there was a good deal of
damage to our vessel, and I apologize for that. But from
here on in, I'll be the skipper, and now here's what I
propose to do . . .''

Altogether, it was the most extraordinary quarterly
report I have ever received. And it was almost worth
losing half of my investment to get it. Bogey would have
loved it.

But New Horizons cruised through the tempest of
1970 without a hint of mutiny and ended up safely in
port in May, 1972. The Lump Sum investor who boarded
with $10,000 worth of stock in January of 1966 was now
worth $33,101, excluding dividends and capital gains dis-
tributions. AIM, by contrast, had gone heavily into cash
at this point—a two to one ratio of cash to stock—with
a net worth of $21,860, excluding dividends and capital
gains distributions. Clearly this is a victory for the fully
invested Lump Summer and a vindication of the theory
of long-term, lock-'em-up-and-forget-'em investing. Or
is it?

Unfortunately, no mythical wizard was around in May
of 1972 to pull the Lump Summer's lapel with the advice
that $15.36 was to be the finish line of this particular
race and that he should get off the track now and walk
around a bit to cool himself off slowly to avoid coming
down with something. Only a year and a month later, in
June of 1973, when the Lump Summer reached over to
fondle his treasure, it had shrunk to only $19,050! When
AIM yawned, stretched, and reached over to fondle *its*
treasure, the pile had so little decreased that the difference was hardly noticeable: it was worth $19,318.

At a price that was still nearly double the original price *of $4.64, Automatic Investment Management, with most of its assets in cash, was running ahead of the fully invested Lump Sum investor!*

In the catastrophic months that followed, of course, it was no contest. Lump Summer nosedived to a jolting crunch at the price of $4.60 in September of 1974. Where once had stood a mighty edifice of $33,101, we perceive dimly through the dust a lean-to valued at $9,913. AIM, with a portfolio holding fast at $14,477, pulls back the curtain, peers at the dismal cold rain outside, and goes back to sleep. Not time to get up yet.

At the end of 1975, fully ten years after the race began, our saga ends and we regretfully close our storybook. The Lump Summer, with a portfolio valued at only $14,352, dreams of the past. AIM, having doubled *its* investment despite the fact that the stock is up only 44 percent from its original, looks hopefully and confidently toward the future. Come what may, AIM will be ready for it.

Defenders of our new AIM religion may rise in protest over this chart and complain bitterly that we have stacked the deck against the Money Machine. Their objections might run something like this: "When all is said and done, given the hypothetical situation you chose to use, Lump Sum investing was the *best method known* for achieving capital gains in a steadily rising market. You not only selected the very top performing mutual fund of all, you not only picked a hysterical, go-for-broke investment period the likes of which we shall probably never see again in our lifetime, but you also matched AIM against some guy who had the incredible luck to plunk down his entire $10,000 at a price that virtually turned out to be the *low* for the whole decade! The stock never went more than 4¢ lower than when he bought it! Who is this mythical genius of yours that you call a Lump Summer? Most investors aren't Lump Summers. The average conventional investor is a 'Hit-or-Misser.' He may buy some today, buy some two months from now, buy again next year and sell in between. And he is far more likely to have bought at the *highs* than at the low *you* pretend he bought at. Why, at the very top of the market, frantic investors were shoveling hundreds of millions of dollars into their mutual fund investments. Many funds couldn't even handle it. They didn't know what the hell to *invest* it in! Especially the go-gos. They'd already bought all the volatile stock around. What were they supposed to do with the new money— buy AT&T? Why don't you compare AIM with the *average* investor who started getting excited about stocks when the New Horizon Fund price was dancing at $10 a share or $12 a share, and especially $15 a share? *That's* when the average investor rushes into the market. And when the price cratered at $4.60 in 1974, your *average* investor was sitting on losses up to 70 percent. Lots of stocks and funds dropped even worse, and many never came back. So your average Hit-or-Miss investor was chopped off at the knees down there. He didn't lose just a hundred bucks or so like your Lump Summer who just happened to buy at the low back there in 1966. He was in there buying and selling and losing all the way up and all the way down. AIM was in there buying and selling the whole ten years and *never* showed a loss! Who do you know who did that? Who do you know besides AIM who held onto a 45 percent profit at the absolute bottom of the market?"

The point's well taken, but there are no figures available showing what the *average* investor did in that decade. We merely wanted to compare what the *best* conventional investor did in the *best* mutual fund. Otherwise, our figures dealing with an "average" result might be open to question. In a way, we are retelling the fable of the tortoise and the hare. And the fact that AIM, the tortoise, wins the race is not as important here as the lesson to be drawn from *how* it won. And the following charts tell the whole story.

As for AIM's final profit, there are two ways you can look at it when comparing it with that of the fully invested Lump Summer: as a percentage of AIM's total original outlay, or as a percentage of the present actual cash outlay from AIM's pocket. In the New Horizons chart, AIM's original investment of $10,000 is now worth twice as much. AIM has a profit of 100 percent. But another way of stating the profit percentage is this: Since AIM presently has $7,312 in its CASH balance, it has actually invested only $2,688 in stock of its original $10,000 ($10,000 less $7,312). But that $2,688 in stock is now worth $12,641—yielding AIM a profit of nearly 400 percent!

We use and prefer the first method because at one point in the charts, AIM held a CASH balance of $15,262—a sum substantially larger than its original nest egg! It also owned several thousands of dollars worth of stock. Since, as a matter of obvious fact, AIM got all its cash back and then some, it had not really laid out a single penny for investment purposes. It would be impossible to calculate the percentage of profit AIM had earned on its investment at this point if we insisted on using the alternate method of calculation, for the simple reason that AIM has not *made* any investment! It has its original cash back—in spades. The stock—well, consider that a gift from Uncle Harry or somebody.

Try telling that to the IRS.

To return to the charts, it might surprise you to learn that although AIM, at the conclusion of the ten-year period, has chosen to hold fewer shares than the Lump Summer's 2,155 shares, the price of the stock must now rise to about $9.50 a share before the Lump Summer can draw abreast of AIM in total worth! If your aim is true, a few shots *at the right time* are all you need to get the job done. But unless the price of New Horizons really hustles to that $9.50 level, AIM will maintain its lead all the way up—because of the interest it is earning on its almost obscenely large CASH balance!*

*New Horizons did not make it back to $9.50 until late 1978, allowing AIM to increase its lead relentlessly.

AUTOMATIC INVESTMENT MANAGEMENT

ROWE PRICE NEW HORIZONS FUND 1966–1975, $10,000 INVESTMENT

YEAR 1—1966

Date	Stock Price	Stock Value	Safe	Cash*	Shares Bot(Sold)	Shares Owned	Portfolio Control	Buy(Sell) Advice	Market Order	Portfolio Value
1/66	4.64	5000	500	5000	0	1078	5000		0	$10,000
2/66	4.72	5088	509	5022	0	1078	5000	(88)	0	10,110
3/66	4.67	5034	503	5044	0	1078	5000	(34)	0	10,078
4/66	4.93	5315	532	5066	0	1078	5000	(315)	0	10,381
5/66	4.67	5034	503	5088	0	1078	5000	(34)	0	10,122
6/66	4.80	5174	517	5110	0	1078	5000	(174)	0	10,284
7/66	4.84	5218	522	5132	0	1078	5000	(218)	0	10,350
8/66	4.58	4937	494	5155	0	1078	5000	63	0	10,092
9/66	4.60	4959	496	5178	0	1078	5000	41	0	10,137
10/66	4.49	4840	484	5201	0	1078	5000	160	0	10,041
11/66	5.07	5465	547	5224	0	1078	5000	(465)	0	10,689
12/66	5.10	5498	550	5247	0	1078	5000	(498)	0	10,745

FIRST YEAR RESULTS
AIM: $745 PROFIT
LUMP SUM INVESTOR: $991 PROFIT

*Interest on CASH Balance: 5¼% per annum.

88

Date	Stock Price	Stock Value	Safe	Cash	Shares Bot(Sold)	Shares Owned	Portfolio Control	Buy(Sell) Advice	Market Order	Portfolio Value
1/67	5.72	6166	617	5270	(96)	982	5000	(1166)	(549)	$11,436
2/67	6.03	5921	592	5845	(55)	927	5000	(921)	(329)	11,766
3/67	6.51	6035	604	6201	(66)	861	5000	(1035)	(431)	12,236
4/67	6.98	6010	601	6661	(59)	802	5000	(1010)	(409)	12,671
5/67	6.84	5486	549	7101	0	802	5000	(486)	0	12,587
6/67	7.42	5951	595	7132	(48)	754	5000	(951)	(356)	13,083
7/67	7.94	5987	599	7521	(49)	705	5000	(987)	(388)	13,508
8/67	7.91	5577	558	7944	0	705	5000	(577)	0	13,521
9/67	8.61	6070	607	7979	(54)	651	5000	(1070)	(463)	14,049
10/67	8.60	5599	560	8479	0	651	5000	(599)	0	14,078
11/67	8.94	5820	582	8516	(27)	624	5000	(820)	(238)	14,336
12/67	8.99	5610	561	8793	0	624	5000	(610)	0	14,403

SECOND YEAR RESULTS
AIM: $4,403 PROFIT
LUMP SUM INVESTOR: $9,373 PROFIT

YEAR 3—1968

Date	Stock Price	Stock Value	Safe	Cash	Shares Bot(Sold)	Shares Owned	Portfolio Control	Buy(Sell) Advice	Market Order	Portfolio Value
1/68	8.46	5279	528	8832	0	624	5000	(279)	0	$14,111
2/68	7.93	4948	495	8871	0	624	5000	52	0	13,819
3/68	8.00	4992	499	8910	0	624	5000	8	0	13,902
4/68	9.33	5822	582	8949	(26)	598	5000	(822)	(240)	14,771
5/68	9.96	5956	596	9229	(36)	562	5000	(956)	(360)	15,185
6/68	9.90	5564	556	9631	0	562	5000	(564)	0	15,195
7/68	9.42	5294	529	9673	0	562	5000	(294)	0	14,967
8/68	9.90	5564	556	9716	0	562	5000	(564)	0	15,280
9/68	10.50	5901	590	9759	(30)	532	5000	(901)	(311)	15,660
10/68	10.65	5666	567	10114	0	532	5000	(666)	0	15,780
11/68	11.17	5942	594	10159	(31)	501	5000	(942)	(348)	16,101
12/68	11.08	5551	555	10553	0	501	5000	(551)	0	16,104

THIRD YEAR RESULTS
AIM: $6,104   PROFIT
LUMP SUM INVESTOR: $13,877   PROFIT

YEAR 4—1969

Date	Stock Price	Stock Value	Safe	Cash	Shares Bot(Sold)	Shares Owned	Portfolio Control	Buy(Sell) Advice	Market Order	Portfolio Value
1/69	10.12	5070	507	10599	0	501	5000	(70)	0	$15,669
2/69	9.40	4709	471	10646	0	501	5000	291	0	15,355
3/69	9.53	4775	478	10693	0	501	5000	225	0	15,468
4/69	9.78	4900	490	10740	0	501	5000	100	0	15,640
5/69	9.94	4980	498	10787	0	501	5000	20	0	15,767
6/69	9.11	4564	456	10834	0	501	5000	436	0	15,398
7/69	8.35	4183	418	10882	48	549	5200	817	399	15,065
8/69	8.93	4903	490	10529	0	549	5200	297	0	15,432
9/69	9.09	4990	499	10575	0	549	5200	210	0	15,565
10/69	9.92	5446	545	10622	0	549	5200	(246)	0	16,068
11/69	9.67	5309	531	10669	0	549	5200	(109)	0	15,978
12/69	9.72	5336	534	10716	0	549	5200	(136)	0	16,052

FOURTH YEAR RESULTS
AIM: $6,052   PROFIT
LUMP SUM INVESTOR: $10,947   PROFIT

YEAR 5—1970

Date	Stock Price	Stock Value	Safe	Cash	Shares Bot(Sold)	Shares Owned	Portfolio Control	Buy(Sell) Advice	Market Order	Portfolio Value
1/70	8.70	4776	478	10763	0	549	5200	424	0	$15,539
2/70	8.91	4892	489	10810	0	549	5200	308	0	15,702
3/70	8.51	4672	467	10858	0	549	5200	528	0	15,530
4/70	6.93	3805	381	10906	146	695	5707	1395	1014	14,711
5/70	6.33	4399	440	9936	137	832	6141	1308	868	14,335
6/70	6.10	5075	508	9108	91	923	6420	1066	558	14,183
7/70	6.49	5990	599	8588	0	923	6420	430	0	14,578
8/70	6.78	6258	626	8626	0	923	6420	162	0	14,884
9/70	7.51	6932	693	8664	0	923	6420	(512)	0	15,546
10/70	7.34	6775	678	8702	0	923	6420	(355)	0	15,477
11/70	7.61	7024	702	8740	0	923	6420	(604)	0	15,764
12/70	8.12	7495	750	8778	(40)	883	6420	(1075)	(325)	16,273

FIFTH YEAR RESULTS
AIM: $6,273   PROFIT
LUMP SUM INVESTOR: $7,499   PROFIT

92

YEAR 6—1971

Date	Stock Price	Stock Value	Safe	Cash	Shares Bot(Sold)	Shares Owned	Portfolio Control	Buy(Sell) Advice	Market Order	Portfolio Value
1/71	8.35	7373	737	9143	(26)	857	6420	(953)	(216)	$16,516
2/71	8.78	7524	752	9400	(40)	817	6420	(1104)	(352)	16,924
3/71	9.47	7737	774	9795	(57)	760	6420	(1317)	(543)	17,532
4/71	9.75	7410	741	10383	(26)	734	6420	(990)	(249)	17,793
5/71	9.62	7061	706	10679	0	734	6420	(641)	0	17,740
6/71	9.99	7333	733	10726	(18)	716	6420	(913)	(180)	18,059
7/71	9.67	6924	692	10954	0	716	6420	(504)	0	17,878
8/71	10.41	7454	745	11002	(28)	688	6420	(1034)	(289)	18,456
9/71	10.76	7403	740	11341	(23)	665	6420	(983)	(243)	18,744
10/71	10.42	6929	693	11635	0	665	6420	(509)	0	18,564
11/71	10.59	7042	704	11686	0	665	6420	(622)	0	18,728
12/71	12.21	8120	812	11737	(73)	592	6420	(1700)	(388)	19,857

SIXTH YEAR RESULTS
AIM: $9,857 PROFIT
LUMP SUM INVESTOR: $16,313 PROFIT

YEAR 7—1972

Date	Stock Price	Stock Value	Safe	Cash	Shares Bot(Sold)	Shares Owned	Portfolio Control	Buy(Sell) Advice	Market Order	Portfolio Value
1/72	13.04	7720	772	12681	(40)	552	6420	(1300)	(528)	$20,401
2/72	13.89	7667	767	13267	(35)	517	6420	(1247)	(480)	20,934
3/72	14.30	7393	739	13807	(16)	501	6420	(973)	(234)	21,200
4/72	14.40	7214	721	14103	0	501	6420	(794)	0	21,317
5/72	15.36	7695	770	14165	(33)	468	6420	(1275)	(505)	21,860
6/72	14.97	7006	701	14735	0	468	6420	(586)	0	21,741
7/72	14.53	6800	680	14800	0	468	6420	(380)	0	21,600
8/72	14.17	6632	663	14865	0	468	6420	(212)	0	21,497
9/72	13.81	6463	646	14930	0	468	6420	(43)	0	21,393
10/72	13.70	6412	641	14996	0	468	6420	8	0	21,408
11/72	14.07	6585	659	15062	0	468	6420	(165)	0	21,647
12/72	14.59	6828	683	15128	0	468	6420	(408)	0	21,956

SEVENTH YEAR RESULTS
AIM: $11,956 PROFIT
LUMP SUM INVESTOR: $21,441 PROFIT

YEAR 8—1973

Date	Stock Price	Stock Value	Safe	Cash	Shares Bot(Sold)	Shares Owned	Portfolio Control	Buy(Sell) Advice	Market Order	Portfolio Value
1/73	12.88	6028	603	15195	0	468	6420	392	0	$21,223
2/73	11.53	5396	540	15262	42	510	6662	1024	484	20,658
3/73	10.79	5503	550	14843	56	566	6967	1159	609	20,346
4/73	9.51	5383	538	14297	110	676	7490	1584	1046	19,680
5/73	9.15	6185	619	13309	75	751	7833	1305	686	19,494
6/73	8.84	6639	664	12679	60	811	8098	1194	530	19,318
7/73	10.20	8272	827	12202	0	811	8098	(174)	0	20,474
8/73	11.44	9278	928	12256	(22)	789	8098	(1180)	(252)	21,534
9/73	10.72	8458	846	12563	0	789	8098	(360)	0	21,021
10/73	10.36	8174	817	12618	0	789	8098	(76)	0	20,792
11/73	8.24	6501	650	12674	115	904	8572	1597	947	19,175
12/73	8.02	7250	725	11779	74	978	8871	1322	597	19,029

EIGHTH YEAR RESULTS
AIM: $9,029 PROFIT
LUMP SUM INVESTOR: $7,283 PROFIT

YEAR 9—1974

Date	Stock Price	Stock Value	Safe	Cash	Shares Bot(Sold)	Shares Owned	Portfolio Control	Buy(Sell) Advice	Market Order	Portfolio Value
1/74	7.87	7697	770	11231	51	1029	9073	1174	404	$18,928
2/74	7.66	7882	788	10875	53	1082	9275	1191	403	18,757
3/74	7.57	8191	819	10518	35	1117	9408	1084	265	18,709
4/74	7.16	7998	800	10298	85	1202	9713	1410	610	18,296
5/74	6.89	8282	828	9731	88	1290	10015	1431	603	18,013
6/74	6.39	8243	824	9168	148	1438	10489	1772	948	17,411
7/74	5.90	8484	848	8256	196	1634	11068	2005	1157	16,740
8/74	5.13	8382	838	7130	360	1994	11992	2686	1848	15,512
9/74	4.60	9172	917	5305	414	2408	12944	2820	1903	14,477
10/74	5.31	12786	1279	3417	0	2408	12944	158	0	16,203
11/74	5.06	12184	1218	3432	0	2408	12944	760	0	15,616
12/74	4.86	11703	1170	3447	0	2408	12944	1241	0	15,150

NINTH YEAR RESULTS
AIM: $5,150 PROFIT
LUMP SUM INVESTOR: $ 473 PROFIT

Date	Stock Price	Stock Value	Safe	Cash	Shares Bot(Sold)	Shares Owned	Portfolio Control	Buy(Sell) Advice	Market Order	Portfolio Value
1/75	5.43	13075	1308	3462	0	2408	12944	(131)	0	$16,537
*2/75	5.82	14015	1402	3477	0	2408	12944	(1071)	0	17,492
3/75	6.46	15556	1556	3492	(163)	2245	12944	(2612)	(1056)	19,048
4/75	6.86	15401	1540	4568	(134)	2111	12944	(2457)	(917)	19,969
5/75	7.27	15347	1535	5509	(119)	1992	12944	(2403)	(868)	20,856
6/75	7.62	15179	1518	6405	(94)	1898	12944	(2235)	(717)	21,584
7/75	7.10	13476	1348	7153	0	1898	12944	(532)	0	20,629
8/75	6.62	12565	1257	7184	0	1898	12944	379	0	19,749
9/75	6.29	11938	1194	7216	0	1898	12944	1006	0	19,154
10/75	6.66	12641	1264	7248	0	1898	12944	303	0	19,889
11/75	6.88	13058	1306	7280	0	1898	12944	(114)	0	20,338
12/75	6.66	12641	1264	7312	0	1898	12944			19,953

TENTH YEAR RESULTS
AIM: $9,953   PROFIT
LUMP SUM INVESTOR: $4,352   PROFIT

*At this point, AIM owns 253 more shares than the fully invested Lump Sum investor, and in addition owns a bank account worth $3,477!

It's traditional among professionals who work with so-phisticated pieces of equipment—be they cameras, tape recorders, or printing presses—to "play" with the device for a while after they buy a new one. It's a kind of shakedown cruise to enable the new owner to familiarize himself with the controls, capabilities, and performance of his new acquisition, so that when he finally places the machine in service, he will make fewer operating er-rors—at a time when errors can be costly.

One way in which you may do this and amuse yourself at the same time is to read the financial ads that appear in our major publications, placed there by financial ser-vices who are proud of their records. An investor who followed their advice on stock selections between such-and-such a date and such-and-such a date would have seen his assets increase by X percent, while the market as a whole was going nowhere.

Simply turn on your Money Machine and, using one of the market averages itself, determine how well *you* would have done. Add to your profit the amount you saved by not paying the financial service its stiff fee. And don't forget the interest on your CASH balance!

While these exciting newspaper ads tend to proliferate during bull markets, however, you may be hard-pressed to find one when the market turns sour, and for obvious reasons. Virtually any investment advisor can look good when the stock market has been in an upward trend for months or even years. The true test—and the one that separates the wheat from the chaff—occurs not only when the market collapses, but even during long stretches of tedium when stocks back and fill and wind up right back where they started. Unfortunately, a great many advisors flunk that test, and they certainly don't care to spend thousands of dollars for newspaper space to advertise the fact that they are, after all, just human beings like everybody else.

For example, in the trying period between May, 1967, and July, 1975, (see charts on pages 100–101) the Dow Jones Industrial Average gained less than ½ of 1 percent in value. It was not the easiest time in which to make money on Wall Street. Understandably, at the conclusion of the period, very few advisors took bows in public for their track records. One who did was the highly respected Holt Investment Advisory in New York. Their advertisement was so unexpected at this point in time that it seemed to warrant clipping and saving.

The Holt Company was justifiably proud of its record in achieving a startling 23.5 percent gain during those eight difficult years, and took out a large ad in the *New York Times* on August 10, 1975, to talk about it. And it was certainly *worth* talking about.

Now, regardless of what you've read, it is no simple matter for a private investor or even for a professional portfolio manager to beat the Dow Jones Average. You might beat it for a year. You might beat it for a string of years. But the Average tends to clobber us all in the end. And that's a sad commentary on the state of investing as it has existed for too many years now. In our high-tech era, investing remains stuck in the primordial mud. For all its vaunted scientific and technological veneer, it's still an art.

Small wonder that the Holt Company was proud of its accomplishment. They could well have been proud if they had done only *twice* as well as the Dow for the eight years in question. But they did much, much better, and their clients were no doubt pleased with the results.

It wasn't easy. The final profit figure was based on a broad sampling of more than 240 securities recommendations by the Holt Company with an average holding period of 1½ years. So in order to achieve that 23.5 percent gain, their clients naturally had to stay on top of things and put forth the required efforts. According to the coupon accompanying the ad, a one-year subscription to the Holt Investment Advisory costs $144 a year. For Holt's clients, it was money well spent. Clients of other investment advisors who came nowhere near to matching the Holt Investment Advisory's record—and may not even have matched the Dow—would, of course,

AUTOMATIC INVESTMENT MANAGEMENT, $10,000 PORTFOLIO

The Dow Jones Industrial Average, Eight Sluggish Years

Date	Price	Stock Value	Safe	Cash*	Shares Bot(Sold)	Shares Owned	Portfolio Control	Buy(Sell) Advice	Market Order	Portfolio Value
5/67	852.56	5000	500	5000	5.865	5.865	5000	—	—	10,000
8/67	901.29	5286	529	5065	0	5.865	5000	(286)	0	10,351
11/67	875.81	5137	514	5131	0	5.865	5000	(137)	0	10,268
2/68	840.50	4930	493	5198	0	5.865	5000	70	0	10,128
5/68	899.00	5273	527	5266	0	5.865	5000	(273)	0	10,539
8/68	896.01	5255	526	5334	0	5.865	5000	(255)	0	10,589
11/68	985.08	5777	578	5403	(.202)	5.663	5000	(777)	(199)	11,180
2/69	905.21	5126	513	5675	0	5.663	5000	(126)	0	10,801
5/69	937.56	5309	531	5749	0	5.663	5000	(309)	0	11,058
8/69	836.72	4738	474	5824	0	5.663	5000	262	0	10,562
11/69	812.30	4600	460	5900	0	5.663	5000	400	0	10,500
2/70	777.59	4403	440	5977	.202	5.865	5079	597	157	10,380
5/70	700.44	4108	411	5896	.799	6.664	5359	971	560	10,004
8/70	764.58	5096	510	5405	0	6.664	5359	263	0	10,501
11/70	794.09	5292	529	5475	0	6.664	5359	67	0	10,767
2/71	878.83	5857	586	5546	0	6.664	5359	(498)	0	11,403
5/71	907.81	6050	605	5618	0	6.664	5359	(691)	0	11,668
8/71	898.07	5985	599	5691	0	6.664	5359	(626)	0	11,676
11/71	831.34	5540	554	5765	0	6.664	5359	(181)	0	11,305

Date	Price	Stock Value	Safe	Cash*	Shares Bot(Sold)	Shares Owned	Portfolio Control	Buy(Sell) Advice	Market Order	Portfolio Value
2/72	928.13	6185	619	5840	(.223)	6.664	5359	(826)	(207)	12,025
5/72	960.72	6188	619	6126	(.219)	6.441	5359	(829)	(210)	12,314
8/72	963.73	5997	600	6418	0	6.222	5359	(638)	0	12,415
11/72	1018.21	6335	634	6501	(.336)	6.222	5359	(976)	(342)	12,836
2/73	955.07	5622	562	6932	0	5.886	5359	(263)	0	12,554
5/73	901.41	5306	531	7036	0	5.886	5359	53	0	12,342
8/73	887.57	5224	522	7127	0	5.886	5359	135	0	12,351
11/73	822.25	4840	484	7220	0	5.886	5359	519	0	12,060
2/74	860.53	5065	507	7314	0	5.886	5359	294	165	12,379
5/74	802.17	4722	472	7409	.206	6.092	5442	637	895	12,131
8/74	678.58	4134	413	7338	1.319	7.411	5890	1308	846	11,472
11/74	618.66	4585	459	6527	1.367	8.778	6313	1305	0	11,112
2/75	739.05	6488	649	5755	0	8.778	6313	(175)		12,243
5/75	832.29	7306	731	5830	0	8.463	6313	(993)	(262)	13,136
7/75	831.51	7037	704	6145	(.315)		6313			13,182

TOTAL VALUE OF PORTFOLIO: $13,182
PROFIT: $3,182
% PROFIT: 31.8%

*Interest on CASH Balance: 5¼% per annum.

101

have entirely different feelings about the wisdom of paying a thousand dollars or more for investment advice over the eight-year period without having much to show for it.

But AIM smiled when it read the Holt Investment Advisory ad. AIM scratched and yawned. AIM said, "Try me. Let's see what *I* would have done. Don't feed me any special stocks. Just slip me the Dow Jones Average."

We protested. The Dow hadn't even increased 1 percent in those eight years. It wasn't fair to AIM. The only proper way to do it was to use the good lively stocks that Holt used, not the sluggish Dow.

AIM remained adamant. "Try me," it said. "Switch me on." So we did, and here are the charts.

After studying and digesting the spine-tingling figures that AIM presented to us, it was several minutes before we could bring ourselves to comment. "You made a profit of 32 percent. You beat Holt, and you probably beat everybody else as well!"

"Could have made more if you'd given me something better to work with than the creaky old Dow."

"It was your idea."

"No matter. Just wanted to show you how easy it is. Look: I'm hardly breathing hard."

"I noticed."

"Did you also notice I did the whole thing on a quarterly basis? I didn't want to be bothered every month. I figured a few seconds of my time once every three months would be sufficient. And it was."

"That's an understatement. But answer me this: you gave yourself only 5.25 percent interest per year on your CASH balance. If you were investing on a quarterly basis, you could have put your cash in a 90-day certificate account in any savings bank and earned a full ½ of 1 percent more. It would have made a tremendous difference in your results."

"I didn't want to be bothered. Besides, I don't believe that interest rate was available on 90-day money back in 1967. If I claimed it *was,* I would be cheating. And I am not programmed to cheat."

"On the other hand, that 5.75 percent rate has been available for several years now and you could have claimed it as soon as it *became* available."

"I said I didn't want to be bothered. I could also, for that matter, have claimed 10 and 12 percent interest per year recently when money market rates were hovering around there. Those rates certainly were available in any so-called money fund. But then somebody might accuse me of hedging. And as you very well know, I am not programmed to hedge. I merely wanted to demonstrate what I could do with a sluggish stock and with the lowest interest rate available. Nothing up my sleeves. No ifs, ands, and maybes. All open and aboveboard. But it's funny how you missed the most important part of my job and the one that, I think, I discharged with uncommon diligence. You completely overlooked it—and I'll bet most other investors will too."

"What's that?"

"Take a look at the last column on the page, the PORTFOLIO VALUE column. Run your eye all the way down that column. What do you see?"

"Just figures. They kinda keep going up, I guess."

"No, my friend. Not that they kinda keep going up. *They never went down.*"

"I don't follow."

"At no time during the entire program did I ever show a loss. Not in the crash of 1969 and 1970. Not in the disaster of 1974. Not ever. You gave me five figures to work with, $10,000, and I *maintained* five figures throughout. Do you know any *other* investor who began investing in 1967 and never showed a loss? I bought $5,000 worth of stock when the Dow opened at 853. And when the Dow subsequently plummeted 27 percent to 619, I *still* had a profit. What do you say to that?"

"I love you."

*   *   *

Not all victories make the headlines, and many an act of heroism is destined for obscurity. Automatic Investment Management will do its thing no matter what kind of portfolio you present to it, but if it had its druthers, it would prefer spicy food, an energetic, swinging portfolio of stocks that bounce from pillar to post, from giddy highs to manic lows. Something it can really get its teeth into.

But what if we offered it a creeping, crawling stock average like the New York Stock Exchange Index which, in a recent decade, snaked from $50 a share to . . . about $48 a share? (See charts on pages 106–115.) Not only that, but it registered a monthly closing high for the decade of only $64.48. That's a gain of only 29 percent. And as for its monthly closing low, the New York Stock Exchange Index touched a ten-year bottom of $33.45, which is a really big 33 percent drop from its original price. Obviously, a foot-dragging portfolio like this doesn't give AIM much room to work in, and while it's unlikely many of our readers could select a half-dozen stocks or so that would behave so lazily, what if someone did? Well, if that someone happened to be a typical buy-them-and-lock-them-up investor who plunked down his entire $10,000 at the start, he would naturally have exited the ten-year period with a loss of $472. And he probably would be relieved and delighted that he almost managed to break even. So many others who came in later did not, and this would include the millions of investors who buy stock when they feel in the mood, or when they have some extra money, or when the booming market lures them into the action. They almost always make their purchases near the highs, with results that are even worse than that of the so-called Lump Summer who makes his single purchase and crosses his fingers.

AIM would have muttered at you under its breath for giving it such a lethargic animal to ride as the New York Stock Exchange Index, but it would nevertheless have gone right to work to run the best possible race for you under the circumstances. At the end of ten years, although the price of the Index is less than it was in the beginning, AIM would have presented you with a profit of $4,459, excluding dividends on stock! If you prefer, the profit can be read as 45 percent of your original $10,000 investment. But, since you still have $5,789 in cash, you theoretically have invested only $4,211 in stock, which is now worth $8,670 . . . for a profit of 106 percent. Either way, it's a comforting return on a portfolio that went nowhere!

Among the other interesting aspects of AIM's performance with this uneventful portfolio is the fact that AIM *did not show a loss at the bottom of the 1970 cave-in or at the 1974 crater!* If you consider that statement at least as significant as the one in which AIM wound up with a final profit while the Lump Sum investor is still a loser, you have the kind of mind that can best appreciate Automatic Investment Management. Because at these crunches, the Lump Sum investor suffered losses of $2,084 and $3,310 respectively!

You would also find interesting the fact that at the very crest of the market, AIM showed a profit of $4,434, while at the end of the ten-year period, with the price of the stock far below its peak, AIM showed an even greater profit of $4,459!

And as for the Lump Summer, AIM led him every year for the entire decade.

Granted, none of us would enjoy seeing our investment vehicle behave as lifelessly as this one over a decade. But if it were our bad luck to construct such a portfolio, which experience would we prefer: the Lump Summer's—or AIM's?

What gives the samurai sword its remarkably superior strength and flexibility is not the metal used, but the way in which it is forged, the metal folded back ,again and again and hammered layer into layer until the craftsman achieves his mathematical goal: 2 to the power of 15, or 30,000 layers. AIM, too, derives its strength from layers of profits folded back and beaten into shape. And for that, one needs a piece of metal—or a swing in the port-

AUTOMATIC INVESTMENT MANAGEMENT

New York Stock Exchange Index, 1965–1975, $10,000 Portfolio: A Decade Going Nowhere

YEAR 1—1966

Date	Stock Price	Stock Value	Safe	Cash*	Shares Bot(Sold)	Shares Owned	Portfolio Control	Buy(Sell) Advice	Market Order	Portfolio Value
12/65	50.00	5000	500	5000	100	100	5000	—	—	10,000
1/66	50.44	5044	504	5022	0	100	5000	(44)	0	10,066
2/66	49.61	4961	496	5044	0	100	5000	39	0	10,005
3/66	48.37	4837	484	5066	0	100	5000	163	0	9,903
4/66	49.29	4929	493	5088	0	100	5000	71	0	10,017
5/66	46.50	4650	465	5110	0	100	5000	350	0	9,760
6/66	45.91	4591	459	5132	0	100	5000	409	0	9,723
7/66	45.29	4529	453	5155	0	100	5000	471	0	9,684
8/66	41.65	4165	417	5178	10	110	5209	835	418	9,343
9/66	41.30	4543	454	4781	5	115	5315	666	212	9,324
10/66	43.16	4963	496	4589	0	115	5315	352	0	9,552
11/66	43.59	5013	501	4609	0	115	5315	302	0	9,622
12/66	43.72	5028	503	4629	0	115	5315	287	0	9,657

FIRST YEAR RESULTS
AIM: ($343) LOSS
LUMP SUM INVESTOR: ($1,256) LOSS

*Interest on CASH Balance: 5¼% per annum.

YEAR 2—1967

Date	Stock Price	Stock Value	Safe	Cash	Shares Bot(Sold)	Shares Owned	Portfolio Control	Buy(Sell) Advice	Market Order	Portfolio Value
1/67	47.30	5440	544	4649	0	115	5315	(125)	0	10,089
2/67	47.56	5469	547	4669	0	115	5315	(154)	0	10,138
3/67	49.52	5695	570	4690	0	115	5315	(380)	0	10,385
4/67	51.54	5927	593	4711	0	115	5315	(612)	0	10,638
5/67	49.17	5655	566	4732	0	115	5315	(340)	0	10,387
6/67	50.27	5781	578	4753	0	115	5315	(466)	0	10,534
7/67	52.65	6055	606	4774	(3)	112	5315	(740)	(134)	10,829
8/67	52.07	5832	583	4930	0	112	5315	(517)	0	10,762
9/67	53.71	6016	602	4952	0	112	5315	(701)	0	10,968
10/67	52.13	5839	584	4974	0	112	5315	(524)	0	10,813
11/67	52.26	5853	585	4996	0	112	5315	(538)	0	10,849
12/67	53.83	6029	603	5018	(2)	110	5315	(714)	(111)	11,047

SECOND YEAR RESULTS
AIM: $1,047 PROFIT
LUMP SUM INVESTOR: $766 PROFIT

p 102

YEAR 3—1968

Date	Stock Price	Stock Value	Safe	Cash	Shares Bot(Sold)	Shares Owned	Portfolio Control	Buy (Sell) Advice	Market Order	Portfolio Value
1/68	51.66	5683	568	5152	0	110	5315	(368)	0	10,835
2/68	49.77	5475	548	5175	0	110	5315	(160)	0	10,650
3/68	50.05	5506	551	5198	0	110	5315	(191)	0	10,704
4/68	54.49	5994	599	5221	0	110	5315	(679)	0	11,215
5/68	55.50	6105	611	5244	(3)	107	5315	(790)	(179)	11,349
6/68	56.08	6001	600	5447	0	107	5315	(686)	0	11,448
7/68	54.78	5861	586	5471	0	107	5315	(546)	0	11,332
8/68	55.44	5932	593	5495	0	107	5315	(617)	0	11,427
9/68	57.70	6174	617	5519	(4)	103	5315	(859)	(242)	11,693
10/68	58.17	5992	599	5786	0	103	5315	(677)	0	11,778
11/68	61.27	6311	631	5811	(6)	97	5315	(996)	(365)	12,122
12/68	58.90	5713	571	6203	0	97	5315	(398)	0	11,916

THIRD YEAR RESULTS
AIM: $1,916 PROFIT
LUMP SUM INVESTOR: $1,780 PROFIT

YEAR 4—1969

Date	Stock Price	Stock Value	Safe	Cash	Shares Bot(Sold)	Shares Owned	Portfolio Control	Buy(Sell) Advice	Market Order	Portfolio Value
1/69	58.38	5663	566	6230	0	97	5315	(348)	0	11,893
2/69	55.19	5353	535	6257	0	97	5315	(38)	0	11,610
3/69	56.85	5514	551	6285	0	97	5315	(199)	0	11,799
4/69	57.49	5577	558	6313	0	97	5315	(262)	0	11,890
5/69	57.87	5613	561	6341	0	97	5315	(298)	0	11,954
6/69	54.13	5251	525	6369	0	97	5315	64	0	11,620
7/69	50.64	4912	491	6397	0	97	5315	403	0	11,309
8/69	52.94	5135	514	6425	0	57	5315	180	0	11,560
9/69	51.69	5014	501	6453	0	97	5315	301	0	11,467
10/69	54.45	5282	528	6481	0	97	5315	33	0	11,763
11/69	52.49	5092	509	6510	0	97	5315	223	0	11,602
12/69	51.53	4998	500	6539	0	97	5315	317	0	11,537

FOURTH YEAR RESULTS
AIM: $1,537 PROFIT
LUMP SUM INVESTOR: $306 PROFIT

YEAR 5—1970

Date	Stock Price	Stock Value	Safe	Cash	Shares Bot(Sold)	Shares Owned	Portfolio Control	Buy(Sell) Advice	Market Order	Portfolio Value
1/70	47.54	4611	461	6568	5	102	5437	704	243	11,179
2/70	50.10	5110	511	6353	0	102	5437	327	0	11,463
3/70	49.87	5087	509	6381	0	102	5437	350	0	11,468
4/70	44.82	4572	457	6409	9	111	5641	865	408	10,981
5/70	41.78	4638	464	6027	13	124	5911	1003	539	10,665
6/70	39.58	4908	491	5512	13	137	6167	1003	512	10,420
7/70	42.43	5813	581	5022	0	137	6167	354	0	10,835
8/70	44.32	6072	607	5044	0	137	6167	95	0	11,116
9/70	46.14	6321	632	5066	0	137	6167	(154)	0	11,387
10/70	45.28	6203	620	5088	0	137	6167	(36)	0	11,291
11/70	47.41	6495	650	5110	0	137	6167	(328)	0	11,605
12/70	50.23	6882	688	5132	0	137	6167	(715)	0	12,014

FIFTH YEAR RESULTS
AIM: $2,014 PROFIT
LUMP SUM INVESTOR: $46 PROFIT

110

YEAR 6—1971

Date	Stock Price	Stock Value	Safe	Cash	Shares Bot(Sold)	Shares Owned	Portfolio Control	Buy(Sell) Advice	Market Order	Portfolio Value
1/71	52.64	7212	721	5155	(6)	131	5167	(1045)	(324)	12,367
2/71	53.19	6968	697	5503	(2)	129	6167	(801)	(104)	12,471
3/71	55.44	7152	715	5632	(5)	124	6167	(985)	(270)	12,784
4/71	57.27	7101	710	5928	(4)	120	6167	(934)	(224)	13,029
5/71	54.92	6590	659	6179	0	120	6157	(423)	0	12,769
6/71	55.09	6611	661	6206	0	120	6167	(444)	0	12,817
7/71	52.81	6337	634	6233	0	120	6167	(170)	0	12,570
8/71	54.74	6569	657	6260	0	120	6:67	(402)	0	12,829
9/71	54.33	6520	652	6288	0	120	6167	(353)	0	12,808
10/71	52.07	6248	625	6316	0	120	6167	(81)	0	12,564
11/71	51.84	6221	622	6344	0	120	6167	(54)	0	12,565
12/71	56.43	6772	677	6372	0	120	6157	(605)	0	13,144

SIXTH YEAR RESULTS
AIM: $3,144 PROFIT
LUMP SUM INVESTOR: $1,286 PROFIT

YEAR 7—1972

Date	Stock Price	Stock Value	Safe	Cash	Shares Bot(Sold)	Shares Owned	Portfolio Control	Buy(Sell) Advice	Market Order	Portfolio Value
1/72	57.71	6925	693	6400	0	120	6167	(758)	0	13,325
2/72	59.24	7109	711	6428	(4)	116	6167	(942)	(231)	13,537
3/72	59.68	6923	692	6688	0	116	6167	(756)	0	13,611
4/72	60.00	6960	696	6717	0	116	6167	(793)	0	13,677
5/72	60.76	7048	705	6747	(3)	113	6167	(881)	(176)	13,795
6/72	59.31	6702	670	6953	0	113	6167	(535)	0	13,655
7/72	59.09	6677	668	6984	0	113	6167	(510)	0	13,661
8/72	61.11	6905	691	7015	0	113	6167	(738)	0	13,920
9/72	60.60	6848	685	7046	0	113	6167	(681)	0	13,894
10/72	61.12	6907	691	7077	0	113	6167	(740)	0	13,984
11/72	63.88	7218	722	7108	(5)	108	6167	(1051)	(329)	14,326
12/72	64.48	6964	696	7470	(2)	106	6167	(797)	(101)	14,434

SEVENTH YEAR RESULTS
AIM: $4,434 PROFIT
LUMP SUM INVESTOR: $2,896 PROFIT

112

YEAR 8—1973

Date	Stock Price	Stock Value	Safe	Cash	Shares Bot(Sold)	Shares Owned	Portfolio Control	Buy(Sell) Advice	Market Order	Portfolio Value
1/73	62.75	6652	665	7604	0	106	6167	(485)	0	14,256
2/73	60.00	6360	636	7637	0	106	6167	(193)	0	13,997
3/73	59.58	6315	632	7671	0	106	6167	(148)	0	13,986
4/73	56.73	6013	601	7705	0	106	6167	154	0	13,718
5/73	55.42	5875	588	7739	0	106	6167	292	0	13,614
6/73	54.84	5813	581	7773	0	106	6167	354	0	13,586
7/73	57.65	6111	611	7807	0	106	6167	56	0	13,918
8/73	55.64	5998	600	7841	0	106	6157	169	0	13,739
9/73	58.51	6202	620	7876	0	106	6157	(35)	0	14,078
10/73	58.28	6178	618	7911	0	106	6157	(11)	0	14,089
11/73	51.18	5425	543	7946	4	110	6257	742	199	13,371
12/73	51.82	5700	570	7781	0	110	6267	567	0	13,481

EIGHTH YEAR RESULTS
AIM: $3,481 PROFIT
LUMP SUM INVESTOR: $364 PROFIT

YEAR 9—1974

Date	Stock Price	Stock Value	Safe	Cash	Shares Bot(Sold)	Shares Owned	Portfolio Control	Buy(Sell) Advice	Market Order	Portfolio Value
1/74	51.64	5680	568	7815	0	110	6267	587	0	13,495
2/74	51.56	5672	567	7849	0	110	6267	595	0	13,521
3/74	50.21	5523	552	7884	4	114	6363	744	192	13,407
4/74	47.93	5464	546	7726	7	121	6540	899	353	13,190
5/74	45.92	5556	556	7405	9	130	6754	984	428	12,961
6/74	44.90	5837	584	7008	7	137	6921	917	333	12,845
7/74	41.55	5692	569	6704	16	153	7251	1229	660	12,396
8/74	37.70	5768	577	6071	24	177	7704	1483	906	11,839
9/74	33.45	5921	592	5188	36	213	8300	1783	1191	11,109
10/74	38.97	8301	830	4015	0	213	8300	(1)	0	12,316
11/74	37.13	7909	791	4033	0	213	8300	391	0	11,942
12/74	36.13	7696	770	4051	0	213	8300	604	0	11,747

NINTH YEAR RESULTS
AIM: $1,747 PROFIT
LUMP SUM INVESTOR: ($2,774) LOSS

114

YEAR 10—1975

Date	Stock Price	Stock Value	Safe	Cash	Shares Bot(Sold)	Shares Owned	Portfolio Control	Buy(Sell) Advice	Market Order	Portfolio Value
1/75	40.91	8714	871	4069	0	213	8300	(414)	0	12,783
2/75	43.07	9174	917	4087	0	213	8300	(874)	0	13,261
3/75	44.21	9417	942	4105	(4)	209	8300	(1117)	(175)	13,522
4/75	46.19	9654	965	4299	(8)	201	8300	(1354)	(389)	13,953
5/75	48.46	9740	974	4709	(10)	191	8300	(1440)	(466)	14,449
6/75	50.85	9712	971	5198	(9)	182	8300	(1412)	(441)	14,910
7/75	47.10	8572	857	5664	0	182	8300	(272)	0	14,236
8/75	46.29	8425	843	5689	0	182	8300	(125)	0	14,114
9/75	44.49	8097	810	5714	0	182	8300	203	0	13,811
10/75	47.05	8563	856	5739	0	182	8300	(263)	0	14,302
11/75	48.24	8780	878	5764	0	182	8300	(480)	0	14,544
12/75	47.64	8670	867	5789	0	182	8300	(370)	0	14,459

TENTH YEAR RESULTS
AIM: $4,459 PROFIT
LUMP SUM INVESTOR: ($472) LOSS

folio—long enough to allow for the process of folding
back time and time again. Be that as it may, if it were
at all humanly possible for the average investor—he of
the notoriously short memory—to recall the unrelieved
gloom of 1974 and the incredible losses he experienced
in stocks he had purchased many, many years ago,
AIM's performance that year as recorded in these charts
is still near-miraculous, even though we purposefully selected them to show AIM in less than the best light. At
the September, 1974, low, AIM still produced a 45-
percent profit for the New Horizons investor and an 11-
percent profit for the fellow with the bad luck to build
a portfolio that matched the foot-dragging performance
of the New York Stock Exchange Index. The safety factor built into AIM was designed to be every bit as
important as its explosive upside potential, for we were
mindful from the start of our own disastrous results playing the Hit-or-Miss game . . . and the equally disastrous
experience of millions of others. Most of us have not
"gotten well." Many of us never will, including a painfully large number of "experts." Said David Babson:
"This was the first wild market in which people supposed
to be professionals got sucked in." He was referring to
1970. For some investors, 1974 was even worse. But
AIM, slogging through the icy waters of those stock market winters, never even caught so much as a cold!

Honored more in the breach than in the observance,
preservation of capital is still the first rule of money
management. This rule became the heart that we, as the
Wizard of Oz, installed into AIM's circuitry, one that
cannot be abrogated, modified, or waived, no matter
what the temptations of a bull market are.

The day will come when you will be glad we did.

Please remember that cash is the fuel in AIM's tank,
and AIM prefers to keep a goodly supply of it at all
times in order to be able to control its own destiny.
Without cash, it would drift almost as helplessly as the
fully invested player. If the market rises, AIM can easily
fill up its tank from the stock market pump by selling

off some of its holdings. But if the market falls further, AIM will be unable to take advantage of the extraordinary bargains in the basement. Even its bank interest, a source of overflowing cash, has dried up. For this reason, we have installed a fuel-injection system in the AIM mechanism that renders it most unlikely for the tank ever to run dry, no matter how severe the demand. We mention this only because a large pool of cash remaining at what, in hindsight, was the bottom of the market, might annoy some overeager investors. The pool is put there for a purpose. It is behaving itself and earning interest.

Siphoning is a punishable offense.

As Victor Hugo advised:

> *Be like the bird*
> *That, pausing in her flight*
> *Awhile on boughs too slight,*
> *Feels them give way*
> *Beneath her and yet sings,*
> *Knowing that she hath wings.*

Those "idle" dollars in your CASH balance are *your* wings.

AIM's results speak for themselves. The old-fashioned investor who made his $10,000 purchase in 1965 and then sat back to wait for his ship to come in was still staring out to sea ten years later. In the meantime, his investment has dwindled to $9,528, while AIM's has mushroomed to $14,459.

But we have good news for the old-timer. One single month after the chart ended in December, 1975, the New York Stock Exchange Index shot up to $53.55 and finally presented him with his $10,000 investment back—plus a little extra compensation for his ten years of patience: $710.

We have *better* news for AIM. One single month after the chart ended, *his* $10,000 investment was worth $15,560!

*   *   *

We have given you what we sincerely believe to be
the finest investment method known—the safest, simplest, most foolproof approach to equity investment ever
devised. You will feel comfortable using it, and you will
be able to sleep nights while your Money Machine goes
on working for you around the clock, faithfully, dependably, consistently. We are convinced that you will feel
such confidence in it after what you have seen that you
will find yourself immediately entrusting to its care—as
we have—a sum much larger than you would dare commit to any other investment method. Because no matter
how large the sum, you know that only *half* is to be
invested in your AIM program immediately. As for the
remainder, AIM will select the time, and you know, too,
that the time will be the *right* time. Uncannily, unfail-
ingly—the *right* time! We did not give birth to a reckless child.

No, not reckless, some might add. Conservative. Careful. Pinchpenny. Why, the child actually *loathes* stocks!
You can tell just by watching it. It buys stocks only when
it absolutely *has* to, and then as soon as it buys them, it
can't wait to get rid of them. He certainly doesn't *trust*
them, that's for sure. Mighty peculiar behavior if you
ask me. Why, just *watch* him sometimes. Half the time
he doesn't even own as much stock as the Lump Summer boy across the street, even though, Lord knows, he
had enough opportunities and the money to buy it. One
would think the child had been *burned* by stocks at some
time in his life . . . And yet, for the life of me I can't
figure out where he gets all that *money!*

We have our Money Machine. We have seen that it
works. All that remains is that we feed it the proper
foods to give it the nourishment, the energy, and the
good sound nerves that every living thing needs.

EIGHT

What to Feed Your Money Machine

On November 4, 1974, the General Motors Corporation, citing a decline in profits and sales and a surge in costs, cut its year-end dividend by 64 percent. The gloomy outlook for auto stocks in particular—recession, energy crisis, etcetera—and the pessimism of the market as a whole in general combined to push GM stock down to a price of 28⅞, the lowest it had been in a decade. Think back. Of all the stocks you would have avoided like the plague that year, the autos—even a quality auto like General Motors—would be right up there at the top of your list. When the consumer doesn't know if he can *get* a tankful of gas, or even what it will cost him if he *can,* he surely won't be in the mood to buy a new car—not at *those* prices! And weren't analysts putting down autos as a "semiregulated" industry whose cost pressures were constantly mounting? And weren't the autos sitting in a political hot seat if they tried to ask for any new price increases?

By October of the following year, 1975, General Motors stock had nearly doubled in price. Surprise! Investors had "suddenly realized" at the price of 30, said one newspaper explanation, that even with a reduced dividend of $3.40 a share, GM offered an attractive yield of more than 11 percent. The fact that the 11 percent was available *only* at the price of $30 was apparently not worth mentioning. At the price of $40, the yield had slipped to 8.5 percent, and at the price of $50, GM was yielding only 6.8 percent—about *half* of its yield at the low. What kept the stock moving up beyond 30, beyond

40, beyond 50? Were investors really buying the dividend? No, what they were buying was the *quality,* the quality of the United States' largest industrial corporation and a component of the Dow Jones Industrial Average. What they had "suddenly realized" was not that GM was yielding 11 percent, or 8.5 percent, or 6.8 percent—a rate obtainable elsewhere at less risk at this time—but that here was a gigantic industrial enterprise with some 1.3 million stockholders, with sales of 30 *billion* dollars annually, and with a record of paying quarterly dividends since 1917, whose stock was now on the auction block at its lowest point in years. They had "suddenly realized" in this critical time of uncertainty that a company as huge and powerful as GM was not going to go out of business regardless of the woes with which it and other auto manufacturers were presently beset. GM would find a way out. GM would *always* find a way out. There are very, very few nations in the world whose budgets even approach the income of General Motors. GM was *quality*, and while it might not be literally true that what is good for GM is good for the nation, the fall of GM would have the psychological impact of the fall of the Colosseum in Rome, where legend holds that such a collapse would spell the end, not only of Rome itself, but of the world.

At the same time that General Motors and other blue-chip stocks were rebounding smartly from the extreme "end-of-the-world" pessimism that infected the investor in 1974, countless other stocks of dubious quality simply fell apart. If, by any chance, the reader has around the house any newspapers or magazines from 1973 or 1974, he need only look at what stocks the experts were recommending for 1974. And if he will then look at what disastrous prices most of those stocks were selling for in October of 1975, he may never again be tempted to trade quality for flash. Come hell or high water, come recessions, inflations, stagflations, energy crises, and material shortages, the rich will survive. They will have their trying moments, and at times the promoters with their new hypes, "new" markets, "new" merchandising techniques, and "new" processes will seem to offer more potential. But when the eyewash clears, they will be gone and the old rich will still be here. Besides, if those "new" approaches really offered any threat, the old rich would use their superior resources to force the upstarts out of the market or, failing that, would simply buy them out. If a small bakery markets a truly superior loaf of bread—a simple task, after all, considering what's presently available at the supermarket—you will wake up one morning and find, inside the wrapper of Aunt Evelyn Rauen's Butterfarm Sweetwheat Loaf, a very ordinary loaf of bread. The big bakeries could easily have duplicated the superior bread, but it would have crimped their profit picture. Good ingredients cost *money!* Far easier to make Aunt Evelyn an offer for her brand name that she cannot refuse.

Go down the list of the corporate giants. A few were born in *your* lifetime. Clout? A mere ten of these monsters—stocks such as IBM, GE, and Microsoft—can account for a *third* of the action of the entire Standard & Poor 500 stocks!

In 1974, as in 1970, the patient and *prepared* investor was presented with the opportunity not only to buy stocks in general at attractive prices but, more important, *the opportunity to buy the best companies at reasonable prices.* A Murgatroyd 4-cylinder at 50 percent off is an interesting proposition, but when you can buy a *Cadillac* at half price, you've really got yourself a bargain! *Quality* at a *discount* is the only bargain worth waiting for. And a square old granddaddy company like GM or Eastman Kodak or Sears or DuPont was a better buy than Dewby Dewby Dew Dynamics—just as a used Smith-Corona is a better buy at $25 than a spanking new $160 Fingerbraken Punchenbeaten Clackenbanger. They are better buys because if your ship is sinking, and you have five seconds to make up your mind, and you see two life preservers hanging in front of you, and one is stamped DuPont while the other bears the imprint

DAN-DEE FLOTE, you will grab the one stamped DU-PONT. These names have a heritage, a tradition, a trust: recognition quality. They will go down on one knee, but they will almost always get back up. They are certain to float.

A point could even be made for selecting your investments from the 30 stocks in the Dow Jones Average, and to further refine your choice by considering only the 15 strongest and most up-to-date companies among them. These tried-and-true companies, which have endured through good times and bad, could make up fully 50 percent of your AIM stock portfolio, for strength, resilience, and reliability. At the trough of a market decline, blue chips are generally the first to stir as burned investors straggle slowly back into the stock market and make their first nervous buys—*quality,* if you please! This activity should supply the yeast to lift your portfolio off the bottom and get it moving again.

We are no longer selecting a stock merely because we want it to go up. We are buying it primarily because we believe that if it goes down, it will have the stamina to rise again. And stocks that are household names usually do come back, at least partially because they *are* household names and have the respect accorded a member of the family. They may not come *all* the way back for a while, but on the other hand, they are not likely to go *all* the way down.

The balance of the portfolio can consist of spicier fare, stocks that tend to shoot up and down faster than the old-line companies, and could even include a speculation or two to satisfy the gambling instinct. (The University of Rochester lumps its "long shots" together under the cryptic definition "Funny Money." A stock called Xerox incubated anonymously here in 1950.) A portfolio structured in this fashion should provide your Money Machine with a tasty, nutritious, and lively diet to enable it to function at peak efficiency.

*   *   *

The *number* of stocks you include in your portfolio is second in importance only to the quality of the stocks. The typical amateur portfolio manager hedges against his ignorance by buying 100-share lots of one stock after another, regardless of price. He has read that "odd lotters"—those who buy fewer than 100 shares of a stock— are not only amateurs but are always wrong about the market's direction (untrue on both counts), and he does not wish to be included among the greenhorns. He imagines that 100 shares of Food Lion and 100 shares of Home Depot are the same, and that if one goes up and one goes down, it will all balance out. He can't quite comprehend that his investment in Food Lion is only $1,800, while his commitment to Home Depot is $6,800! There is no balance whatever in these selections. If he were four times more certain that Depot was headed up, such a bold play could be justified; but nobody can be four times more certain of anything in the stock market. He cannot even be *twice* as certain! This unwillingness to appear amateurish and the pursuit of diversification to its outer limits leads to such unfortunate examples as a $250,000 investment club portfolio consisting of an incredible 50 stocks—100 shares of each! The end result is both amateurish *and* silly, and, of course, unrewarding. As the man said, if you want a mutual fund, buy one. The University of Rochester's brilliantly managed $500,000,000 portfolio contains little more than 25 common stocks! (From the vantage point of our new AIM discovery, we must nevertheless admire excellence wherever it is found. Ingenious craftsmen, working with what we believe now to be primitive tools, can still produce results that astonish us.)

Ignore round lots. Ten $100 shares equal $1,000. One hundred $10 shares equal $1,000. That is the way you make an equal investment in two stocks, by buying 10 $100 shares of Company A and 100 $10 shares of Company B. And, since nobody knows which of the two stocks will go up most in the future, it makes sense to take profits from the rising stock and make future investments in the falling stock. Try to keep roughly the same amount invested in each stock in the "blue chip" half of your portfolio. This is your "first string" team, and when one stock falters, a stronger stock should lend a hand. The day will almost certainly come when their positions will be reversed. And the weaker stock, thanks to the timely transfusion, could become so robust it might eventually lend a hand not only to the stock that unselfishly came to its aid, but to other stocks as well. And isn't that what charity is all about? Think about it.

For all you know, the same specialist could be handling *both* of those stocks on the floor of the Exchange, and when he has squeezed all the juice out of Stock A, he might then decide to nurse it back to health while squeezing the juice out of star performer Stock B. As to whether all this is on the up and up, it is of no concern to the AIM investor. He *wants* his stocks to fluctuate, and he will be taking profits when the swings are to the upside. More traditional investors may have a different viewpoint; they do have our sympathy.

There are a couple of investment companies that do try to keep the same amount invested in each stock in their portfolio—as well as some that concentrate exclusively on "out-of-favor" stocks—and their results do not seem to suffer by comparison as a result of this unusual, simple, but sensible approach. The technique seems particularly suited to AIM, where all we want is fluctuation. Growth can go hang, for all we care. If you disagree with this philosophy and still insist on committing a larger investment to Blue Chip Stock A than to Blue Chip Stock B, by all means do so. *But do not let the price of the stock itself determine your investment in that stock.* If Stock A is priced lower, you may have to buy 200 shares of it and only 50 shares of Stock B to achieve a larger investment in Stock A. If Stock A is priced higher, you may have to buy only 50 shares of it and 200 shares of Stock B in order for you to have a greater investment in Stock A. It's the dollar commitment—not the number of shares—that counts. Elementary, maybe, but thousands of amateur investors never grasp it.

By keeping the stocks in the "blue-chip" half of your portfolio fairly even in value, you can direct your real attention and thought to the more volatile half. You may own some speculative stocks in this section whose outlook appears so bleak that you would not care to commit more capital to them as they decline. You may even decide to eliminate some of your poorer-performing "second string" stocks from time to time. It is one thing to buy more General Motors on the way down, but quite another to send good money chasing after a speculative stock gone sour.

Your "first string" team can pretty much call its own signals, but the "second string" needs all the coaching direction it can get.

What, after all, is the purpose of diversification? Very simply, it is a means by which we attempt to reduce the risk of investing while increasing our opportunities for profit. *Opportunities* for profit, not *amount* of profit. Obviously, *maximum* profit would be available in a single stock whose scenario has slated it for a spectacular leap into the stratosphere—provided that we, by hook or crook, were able to obtain an advance copy of the script. And, just as obviously, *maximum* losses could be nimbly avoided by bypassing a single stock marked for market mayhem if we but knew in advance exactly *which* security was due for the beheading. Not knowing all this, we traditionally hedge our bets on a number of stocks in the hope that more of them will rise than fall—or that the ones that *do* rise will more than atone for those that drop.

But AIM, as we have seen, performs to a large degree the same functions previously served by orthodox diversification. By timing our sales and investments—buying low and selling high—it automatically reduces our risk while increasing our opportunities for profit. And by substantially fulfilling those requirements, AIM has reduced the importance of actual physical diversification.

We need a *few* stocks, true—a single security could possibly drop like a stone and leave us stranded for years at its low—but we no longer need anywhere near the number of stocks that prudence formerly dictated.

Again: Overdiversification leads to underachievement. Keep your portfolio lean and lively. Ten stocks should be sufficient for all but the very largest portfolios, and even that number might be considered excessive by some professionals in the field.

What's more important is that long-term investing can no longer be viewed as a viable concept. Too many changes have occurred in the nation and on Wall Street itself. Stock volatility alone has intensified alarmingly— the Dow runs up several hundred points and then just as quickly reverses itself and erases all its gains. Institutional investors, who now account for 70 percent of trading activity, have seemingly abandoned their long-term, faith-in-America's-economy approach of a decade ago and have now become as nervous as a long-tailed cat under a rocking chair. What happens when one of these giants decides to unload a cargo of Stock A just after you bought your 100 shares? Your stock could be pulverized. Remember, pension funds and certain other privileged institutions pay no tax on their profits. While you're paying full taxes on all your stock market profits, dozens of members of this elite group could be dumping truckloads of your stock onto the market only weeks after acquiring it. Even mutual funds aren't hamstrung by tax considerations when it comes to selling: they simply pass along their tax liabilities to their shareholders.

Don't be the last on your block to recognize what's going on. Long-term investing, in this era of economic emphysema, bears a warning that continued use may be hazardous to your financial health!

Extremism in the defense of your savings is no vice.

The CASH balance in your Automatic Investment Management program can be kept in an account in any federally insured savings bank or savings and loan association. A day-of-deposit-to-day-of-withdrawal account, which currently pays less than 3 percent per annum, may prove ideal for some investors. The advantages of such an account are these:

1. No penalty for withdrawal at any time.
2. No minimum deposit.
3. No minimum withdrawal.
4. Deposits are insured up to $100,000.
5. Interest is paid on every dollar for every day it remains on deposit. In other savings accounts, money withdrawn before the end of a quarter loses all the interest it has accumulated during that quarter. With the "day of deposit" account, the interest *already earned* on the money you withdraw will be paid to you at the end of the quarter, provided you keep your account open.

Unfortunately, even with inflation running only about 3–4 percent yearly, this interest rate is far from satisfactory—particularly since you may have many thousands of dollars in your CASH balance. This money should be *working*. At 3 percent, it is merely leaning on its shovel, watching the world go by.

An alternative is the 90-day certificate account, offered by some savings banks and savings and loan associations, which pays somewhat more. The *disadvantages* of such an account are these:

1. Money withdrawn from this account before the 90 days are up loses all interest it has earned.
2. Each deposit you make renews the maturity date of this account to its full 90 days. Thus, if you make a deposit 30 days after you open the account, the maturity date is extended by one month. The new maturity date is 90 days away.

You can sidestep these drawbacks by operating your AIM program on a quarterly basis. Your withdrawals and deposits will then coincide with the maturity of your certificate. At the end of each quarter, you make your deposit or withdrawal as AIM dictates. If AIM gives a "no action" signal, your certificate will still automatically be renewed for 90 days. Either way, there is no penalty. And you will be earning more than 3 percent on your idle funds.

Longer-term certificates of one year and more yield higher interest rates, but penalties for premature withdrawals are so severe as to render them totally impractical for our purpose.

Earlier we had some fun by deprecating the interest AIM had earned on its Cash Reserves, suggesting that the amount was so small and so insignificant compared with AIM's huge trading profits that it really wasn't worth bothering about. I think most investors would agree. Give *me* a huge capital gain and I promise not to complain about missing out on an extra 1 or 2 percentage points in interest on my Cash Reserve. On the other hand, if our profits tend to be on the modest side, the interest rate would loom larger in our thoughts than in our ledgers: a higher rate might have bought us at least a Saddamino's Pizza ("We don't deliver but we'll Scud one to you")! I've not done any experiments to determine whether the interest dollars earned by our Cash Reserve make a very real difference in our final figures, but now that the cash in my own AIM program exceeds the stock portion, I suspect that it can. But whether it does or it doesn't, it's only prudent to place your Cash Reserves in a position to earn the maximum interest possible consistent with safety, convenience, and ease of withdrawal. You might decide that considerations of safety outweigh all the others, in which case you'd pick a bank account. But remember that even though Money Market Mutual Funds are not federally insured, no one has ever lost a penny in them; and that record should comfort all but the most timorous souls.

For convenience, flexibility, and the possibility of attractive yields, it would be hard to beat the so-called "money funds" as a repository for your CASH balance. These funds invest solely in bank certificates of deposit and/or U.S. Treasury bills, top-quality commercial paper, and other money market instruments. Although your money is not insured, these funds are relatively safe. Many money funds keep the price per share fixed at $1 a share or $10 a share. Should the fund earn trading profits (as opposed to interest), they are passed on to the shareholders as an increased dividend that month. If the fund experiences trading losses, these are deducted from the shareholder's dividend that month. Other money funds do not follow this practice, but rather allow the price per share to fluctuate to reflect any trading profits or losses. This comparatively rare fluctuation is generally very slight—a penny per share increase this week, a penny per share decrease the next week on a per share price of $10.

Late in 1974, when money was tight, yields of 10 percent and better were available from money funds. But by the end of 1975, these yields had tumbled to less than 6 percent. A year later, some were yielding less than 5 percent.

A REPRESENTATIVE "MONEY FUND" YIELD

1986	1987	1988	1989	2000
7%	6%	6%	8%	6%

That being the case, what possible justification could there be for keeping our CASH balance in a money fund rather than in an ordinary bank account even when at times, rates are similar? One reason is that money fund yields go up as well as down; our bank account yield remains the same. Second, there is never any penalty for withdrawing from a money fund. Dividends are paid on your money for every day it remains with the fund. Third, money funds declare dividends every month and credit our account accordingly. We know month by month exactly how much CASH balance we have. Fourth, most money funds offer free checking privileges. They send us free checks, which we can use just like a checking account. There is only one catch: the smallest check we can write against our account is $500. (Some funds allow $250.)

If AIM should ask us to invest only $250, how can we use a money fund check to draw against our CASH balance? Simple. We write a money fund check in the amount of $500, deposit it in our own bank checking account, and write two checks on our bank for $250. One check we send back to the money fund for deposit, the other we send to our broker or mutual fund to buy stock for us. Nothing could be more convenient. And it is profitable as well, for the money fund continues to pay interest on the $500 check we have just written until it clears through our own bank and reaches the money fund's bank, a process that could take as long as a week. Not only have we not lost any interest by this technique, we actually can pick up a couple of days of free interest before the money fund check is presented to its own bank for payment!

In making your choice from among the many money funds available and advertised in the financial sections of newspapers, consider the following to determine if the fund's requirements match your own needs:

1. Does the fund require an *initial* deposit greater than our initial CASH balance? If so, we'll have to make up the shortfall and then withdraw the excess.

2. Does the fund require subsequent deposits greater than $100? If it does, you will not be able to sell $100 worth of stock when AIM asks you to and deposit the proceeds in your money fund account. If the fund requires a minimum subsequent deposit of, say, $250, the difference is not so critical as to make the fund unusable for you. You would simply wait until AIM asks you to sell $250 or more worth of stock before taking any sell action. Some money

funds, however, require subsequent deposits of $1,000 and more. Unless your portfolio is of very substantial size, your sale transactions will ordinarily not approach this figure; and the $1,000 limitation might prevent AIM from functioning at its peak efficiency.

3. Does the fund require that a *minimum balance* be maintained in your account? If the minimum balance is quite small, perhaps a couple of hundred dollars, it is not likely that the CASH balance of a moderately sized AIM program will fall to that level. But if the minimum balance required is several thousands of dollars, your CASH balance may easily sink below that level—and the fund's computer will send you a warning to make up the difference within a month or your account will be closed.

Money funds, then, are recommended as a depository for your idle investment dollars. In 1984, money market mutual funds were once again yielding about 12 percent, as they had back in 1982, and 1980 as well. And at 12 percent, money doubles in six years!

As heartwarming as 12 percent would be to the AIM investor who, unlike most other investors, generally has a substantial portion of his portfolio in cash and enjoys the best of both worlds, AIM's mechanism is not so unsophisticated as to be content with simply a generous return on its CASH balance. *Even if its CASH balance earned no interest at all, these reserve funds are always generating a hidden power all their own.* How? Because the dollars themselves are constantly changing value according to the number of shares they will buy. When a stock sells at $10 a share, for example, it takes ten dollars to buy a single share. But if the stock declines to $7 a share, it takes only *seven* dollars to buy a share. AIM is so constructed as to make maximum use of its CASH balance: it makes its major purchases at bargain-basement levels. When it sells a share of stock for $10 and transfers the proceeds to its CASH balance, it increases its CASH balance by $10. Then, and only then, is that $10 bill worth exactly $10. It is worth $10 because AIM can buy a share of $10 stock with it.

Should the stock decline to $7 a share, that $10 can now buy 1.43 shares! *Without earning any interest* whatever, the $10 has leaped in value, relative to what it can now buy, by 43 percent. Any interest it does manage to accumulate in the meantime is just so much gravy.

Although there seems to be no compelling reason for doing so beyond the pleasure involved, we operate our own Automatic Investment Program on a *monthly,* rather than quarterly, basis, even though in the several tests we have done comparing monthly operation with quarterly operation, the final results do not appear to differ appreciably. As noted earlier, we generally keep our CASH balance in a money fund for the higher interest rates that may be available in these instruments. When money market yields declined in 1976 to levels below those obtainable in savings accounts, prudence dictated "disintermediation"—a financial term used to describe the shifting of assets to more lucrative areas. We chose the 90-day savings certificate with an effective yield of 6 percent (5.75 percent compounded continuously). Although the savings banks we queried do not permit additional deposits to these certificates—requiring the depositor to go to the trouble of opening a new account for each subsequent deposit—the federally insured savings and loan associations we contacted do.

These certificates can yield much more, but the mechanics remain the same at most Savings and Loan Associations that we checked out. If there is no activity in our savings account for the original term of 90 days, the bank automatically extends the maturity date by 90 more days at the conclusion of each quarter. Should AIM direct us to sell stock, we would simply deposit the proceeds of the sale into our savings account. Such activity also automatically extends the maturity date of our savings certificate by 90 days.

If we should have to withdraw funds from our savings

account in order to buy stock—a relatively infrequent occurrence—the bank imposes a small penalty: no interest is paid for the period on the amount withdrawn. However, we are permitted to withdraw our accumulated interest at any time without penalty.

True, savings banks and savings and loan associations levy no penalties whatever on withdrawals from ordinary day-of-deposit-to-day-of-withdrawal accounts paying 5.73 percent (5.50 percent compounded daily)—but a 90-day account can increase the earnings on your CASH balance by 13 percent! We believe the extra earning power justifies the small penalty risk.

GROWTH OF A $10,000 CASH BALANCE

Year	5.50% Passbook Account	6% 90-Day Certificate Account
1st Year	$10,573	$10,627
2nd Year	$11,179	$11,293
3rd Year	$11,820	$12,001
4th Year	$12,497	$12,753
5th Year	$13,213	$13,553
6th Year	$13,970	$14,403
7th Year	$14,770	$15,306
8th Year	$15,616	$16,266
9th Year	$16,511	$17,286
10th Year	$17,457	$18,370
11th Year	$18,457	$19,522
12th Year	$19,515	$20,746

After a dozen years, the 6 percent savings account has doubled in value. At this point, although it is still yielding 6 percent interest, it is earning 16 percent more dollars annually than the ordinary passbook account:

$$6\% \ (6.27\%) \times \$20,746 = \$1,301$$
$$5.50\% \ (5.73\%) \times \$19,515 = \$1,118$$

During long stretches of dullness in the stock market, a CASH balance consistently growing at the rate of 6 percent per year can soothe many a troubled brow. And, of course, should money market rates turn upward again, it is a simple matter to transfer our CASH balance back into a money fund to take advantage of the higher yields.

A word of caution: Some savings institutions *appear* to offer the kind of convenient, flexible 90-day certificate we have been discussing, when in fact they do not. While they do permit subsequent deposits to the account, the legal jargon in which their rules and regulations are written may conceal truly hellish punishments for the unwary depositor. Each time you renew your account for another 90 days, the interest you have earned over the past 90 days *stops* being interest and becomes a part of your new principal. You may therefore not withdraw those interest dollars, should the need arise, without paying a penalty. This will never do. It is one thing to penalize us for withdrawing from our *principal,* but quite another to slap our wrists when we dip into our pool of interest dollars. Worse yet, some savings institutions may impose a *double* penalty on ordinary withdrawals from your principal: regardless of how long you have held your account, if you dare to make a withdrawal the bank not only cuts the interest this amount has earned to 5.50 percent, but penalizes you a full 90 days' interest on the amnount withdrawn!

The kind of 90-day account *you* want offers the following advantages:

1. It automatically renews itself every 90 days.
2. It permits subsequent deposits.
3. Accumulated interest does *not* become a part of the new principal every time you renew the account.
4. The only penalty imposed is the forfeiture of all interest earned by the amount withdrawn from the beginning of the most recent 90-day term.
5. The account is federally insured.

With such an account, an investor who operates his AIM program on a quarterly basis would never have to pay any penalty whatever, since his withdrawals—when they are required—would occur quarterly at the same time his 90-day bank account matured.

An investor who prefers to operate his AIM program on a monthly basis risks only a very slight penalty. To the extent that the accumulated interest in his account will accommodate him, he is not penalized for dipping into this ever-growing pool of cash reserves. Should he need funds in excess of his accumulated interest, and should this need occur at the end of the first month of the 90-day term of his bank account, he will lose one month's interest on the amount he withdraws. If the need occurs at the end of the second month of the 90-day term of his bank account, he will lose two months' interest on the amount withdrawn. And, obviously, if the need should occur at the end of the third month of the 90-day term of his bank account, he will lose *no* interest on the amount withdrawn, because his 90-day account is now mature and he may withdraw his entire account, if he so desires, without penalty. Thus, regardless of the length of time the AIM investor holds his 90-day account and regardless of the number of times he renews it, the *maximum* penalty he risks is 60 days' interest on the amount he withdraws—and this would occur only rarely.

Personally, I prefer the standard, plain vanilla money market fund offered by most mutual fund companies. I have enough to worry about.

NINE

Better Than Gold as an Inflation Hedge—at 4¢ an Ounce!

Feisty little President Harry S. Truman. Lean, tall General Douglas MacArthur with his filigreed campaign cap brushing the clouds. In ABC-TV's drama "Collision Course," depicting the conflict between these two historical figures, compact E.G. Marshall portrayed the late President while lanky Henry Fonda was given the role of General MacArthur. A publicity photo shows the two of them together, with Hank Fonda towering over E.G. Marshall.

Anything wrong with that? Nothing—except if you had seen the *real* Harry S. Truman standing next to the *real* Douglas MacArthur, it might have taken you awhile to determine just who was towering over whom! The General, of course, had a way of directing camera angles to make himself appear gargantuan, and thus that was the image he successfully projected. Harry Truman, the "underdog" in the presidential race against Tom Dewey, entered our consciousness as a little David battling Goliath: "Give 'em hell, Harry!" We thought of him as small in stature. We thought of General MacArthur as much the taller of the two—at least partially because, in those critical early war years against Japan, we *wanted* him to be tall. Nonetheless, the fact remains that only an inch or two separated the two men!

In much the same way, we have been conditioned in recent years to think of gold as the miracle metal that will protect us from disaster in the economic collapse that is sure to come. Numerous Jeremiahs have warned us that paper currencies, so rapidly depreciating in value, will shortly become worthless—and that we had better buy up all the precious metal we can, regardless of price. Otherwise we will all starve to death, because the farmer isn't going to exchange any of his precious vegetables for worthless paper and the grocer isn't going to sell us a loaf of bread for those clunky coins in our pockets from which all the silver has been removed. Gold represents the only true value, they tell us. It always has and it always will.

Any GI who has served abroad could tell you a different story. In the shattered economy of Japan in 1947, needing some Japanese currency with which to buy film, I sold my gold school ring in a Tokyo jewelry shop for 300 yen. At the official exchange rate, this amounted to about $5. The ring had cost three times that. "Plenty gold," the jeweler said, shaking his head sadly when I protested the price. "Plenty gold. Everybody want to sell. Nobody want to buy." When I mentioned the experience to one of my superiors, a top sergeant, he laughed. "I'm going into Tokyo tomorrow," he said. "Come on in with me. I'll show you something."

We stopped first at the post exchange, where the sergeant purchased a carton of cigarettes and some soap and handed the female Japanese clerk his ration card. *"Anata-wa taihen utsukushi kami no ke o motte imasu,"* he said to the girl. She giggled. *"Honto?"*

"Honto," he said.

"Arigato gozaimasu," she giggled, handing him back his ration card—unpunched.

"What did you say to her?" I asked him outside.

"I told her she had pretty hair, that's all."

"But they *all* have the same hair. They all have pretty black hair."

"You don't know *anything* about women, do you?"

In Tokyo we headed for the Dai-Ichi Building, General MacArthur's headquarters. We entered an elevator, and the sergeant pressed the Basement button. Down we went.

The door opened and we stepped out. A Japanese, possibly an employee of the building or a relative of someone who was, greeted us effusively. The sergeant, who had no doubt dealt with the gentleman before, spoke a few words to him and then emptied his pockets of soap and cigarettes. In return, the Japanese counted out *thousands* of yen and handed the bundle of currency to the sergeant.

"Here," the sergeant said as we left the building, thrusting a wad of bills into my hand. "You'll need some yen."

We did the hick-in-the-big-town routine: shoeshine, haircut, facial massage, manicure, another shoeshine, rickshaw rides, souvenirs, etcetera. When the day had ended, I discovered to my surprise that I had managed to squander only 10 or 20 yen. I'd spent a day living like a pampered playboy on the proceeds of only a couple of cigarettes!

Unfortunately, there was a flaw in my character that did not permit me to enjoy being rich among the many poor, and since the Army provided me with the necessary food and shelter, I didn't really need anything that could be purchased with yen. But I remembered the grim lesson I had learned in the Tokyo jewelry shop: "Plenty gold. Everybody want to sell. Nobody want to buy." I had learned that in a busted economy in which everybody is scrambling to survive, gold might bring only a fraction of its cost while a bar of soap or a package of cigarettes could command hundreds of times their value! Why? Because a bar of soap can be *used*. A package of cigarettes can be *used*. And if one were too poor to consume the luxury himself, it could be used as a medium of exchange. When everybody has gold, what will they *buy* with that gold? You are in a lifeboat full of survivors, and each has managed to escape with a bag of gold. Except you. You have a bar of soap and a package of cigarettes. Who is the wealthiest individual in the boat? *You* are, because you have something all the rest *want*. If you wished, you could demand all the gold in everybody's possession in return for a cigarette or a sliver of soap (and afterwards, of course, sleep with one eye open). Gold has no day-to-day utility beyond its representational value: you can't eat it, smoke it, or wash your face with it. Cigarettes and soap have other advantages as well: they do not have to be weighed or assayed. They come in convenient, printed packages with built-in recognition factors. And as any GI knows, the black market price for these items in Japan tended to remain fairly stable from dealer to dealer and over a long period of time.

In the kingdom of gold, soap and cigarettes are king.

When the factories are shuttered, when the tobacco fields are overgrown with weeds, it is the usable item, not gold, that will enable you to survive. Any remaining farmer will exchange food for a bar of precious soap or a package of cigarettes. Any grocer—if there are any left—will give you some bread or a few slices of meat for your soap or cigarettes, provided he makes a profit on the transaction. A friend or neighbor would most likely trade you a can of food or a few potatoes for your bar of soap or your cigarettes. With gold bars or gold coins—even if they *are* acceptable as value in this cataclysm predicted by the prophets of doom—you would have to make a *major* purchase each time you went forth seeking food. The grocer, the farmer, or your neighbor certainly can't give you "change" for your gold coin. What would they use for change?

Of the two items, we prefer soap as the perfect medium for barter. Its shelf life is far longer than that of cigarettes, which tend to dry out and become stale over a period of time. *Everybody* uses soap, and even in chaos, unless people want to sink to the level of savages, everybody will need soap almost as much as they need food. And although it has soared in cost over the past two years (grain shortage equals livestock shortage equals fat shortage equals expensive soap), its still modest price does not reflect the multitude of state and federal taxes that are levied on cigarettes.

We do not envision a calamity on the scale predicted by the doomsayers, but even if we are wrong, we would far rather have laid in several cases of soap at a cost of a couple of hundred dollars than to have tied up a good part of our investment capital in a few bars of gold. Remember the story of King Midas. Gold can be a mighty cold companion.

And if worse doesn't come to worst, we can always use our soap. We would have to buy it anyway, and chances are quite good that the price of soap will have risen sharply in the meantime. So that investment in soap has actually been earning interest for us!

"GOLD IS THE ONLY TRUE WEALTH!" screamed the ads in the financial section of the *New York Times* back in gold-feverish 1974. But if you turned back a few pages, you would find an inch-and-a-half news item buried somewhere inside:

SOAP RUSH KILLS 2 IN EGYPT

CAIRO, Aug. 10 (Reuters)—Two people were killed and five injured in the rush to buy a piece of soap, which is scarce in Egypt these days, the newspaper *Al-Ahram* reported today. In a fight over the last piece of soap in a shop in Rozeik village, the grocer and his son were killed, the newspaper said.

"GOLD AT $400 AN OUNCE?" cried the ads in the financial section of the *Times* on yet another day of that wonderful year, 1974. Again, if you turn back several pages, you will find a news story slugged "India Begins Drive Against Tax Evaders." Following are excerpts:

NEW DELHI, July 27—Prime Minister Indira Gandhi's Government has begun a vigorous drive against hoarding and tax evasion.

In cities and towns around the country, police officials and internal revenue men have raided shops,
business houses, and bank safety deposit vaults to
bring out hoarded grain, steel, paper, kerosene, soap,
cigarettes, and other fast-moving consumer goods.

The two-week-old drive is aimed at bringing into
the open the huge amount of income that had evaded
taxation, estimated at nearly $10 billion. Fifty percent
of all transactions in real estate, transport, industry,
and trade are said to be financed by untaxed funds. . . .

Few people were found to hoard their wealth in the
form of currency notes or gold. . . . In Bombay the
favorite hoarding commodities are soap, toothpaste
and even combs. . . .

"As long as they kept the black money in paper
currency it didn't bother us much," said an official.
"But now they have started using that money to buy
up fast-moving consumer goods, pushing up their
prices enormously."

The official also said that with the rupee losing
value—a rupee is worth today a quarter of its value 15
years ago—people want to dump paper currency in exchange for more durable goods. Gold and jewelry used
to be the favorites, but these are becoming more and
more difficult to negotiate because of their skyrock-
eting prices.

"So the natural choice is something which is more
in demand and can produce money in the quick," the
official said.

In the United States at about that time, a bar of giant-
size Ivory soap was selling for about 21¢ in the supermarkets. A couple of years later, the price had nearly
doubled, while the price of gold had steadily declined
from its all-time high of approximately $200 an ounce to
about $130. As Green's Commodity Letter had noted
earlier: "Of course, as long as the gold pool bankers,
aided by the merchants of fear . . . found ready buyers,
the price of gold has a rise like any other glamour

stock . . . then, like in most stock promotions which soured when a few holders, simultaneously awakened to the idea of taking profit, the friendly Swiss bankers, when instructed to dispose of the coveted yellow metal at the $120–$130 level, scratched their gnomish heads and asked the world's oldest question: 'Sell at those prices? To whom?' "*

On December 19, 1975, I walked into a local grocery store with a giant-size bar of Ivory soap I had purchased two years earlier at a supermarket for 21¢.

"How much will you give me for this?" I asked the owner.

"Thirty-five cents," she replied.

"How could you afford to pay me thirty-five cents for it?

"Because it sells for more than that, and I'd have to make a profit."

"I'll take it," I said. "But instead of the money, I'll just take this can of vegetables."

I had just exchanged a bar of soap for food! And over the two-year period, my bar of soap had increased in value 67 percent!

In the meantime, a new breed of thieves had been stealing barrels of cooking fat from the rear of restaurants in Manhattan. Way back in World War II, if you remember, butcher shops were paying housewives 4¢ a pound for the rendered fat they brought in. And that's what soap is made of—fat saponified with an alkali.

You can't really construct a disaster-proof portfolio or invest in anticipation of economic collapse. But with Automatic Investment Management handling your stocks and a few cases of soap tucked away in your cellar or garage, you're as prepared as anyone could be for the worst that could happen. And if gloom-prophet Harry Browne is right and a pound of beef does sell for $80

*We live in nervous times. Gold subsequently soared over $800, then drifted below $300 in 2000.

billion in the middle of the crisis he and other writers see ahead, so will a pound of soap!

You can't buy and store beef in preparation for that eventuality—but you can buy soap!

Besides, when the Treasury's gold is depleted, the government can always confiscate your gold as they did in the thirties at $35 an ounce. And then they could sell it back to you some years later, as they did in 1975, at something like five times what they paid you for it.

But what in the world could the government do with all that Ivory Soap?

At this point, if you have come to feel about AIM as we do, you may be tempted to build a shrine in its honor. In the beginning, understandably, you might have been skeptical. You had heard it said, "There is no such thing as a free lunch." But AIM brings forth a new doctrine: "People who say that usually own the restaurant!"

Now *you* own the restaurant. AIM will not only manage your investments for you better than most of the "experts"—at no charge—but allows you to deposit new funds into your program anytime you feel like it. And it manages these new funds with the same care and devotion that it applies to your original nest egg. All AIM asks of you is a few minutes of your time once a month.

If that isn't a miracle, I'd like to know what is.

But there is even more to come: AIM is not a finicky eater. You can feed it blue chips, you can feed it dogs, *you can even feed it gold!* That's correct—AIM thrives on equity of any kind: gold, silver, any item that fluctuates in value. If you feel that our economic system is on the verge of collapse and that only those who own gold or silver will survive, AIM will be pleased to manage your portfolio of precious metals. And if you have faith in our economy and yet want to hedge your bet by adding *some* gold or silver to your portfolio, AIM will accept those terms as well.

Gold and silver are presently available in a variety of

forms and quantities. Banks and coin dealers can give you all the information you need, whether you are interested in one-ounce gold coins like the Krugerrand, widely available and a big favorite among "gold bugs"; gold wafers—tiny bars of gold weighing anywhere from ⅙ of an ounce to 3 ounces; or silver coins minted by the U.S. prior to 1965. You will have to pay many times the face value of these silver coins, but there are those who maintain they still represent great value. When the end comes and paper money becomes worthless, they say, you will need these silver coins to buy your daily bread.

Larger portfolios may want to investigate gold and silver bullion, the purchase of which requires substantially larger outlays.

With Automatic Investment Management, gold and silver are bought and sold exactly like stocks. If AIM gives a $500 buy signal, you would buy $500 worth of gold or silver. If AIM says sell $500, you would sell $500 worth of gold or silver. There is no better way of investing in these precious metals, and avoiding disaster, than letting AIM handle it for us. It can be a volatile and treacherous market, as many investors have discovered to their loss and dismay, but AIM understands all this and is not intimidated. AIM will smooth out all the highs and lows for you. It will buy in times of pessimism, and it will sell in times of overenthusiasm. Automatically.

If you believe, as we do, that stocks *still* offer the best opportunities for capital gains *if* we use AIM to handle our investments, you may nevertheless think it prudent to consider substituting gold for one of the stocks in the blue-chip half of your portfolio. Stocks in this portion may be kept at roughly the same value and require no other attention. Thus, as the price of gold rises and falls and conventional investors are run ragged by missing the boat at either port, this unit of your AIM program could generate some exciting profits for you through the years. Automatically!

With a portfolio consisting of blue-chip stocks, gold,

and an assortment of spicier stocks, and with Automatic Investment Management handling the whole affair, you are just going to have to find something *else* to worry about than your investments!

TEN

In Case of Emergency—Stay Put

Your Money Machine would welcome a crisis a good deal more than you might. As long as there's a stock market left when the smoke clears, AIM will emerge sweaty but happy. AIM positively loves a good solid disaster—something it can get its teeth into.

The crash of 1974 was a nice appetizer, as was that of 1987. For most investors, professional and amateur alike, a crash is a trauma from which they will never fully recover. For AIM, 1974 was an interesting year. Nothing to get excited about, but an *interesting* year. The month-end Dow Jones Industrial Average lost 28 percent, although many individual stocks lost far more than that.

A hypothetical investor who invested $10,000 in the Dow Jones Average at the beginning of 1974 suffered the same 28 percent loss as the Dow. Helpless as a hog on ice. By contrast, Automatic Investment Management emerged with an insignificant loss of only 12 percent! The ordinary investor has only $7,203 left of his original $10,000. AIM has $8,755.

Three short months after this horrendous year gasped to a close, AIM had moved briskly into the profit column! The ordinary investor did not surface until June, and when he did it was with a capital gain of only $274. By that time AIM had powered *its* portfolio into a profit of $1,042!

How AIM would have loved to see the stock price drop further in 1974! What a job it could have done if the market had become so demoralized as to fall completely apart!

"DOOMSDAY PREVIEW"
THE DOW JONES INDUSTRIAL AVERAGE, 1974

AUTOMATIC INVESTMENT MANAGEMENT: $10,000 INVESTMENT

Date	Stock Price	Stock Value	Safe	Cash*	Shares Bot(Sold)	Shares Owned	Portfolio Control	Buy(Sell) Advice	Market Order	Portfolio Value
Jan.	855.55	5,000	500	5,000	5.844	5.844	5,000	—	—	$10,000
Feb.	860.53	5,029	503	5,022	0	5.844	5,000	(29)	0	10,051
Mar.	846.68	4,948	495	5,044	0	5.844	5,000	52	0	9,992
Apr.	836.75	4,890	489	5,066	0	5.844	5,000	110	0	9,956
May	802.17	4,688	469	5,088	0	5.844	5,000	312	0	9,776
June	802.41	4,689	469	5,110	0	5.844	5,000	311	0	9,799
July	757.43	4,426	443	5,132	.173	6.017	5,066	574	131	9,558
Aug.	678.58	4,083	408	5,023	.847	6.864	5,354	983	575	9,106
Sept.	607.87	4,172	417	4,468	1.258	8.122	5,737	1182	765	8,640
Oct.	665.52	5,405	541	3,719	0	8.122	5,737	332	0	9,124
Nov.	618.66	5,025	503	3,735	.338	8.460	5,842	712	209	8,760
Dec.	616.24	5,213	521	3,542		8.460	5,842			8,755

AIM: $1,245 LOSS (12%)
ORDINARY INVESTOR: $2,797 LOSS (28%)

*Interest: 5¼% per annum.

147

"DOOMSDAY PREVIEW"
THE ROWE PRICE NEW HORIZONS FUND, 1974

AUTOMATIC INVESTMENT MANAGEMENT: $10,000 INVESTMENT

Date	Stock Price	Stock Value	Safe	Cash*	Shares Bot(Sold)	Shares Owned	Portfolio Control	Buy(Sell) Advice	Market Order	Portfolio Value
Jan.	7.87	5,000	500	5,000	635.324	635.324	5,000	—	—	$10,000
Feb.	7.66	4,867	487	5,022	0	635.324	5,000	133	0	9,889
Mar.	7.57	4,809	481	5,044	0	635.324	5,000	191	0	9,853
Apr.	7.16	4,549	455	5,066	0	635.324	5,000	451	0	9,615
May	6.89	4,377	438	5,088	26.851	662.175	5,093	623	185	9,465
June	6.39	4,231	423	4,925	68.701	730.876	5,313	862	439	9,156
July	5.90	4,312	431	4,506	96.610	827.486	5,598	1,001	570	8,818
Aug.	5.13	4,245	425	3,953	180.897	1008.383	6,062	1,353	928	8,198
Sept.	4.60	4,639	464	3,038	208.478	1216.861	6,542	1,423	959	7,677
Oct.	5.31	6,462	646	2,088	0	1216.861	6,542	80	0	8,550
Nov.	5.06	6,157	616	2,097	0	1216.861	6,542	385	0	8,254
Dec.	4.86	5,914	591	2,106	0	1216.861	6,542	628	0	8,020

AIM: $1,980 LOSS (20%)

ORDINARY INVESTOR: $3,823 LOSS (38%)

*Interest: 5¼% per annum.

Maybe next time . . .

Comparative results with the New York Stock Exchange Index for this period were virtually identical.

More aggressive portfolios, of course, experienced steeper drops in 1974, allowing AIM's reserves greater opportunities to move in for the kill at the bottom. When the more speculative Rowe Price New Horizons Fund dived 38 percent, the conventional investor who bought $10,000 worth of the fund's shares at the beginning of the year also lost 38 percent of his investment: $3,823. By the end of April 1976, he had *still* not recovered his original investment.

Automatic Investment Management held *its* loss to a much more tolerable 20 percent, $1,980, in this ferocious shakeout. Equally heartwarming, *AIM moved into the profit column four short months later, in April of 1975, at the price of $6.86!*

Our Doomsday previews presuppose that Armageddon will occur virtually as soon as we switch on our Money Machine, without allowing AIM's CASH balance to grow fat on sales of stock and on the interest it earns. Given a fair amount of time to increase its CASH balance, AIM will perform even greater miracles for us when stocks collapse for real.

It's something to look forward to.

ELEVEN

The Future of Investing

"I'm certainly not advertising the end of the world," *Newsweek* quoted a highly respected economist as saying in the midst of the gloom of 1974, "but I do think it's amazing that for the first time, I'm considering possibilities I never dreamed I would have to consider."

The world did not end, but many of the problems that inspired the melancholy did not result in the worst. Yet despite the lessons of that year, 1987 witnessed another debacle. The optimists predict that most of the problems are being overcome. The pessimists insist that we have merely been given a respite and that perdition lies just around the next bend: terrifying inflation, perhaps on the order of Germany in the twenties, during which lunch in a Gasthaus cost 20 billion marks, equivalent to 140 gold pfennigs, and the dollar—today worth about 2 marks—was fixed at 4.2 *trillion* marks; or an equally terrifying Depression such as the one that scarred the world in the thirties with its even more disastrous political and military consequences. Well, inflation proved to be a problem in the late seventies but nowhere on the order of that.

Nothing—including gold coins, antiques, art collections, and stocks and bonds—can really protect us against Doomsday. And, as we indicated earlier, it is not possible to invest in anticipation of disaster, particularly since we do not even know what *kind* of disaster we are anticipating. A rational approach is of little help here because we are not living in rational times. Even if we were, we could not be forearmed and comforted by the fact that history repeats itself while at the same time ignoring Edson Gould's wise observation that, while history does repeat, the *details* change—and the details are what trap generation after generation. The German father back in the 1900s was being quite rational when he left his two sons a large sum of money and cautioned them to spend it wisely. The good son, a sensible young man, invested his inheritance in safe German government bonds. The other son promptly went out and blew his share on wine, women, and song. When inflation struck and it took wheelbarrows full of paper marks to buy a loaf of bread, the prudent son found that his bonds were worthless. The prodigal son, discovering that glass was now in short supply, sold his cellar full of empty champagne bottles for a very tidy sum of money.

A little luck and bold new approaches are likely to be the ingredients for investment success in tomorrow's climate. For what are we to do when Franz Pick, the international currency expert, predicts: "Banking holiday. Moratorium on all debts except mortgage debts. Closing Wall Street for good, including the bond markets. Exchanging dollar bank notes for new dollars at a rate of ten for one or twenty for one"? What can we think when C.V. Myers, editor of Myers' Finance and Energy Letter of Zurich, Switzerland, says, "I believe the road to deflation now stretches before us. That means the reduction of the money supply by the reduced values of equities—in other words, the crashing market. It means the liquidation of debt through deflation. The big bad day that we have known is surely coming, is now drawing very close"? How are we to plan our defense when Frank Ogden of the Survival Institute of the Future looks at his "economic collapse indicators"—including the price of gold and luxury foods, crop failures, soil depletion, terrorist activities, labor unrest, public service breakdowns, industrial damage to the environment, and police and political corruption—and predicts "massive, catastrophic economic collapse"? Where do we turn when stock market letter writer James Dines, who was reportedly planning a move to Switzerland, predicts a huge market shakeout down to 400 on the Dow, a massive collapse of pension funds, bank and utility failures, a busted Social Security system, followed by a sound economy based on gold and a new political system, either of the right or the left?

If these distinguished gentlemen are correct, what's the sense in kidding ourselves any longer? Why go through the motions of earning and investing and hoping for a brighter tomorrow when we *know* the clock is ticking? Well, for one thing, the predictions may not come true. For another, we've got to do *something*—however useless—like the husband ordered by the doctor to run out and boil some water while his wife is in labor. And finally, the great sportswriter Damon Runyan once said that where the human race is concerned, the odds are 9 to 5 against. We know the odds are against us—always have been—but we keep plugging away anyway. What's the alternative?

This time around, however, even in the face of the seemingly overwhelming obstacles that confront us, we have a valiant and dependable ally we have never had before: Automatic Investment Management. Unless the market crumbles to powder and stock certificates aren't worth the paper they're printed on—in which case money itself will probably be worthless—AIM will wage war on our behalf to achieve its twin objectives: to protect our original capital, and to make that capital *grow* as rapidly as possible consistent with safety. We have already seen AIM's performance in the field during declines of considerable magnitude, but it may yet turn out that these were only war games and that the true test is yet to come. If so, the evidence is before us that AIM will not only rise to the challenge but could achieve results for us on a scale we can scarcely imagine. With almost uncanny foresight, AIM shuttles its assets back and forth between equity and cash, moving heavily into cash at the highs and thunderously into equity at the lows—precisely the opposite behavior of most investors, both professional and amateur, who buy at the highs and sell at the lows. So widespread and so dependable is this idiocy that mutual fund cash balances are closely watched as an indicator of the market's next move: a large cash position means the bear market is over. In like manner, when most investment advisors are bearish, the market can be expected to explode upward.

In the final stages of a bull market, mutual funds maintain an almost insignificant cash balance. With their stockholders cheering them on in the performance derby, they dare not move into cash and thereby slow the increase in their per share asset value. At all costs, they *must* stay fully invested, they *must* stay in the race and keep their momentum going. The penalty for not observing this routine is investor disenchantment and a subsequent decrease in fund shares sold. The penalty for *following* such a disastrous philosophy, of course, is a demolition of the investor's capital when the crunch comes—but that's not quite as painful to the fund managers. "By and large in such circumstances," wrote Robert Metz in the *New York Times* on October 5, 1973, "all mutual funds will stay on the equity-investment pond like sitting ducks and take a royal beating, short term anyway. That is to say, the shareholders of the funds will take a beating.

"Management rides out the storm in the comfort of well-appointed offices. The fee may drop a bit as anxious shareholders cash in, but the major managements will survive more or less intact. Individual portfolio managers may be fired, taking the rap for matters that are essentially beyond their control. . . .

"Take the recent bear market. There could hardly have been any doubts six months ago that the market was unfavorable in the extreme—especially for the broad list of stocks. Yet at no time did the combined cash level of the mutual funds rise above 9 percent."

You can depend on it. At the close of 1969, just before the stock market began to fall apart in earnest, mutual funds held only $3.8 billion in cash or cash equivalents, which worked out to only 7.96 percent of their $48.2 billion in assets! This cash position is far too small to protect a portfolio from severe damage in a market dive and to enable a mutual fund to take effective advantage of firesale prices at the bottom of the slide.

With the market well into its death throes, mutual funds finally make the effort to pull in their horns and build up their cash positions. Here, at least, one would suppose mutual funds would try to atone for missed opportunities by shifting some of their cash reserves into bargain-priced equities. But, like a spent fighter on the ropes who covers up while his opponent batters him unmercifully, mutual funds tend to hang on to their cash in self-defense against the market's pummeling. Long after the market, its arms weary, backs away to catch its breath, mutual funds are still covering up on the ropes, wincing under imaginary blows—even though a good solid punch would floor the wobbly-legged market at this point. By the time mutual funds decide to come out of their shell and throw some leather, it's too late. The bell has rung and the market has won on points.

After one of the most brutal poundings in history, the Dow Jones Industrial Average closed at 616 on December 31, 1974. Obviously, this presented one of the great opportunities of a lifetime to accumulate quality stocks at giveaway prices and build a fortune on them. Warren Buffet, one of the shrewdest and most successful investors in America, who called it quits in 1969 because the market was overpriced, told *Forbes Magazine* late in 1974 that he now felt "like an oversexed guy in a harem. This is the time to start investing."

It was. It was. But at the end of 1974, even as the market had begun to rally off its low, many mutual funds and other "professional" investors were still sitting on enormous cash hoards. The two common stock mutual fund annual reports we happen to have on hand speak for themselves:

	% of Common Stocks Held	Price Per Share 1974	1975
FUND A	56%	$6.38	$7.95
FUND B	94%	$4.82	$7.76

At one of the most historically attractive buying points ever, Fund A had only 56 percent of its assets in stock! Fund B, whose wisdom in retrospect was due more to its policy of remaining fully invested at all times than to adroit market timing, held 94 percent of its assets in equities. In 1975, the Dow soared 35 percent. Fund A failed even to keep up with the averages for the simple reason that it was heavy into cash instead of stocks. Fund B's performance far surpassed that of the Dow both because it was virtually fully invested and because it specializes in high-growth securities. But at the end of 1975 both funds were still selling below their 1969 prices, despite a number of extraordinary buying opportunities along the way. Therefore, neither fund can be said to have given its shareholders professional management in the sense that all buy and sell decisions have been made for them, and in this failing, the two mutual funds are not alone. No mutual fund can possibly furnish this service with any consistency. If it is the fund's policy to be fully invested at all times, its portfolio will tend to move up and down with the market—and its performance at any given time will depend almost entirely upon the direction of the market itself. If the mutual fund has more flexibility and can adjust its cash-to-equity ratio at will, the situation can be even more fraught with peril and frustration: the market may go on to make new highs while the shareholders of such a fund, whose managers have erred in judgment, are still suffering from the results of that mistake.

Mutual funds can be a valid and profitable tool in your investment program, but do not expect the tool itself to do the whole job. It is your *use* of the tool that can get the job done.

Because AIM has no fear and no greed, and because it does not listen to idle gossip, it *cannot* misjudge the direction of the market. At each stock-value level, it has a certain, definite job to do. This job it discharges with diligence and efficiency. And if there is a cataclysm lurking somewhere out there in the shadows and $50 stocks are selling at $5, AIM will automatically come down with both feet on the buy side and scoop up mountains of stock.

Enough to make you one of the leading citizens of the new society that will spring from the rubble.

You can bet on it.

We have suggested, immodestly perhaps, that the future belongs to Automatic Investment Management, and that AIM could positively shine in the turbulent kind of market many observers see ahead. The future investing climate, they say, is going to be quite different from the past. Those who do not recognize the changes that have occurred and the new problems we face and will continue to face are simply placing their heads on the chopping block.

Back in 1972 when the ebullient Dow had thrust through 1,000 and God was in his heaven and all was right with the world, the talk was that we were in a new era of perpetually rising stock prices (where have we heard *that* before?) that could rival the great post-World War II bull market. Gerald S. Jeremias, president of the Empire Planning Corporation in New York City, did not agree. "On February 9, 1966, when the Dow-Jones Industrials made an intraday high of 1,000.1, the post-World War II market, which stretched from mid-1949 when the Dow was 161, was over," Mr. Jeremias mantained. "This was a gain of 520 percent and reflected the fact that all the conditions in 1949 were uniquely right for a gigantic boom. Until then, the United States had been under the impact of war; the painful memory of the Depression and the economic insecurity of the 1930s was still vivid."

Those days are gone forever, Mr. Jeremias said. The problems are different now. And the solutions do not lie in stepped-up production of consumer goods but in expensive remedial measures to correct environmental excesses, racial inequities, educational deficiencies, and a variety of social dilemmas.

Mr. Jeremias pointed out that while the solutions themselves would create new businesses and new jobs, they almost certainly would not produce explosive growth and profits. "To get the same kind of growth that we got between 1949 and 1966, we would have to expect by 1982 a Dow-Jones average of 5,200. This is manifestly impossible. In fact, I foresee a severe setback for the Dow by 1974 when it could retrace its steps to the levels of the 1970 bear market."

Mr. Jeremias was right about 1974. And a growing number of other stock market watchers would agree that he is probably right about his other views as well. Charles W. Buek, president of the United States Trust Company, addressing a conference sponsored by the American Bankers Association in 1968, zeroed in on 1967, the vintage year for hot-shot mutual funds. While the Dow crept up a modest 15 percent, performance funds were logging spectacular gains of 50 percent and more.

But, Mr. Buek told the conference, th-th-that's all, folks! What helped the mutual fund managers look like ultrastars was "something unique and nonrecurring"; 1967 was the year in which "pale blue chips" were awarded substantially higher earnings multiples, just as blue chips had been so honored in the period between 1957 and 1961.

Under a cloud of distrust in the post-Depression years, common stocks didn't achieve complete respectability until 1958. "It was then that the long-awaited 'post-war depression' was permanently laid to rest," said Mr. Buek. "Avoided in 1948, postponed by the Korean War, it was widely anticipated and long overdue in 1958. When the test came, corporate management took timely action, the Government played its part, consumers displayed exceptional equanimity, and our economic instrumentation helped us navigate through a critical period."

At this point, pension funds, endowment funds, mutual funds, and even life insurance companies made the daring decision to "get their feet wet in common stocks. The blue chips responded to this new interest. Stock prices advanced without a corresponding increase in earnings—and price-earnings ratios of the key stocks moved up sharply. To name a few: General Foods' price-earnings ratio went from 11 to 30, Sears' from 12 to 25, U.S. Gypsum's from 13 to 23, American Home Products' from 15 to 35, International Nickel's from 15 to 24, American Electric Power's from 16 to 27, Procter & Gamble's from 19 to 33.

In 1967 the stock market's new respectability spilled over into the "pale blue chips." This second echelon of equities responded to the buying in the same manner as had the blue chips a decade earlier—even more vigorously because of their small size. Between 1966 and 1967—in one year—Simplicity Pattern's price-earnings ratio leaped from 13 to 30, McDonald's from 16 to 26, Holiday Inns' from 21 to 33, Papercraft's from 12 to 20, P.A. Hunt Chemical's from 21 to 33, and Dr. Pepper's from 11 to 18.

And that's what made 1967 the golden year we all look back on fondly. Will it come again? It is so far in the future that it may not be worth waiting for, said Mr. Buek.

Back there in 1968, it was anybody's guess.

Arthur Burns, chairman of the Federal Reserve Board, suggested later that the U.S. economy may have entered a new "long cycle" of sluggishness, with deeper recessions than have been experienced since World War II, greater unemployment, and recoveries that do not bounce upward as high. In short, the modern equivalent of the grim 1930s. "There has been a blow to confidence so sharp that you do not recover fully from it for a good while," he said.

Fred Alger of Fred Alger & Co. observed in 1971: "The sixties saw some permanent changes in investment approach," and indicated that portfolio managers no longer buy stock and lock it up in the expectation of growing with the economy. Rather they demonstrate "a willingness to move assets around with more intensive, more energetic management. There is no question that we will have a more speculative stock market."

This turned out to be an understatement as the nineties witnessed the rise of the day trader.

Look back to the shuddering seventies: Despite the conventional wisdom that the small investor is always wrong, the odd-lotter, who buys or sells fewer than 100 shares at a time, also regards the future with pessimism. Total odd-lot activity has been declining steadily over the years, a trend that not only threatens to undermine the liquidity of the market, but also suggests that the small investor has had it with stocks and is pulling out what's left of his investment dollars. In 1972, for the first time in history, investors redeemed more mutual fund shares than they bought. And the trend has persisted, although the so-called money funds have taken up some of the slack. Strictly speaking, money funds do not represent investment dollars, but idle dollars waiting for a better opportunity. Such was the dire situation in the seventies.

Thus, the Second Era of investing died, not with a bang but a whimper. In the First Era of investing, prior to World War II, dividends were the primary reason for buying stocks. Investors hoped to earn more income on their money than they could in a savings account, and if the stocks they bought just happened to rise in price after ten years or so and give them a long-term gain as well, that was just so much sweeter. In the Second Era of investing, after World War II, capital gains became the paramount reason for buying stocks, with dividends being relegated to a position of insignificance. For two decades, during which the U.S. experienced the greatest period of well-being of any nation in modern history, the search for long-term capital gains evolved into a gold rush. And then, toward the end, *short-term* capital gains became the goal—the shorter the term, the better.

The Second Era of investing met its frightful end in 1974. From the ashes of its pyre, we felt, must now arise a Third Era of investing, an investment philosophy totally different from any that has gone before. It cannot be a search for dividends; the modern investor has been too badly scarred to risk losing a large portion of his investment capital in return for a dividend perhaps only one or two percentage points higher than would be available in a savings bank with perfect safety. Moreover, even the higher yields that may from time to time become available in stocks will not offset the ravages of inflation. If "breaking even" is the best one can hope for in stocks, the extra risk to the investor's capital cancels out the advantage. One might better accept a bank's lower interest rate and allow inflation to nibble at his savings than to risk losing most of his capital in a single year in the stock market.

The Third Era of investing, we believed back then, cannot be a self-deluding concentration on capital gains—short-term *or* long-term. Here again, the risk is too great, particularly now when the institution-dominated investment landscape is charged with nervousness, manic-depressive swings in mood, and an overriding distrust about the future. Growth stocks? Why has it never occurred to us that, throughout nature, growth beyond that which occurs gradually and within well-defined limits is a disease? When our broker sent us a list of stocks whose growth rates were phenomenally high—the Equity Fundings, the Levitz Furnitures, the nursing homes, the fast-food franchises, the conglomerates, the electronics—why did we not groan in sympathy and reply, "Don't you have anything healthier?" Rapid growth is unnatural—and too often *unreal.* "That isn't the way business works," the president of one firm complained. "Every year *can't* be that much better than the last." Less honest companies say, "If they want growth, we'll give them growth," and in the wink of an accountant's eye, you got your growth.

And even if the growth is legitimate, high-profit companies tend to carry within themselves the seeds of their own destruction. Mr. Steve Robert, helmsman of the Oppenheimer Mutual Funds: "Union Carbide earned $2.66 on a book value of $17.65, or 15 percent back in 1962. The company earned $2.53 in 1971 on a book value of $30.33. The rate of return has thus dropped to about 8 percent. Obviously the high rate of return drew increased competition, while capacity grew apace and soon outstripped demand. As a result, chemical prices fell and the company's rate of return had to suffer. Similar phenomena developed in the bowling industry, the paper industry; it has happened in the computer-leasing industry, the color television industry, the double-knit industry, and it will happen to some of the darlings of the present as well."

That was in 1972 . . . and it did.

Growth stock and blue chip, all securities swing like planets through their mysterious cycles of favor and disfavor, of love and hate; and many luminous stars of yesteryear still languish in the cosmic depths long, long after reaching their zeniths in the dimly remembered past. Pretend it's January, 1977. The Dow Jones Average stands at a lofty 959. But look at the stocks you bought way back when: the AT&T you purchased in 1964 at $75 a share is now worth only $63! Your Aluminum Company of America, bought at $134 a share in 1956, is now $57. Bethlehem Steel, $59 in 1959, stands at $38 now. Your Con Edison, $49 in 1965, is now $22. General Motors peaked at $114 in 1965, is now $75. Great Atlantic & Pacific is now $12, but was $71 in 1961. Hershey Foods crested at $41 in 1961 and now sells at $21. Lockheed, $74 in 1967, has dived to $10. R.C.A. at $26 is a long way from its 1967 high of $66. Ditto Scott Paper at $18 from its 1961 high of $48. Sherwin-Williams looks pale at $39 compared with its colorful $77 high in 1961.

Singer Co. sings the blues at $21 now, but hit its high note in 1962 at $129. U.S. Steel at $46 has yet to return to its 1959 high of $109. . . .

If you had bought them and locked them up, you would have locked up an intolerable loss for yourself, a loss compounded by inflation that magnified the erosion of your capital. Because of the sharply reduced purchasing power of the dollar, what you had left in 1977 was less than you thought.

We look for Automatic Investment Management to protect us against such chilling long-term slides in even the best stocks. It will do this by *taking profits* as the security booms under the impact of bull-market excitement and greed, gradually reducing our commitment to the inflamed stock. While others are buying, Automatic Investment Management will be *selling* and locking up its profits in its CASH balance. At this point, AIM's CASH balance will normally be earning only a modest interest rate. Easy money tends to fuel stock market booms, and when money is easy, interest rates are low. But when the Federal Reserve turns off the spigot, stocks decline and interest rates climb. Thus, AIM's CASH balance, gorged and swollen with profits at the very peak of the market, will respond instantly to the new rates and will begin to generate thrilling amounts of interest dollars for investment use in the stock slump. And then, at the bottom of the market, as interest rates begin to drift downward and AIM's CASH balance has a thready pulse, AIM will get set for the market's recovery and prepare to build up its CASH again by taking profits. In recent history, the market has tended to hit bottom, on average, three months after short-term interest rates have peaked. AIM knows this. AIM knows many things it doesn't care to boast about.

"If investment analysts knew more about probability theory," wrote Paul A. Samuelson, "they would realize that each stock can at most drop by 100 percent. But each may increase by 200, 500, or any positive percent.

Therefore, a portfolio of many stocks rises even when most of its holdings drop. The way fortunes grow is by losing a little on several items while making a lot on a few!"

This is not exactly AIM's way of doing things, but it does yield a rare and vivid glimpse of portfolio mathematics. Your winners can more than make up for your losers—even though you hold more losers. AIM's strategy involves keeping *all* its first-line troops healthy for the major assaults. Those who fall in battle receive immediate medical attention. Shock troops do their job up front, are relieved for R & R, and replaced by fresh troops from the rear. Like the thousands of teeth in a snail's mouth that constantly march forward on their assembly line to replace worn-out teeth at the front, AIM hurls wave after wave of fresh reserves into combat. And the casualty of today often becomes the hero of tomorrow.

A & P became a casualty in 1961. AIM, of course, would have reduced its holdings in the stock as it climbed. If, at the top, AIM still held 50 shares of A & P, every point advance in the stock would have earned AIM a profit of $50. As the stock fell, AIM would have bought more. Today, it might own 500 shares of A & P—and every point advance in the stock earns AIM a profit of $500!

What must be resolutely resisted is the urge to over-diversify, with a resultant blunting of investment results. Vice President Nelson A. Rockefeller, one of the nation's richest men, was life beneficiary of two trusts managed for him by the Chase Investors Management Corporation, a subsidiary of the Chase Manhattan Bank, of which Nelson's brother David was chairman. In the fall of 1974, Trust No. 1 was valued at $106,272,184. Trust No. 2 was worth $10,231,574. Mad money, perhaps. These two trusts did not reflect *all* of Mr. Rockefeller's stockholdings, of course, but they appeared to constitute the largest portion of his stock ownership. He and wife Happy also owned $13 million in stocks outright. Then

Happy has a $4 million trust from which she receives income for life. And then there's $36 million in stocks and bonds held outright or in trust for his six children.

Two things are striking about Mr. Rockefeller's two trusts: they both boast incredibly lean selections of common stock, and they both had the overwhelming majority of their assets invested in common stock. In the fall of 1974, remember, stocks were very near their lows in one of the worst declines in history. *It was the absolutely ideal time to be heavy in stocks and light in cash—as AIM itself would have been.*

Trust No. 1, the larger, held only 12 common stocks with a combined value of $89,244,557—84 percent of the total value of the portfolio! There are two corporate bonds and one preferred stock amounting to less than $1 million. U.S. Treasury bills and cash in the amount of $2,699,665 provide a wisely small reservoir of buying power at this point. The balance of the portfolio consists of state and municipal bonds.

TRUST NO. 1, Common Stocks

DuPont	$ 358,050
General Electric	$ 2,185,994
Realty Growth Investors Benefit	$ 450,000
Exxon	$20,726,450
Standard Oil Co. of California	$ 5,055,575
Merck & Co.	$ 5,353,050
Eastman Kodak Co.	$ 9,615,000
Caterpillar Tractor Co.	$ 2,706,439
IBM Corp.	$15,076,224
Minnesota Mining & Mfg. Co.	$ 1,296,000
International Basic Economy Corp.	$ 922,275
Rockefeller Center, Inc.	$25,499,500

Trust No. 2, the smaller, held only seven common stocks worth $8,445,941 and representing 83 percent of the entire portfolio. Again, there are two corporate bonds and one preferred stock, amounting to only a couple of hundred thousand dollars. State and municipal bonds round out the portfolio. The cash balance in this trust stands at a slim $72,318.

TRUST NO. 2, Common Stocks

Monsanto Co. ....$	383,382
International Telephone & Telegraph Corp. ....$	10,800
Motorola, Inc...$	158,400
Exxon Corp. ....$	4,371,250
Standard Oil Co. of California...............$	3,450,384
Upjohn Co. ....$	31,500
S.S. Kresge Co. ....$	40,125

Without having access to the previous histories of these two portfolios, there is no way of knowing whether their managers actually followed a set policy of adjusting the ratio of cash to stock in line with the philosophy of our own Automatic Investment Management, or whether the optimum ratio that exists before us is simply coincidence. What is clear and unequivocal is the quality of the securities held and the extremely small number of stocks that make up the portfolio. If anything, the common stock selection in the two trusts—particularly in the $106 million Trust No. 1—is daringly sparse. But then one must consider the fact that Mr. Rockefeller was not risking *all* his assets in these trusts and that safety of principal may not be as critically important here as it would be to most of us.

Incidentally, there are a couple of clunkers in the portfolios. The same two corporate bonds appear in both trusts: Farrington Manufacturing and Photon Inc. The $550,000 face amount of Farrington Manufacturing is carried at 20 cents on the dollar. The $500,000 face amount of Photon Inc. is carried at 5 cents on the dollar.

Nobody's perfect.

Automatic Investment Management does not require for its fuel the kind of hot stock everyone else seems to seek—in vain. It requires only securities or mutual funds that have proved over the years that they can "take it" on the chin and at least get back up off the canvas. As we have seen in the million-dollar portfolio, *it is not even necessary that the stocks rise above our original purchase price.* Incredible, but true. And if our stocks should decline and fail even to come back to within shouting distance of our original purchase levels, AIM can generate truly amazing profits for us down there near the bottom simply by using the market's dependable fluctuations!

Come what may, we have a powerful new weapon in Automatic Investment Management, one that actually combines safety, reliability, and performance in every kind of market. And *you* are no happier to see it arrive than we are ourselves. It has worked, it is working, it will work forever as long as there are stocks to buy and stocks to sell. Turn it on and put it to work for you. Then sit back and watch the unbelievable profits come churning out—perhaps the first investment profits you have earned in ages—and laying the foundation for a fortune you might not have believed possible.

Then, and only then, will you realize that you *do* have in your possession what, until now, has been only a joke and a dream.

The joke is over. The dream has come true—at this very moment. Believe!

You've got yourself a *Money Machine!*

TWELVE

Money, Money, Money Funds

Since the original publication of this book, assets of the nation's money funds, fueled by the lure of soaring interest rates, have mushroomed to more than $900 billion. When banks received the green light from Washington some years back to offer their own so-called "money market funds"—with federal insurance to boot—there was some concern within the real money market funds that they might be on their way out. Their fears proved groundless. Investors, by and large, decided that for service, convenience, and top interest rates, real money market funds were the best bet even without insurance. And although money market fund assets dipped as some investors switched over to banks, many investors returned to the fold. This loyalty is further evidence of the widespread acceptance of the money fund idea. And as far as the AIM investor is concerned, money funds as a substantially safe, splendidly convenient, and often highly productive repository for idle cash now appear to be "the medium of choice."

In Dec., 2000 money market funds were yielding a zesty 6 percent. But bank money markets were paying a paltry 3 percent!* As with money funds, you may withdraw funds at any time without penalties of any kind and still receive the interest your funds have already earned. Unlike money funds, however, your money is insured by the federal government. Although there are

*Banks pay more on certificates of deposit—but withdraw prematurely from these certificates and banky spanky!

those authors who warn that there is precious little real
backing in the insurance pot for your savings accounts,
and that in the event of a bank panic occasioned by
the failure of a couple of big banking institutions and a
resultant stampede among savers clamoring for their
money at every bank, the government will simply pull
the plug on you and let you go down the tubes, I am
still ingenuous enough to believe that your CASH balance would be technically safer in a federally insured
bank than in a money fund.

But safety is relative. There is no such thing as a risk-
less investment. With the rate of inflation sometimes
running in the double digits, even if there were no question in the world about the safety of the *dollars* in your
bank savings account, you are still suffering an alarming
loss of your buying power—though you have not lost
any *dollars.* In May, 1979, Citibank, one of the nation's
largest, ran a full-page ad protesting the government lid
on the passbook interest it was allowed to pay, in view
of inflation's toll on buying power. The headline read:
"Deposit $500 with Us Today and We'll Give You Back
$475 Next Year."

When I can get a much more attractive return, the
convenience of free checking, and still feel that my
money is pretty secure—given the fact that money funds,
like all mutual funds, operate in a kind of legal goldfish
bowl with the government always lurking in the background—I'll opt for money funds over a savings account
for my AIM CASH balance. But each investor has to
decide this issue for himself, based on his own circumstances and philosophy.

*Comparison Between 5.5% and 13% Simple Interest
on a Hypothetical CASH Balance of $10,000 for 1 Year*

5.5%	13%	Money Fund Advantage
$550	$1,300	$750

Remember, though, money funds do not guarantee their yields. They can go down as well as up. This applies to the "money market funds" offered by banks as well. But where the real money market funds pay the best rate they can obtain for you by purchasing money market instruments in the open market, bank money market funds are not compelled to buy any such thing. They can pay you as much or as little as they want—and their rates are now trailing their "legitimate" cousins, the real money market funds.

In 1981, with money rates floating at pathological heights, money market funds were yielding an annualized rate of 16 percent. Imagine the tremendous additional advantage such yields afford the AIM investor who, unlike most other investors, considers cash an integral part of his investment program.

Most money funds now follow a policy of "stable net asset value" of $1 per share. Although there can be no absolute guarantee that the $1 price will be maintained forever, it is reasonably assured since the fund is permitted by regulations to "round off" the value of each share to the nearest full penny. Additionally, the market value of the fund's investments experiences only minimal fluctuations as a rule, thanks to quality money-market instruments and an average portfolio maturity of 190 days or less.

Some money funds do not maintain a "stable net asset value," but rather allow their net asset value per share to fluctuate. The fluctuations, as has been pointed out elsewhere in this book, tend to be insignificant. But most investors seem to feel more comfortable with funds that fix their net asset value per share at $1. For one thing, it's easier to figure. 1,000 shares = $1,000. You know at a glance how much your money fund shares are worth. Not so easy if the price per share is 0.996 or $9.96. Fortunately, most "fluctuating" money market funds have changed their policy and now sell at a fixed $1.00 a share.

For what it's worth, some funds let you write checks

in the amount of $250—half what other money funds fix as the minimum. These include the giant Vanguard money funds. Scudder permits $100 checks!

Most money funds pay dividends monthly and send you a statement with your dividends reinvested in additional shares, if that is your wish. AIM investors particularly will find this practice extremely convenient, since their CASH balance is kept right up to date. If you operate your AIM program on a monthly basis—as most of us do—you will appreciate having an updated new statement of your CASH balance sent to you each month, informing you of your exact current buying power.

Some money market funds require an initial deposit that may be larger than your AIM program requires. Simply send the fund the initial investment they require, then withdraw the excess from the fund. If the fund requires a $5,000 minimum initial investment, and you wish a CASH balance of only $2,500 to begin your AIM program, send the fund $5,000 and then withdraw $2,500.

Most funds, though, require an initial investment of only $1,000 to $3,000, so even modest investors should have no trouble finding one to accommodate them.

But don't buy a money fund *just* because it provides a unique service, or because it offers beautifully designed checks. We should look for the best yield possible consistent with preservation of capital and liquidity. Comparing the yields of various money funds is a step in the right direction, but it's not the whole trip. Funds figure their yields in different ways (the SEC has proposed that money funds use a standardized method of calculating their yields), so one fund's yield superiority over another might prove as fuzzy as a film star's memory of how he really got into the movies. A very few funds levy a monthly service charge that may appear nominal. But if your account is $5,000 and you're paying a service charge of $3 a month—$36 a year—your annual yield will not be at all what you thought it was. If the fund claims its yield for the year was 13 percent, you will not have earned 13 percent of $5,000 ($650), but rather $650 minus the $36 service charge: $614. The true interest you earned was only 12.28 percent—at a time, perhaps, when a *real* 13 percent was obtainable in a dozen other funds.

So if the fund in which you are interested does happen to levy a service charge, remember that the larger your balance the smaller the effect a service charge will have on your final results. Such a fund structure obviously favors large accounts. A more substantial account of $10,000 would see its true yield reduced only down to 12.64 percent. And an investor with $100,000 would realize a yield of 12.96 percent after deducting for the service charge. *He* wouldn't notice the difference.

For that matter, some money funds don't even enclose a postage-paid envelope for your next investment whenever they send you a statement. So what's a 34¢ stamp, you say? Suppose you spend 34¢ to mail them an investment of $100. A year later, although your fund yielded 6% for the year, your $100 did not earn 6%—$6. It earned $6 minus 34¢, for a net yield to you of 5.7%! In the hotly competitive money fund industry, in which Fund A's advertised yield advantage over its rivals' average for a given period may amount to a *smaller* fraction than 3 basis points, it is amazing to reflect that a simple postpaid envelope might make a very big difference to some investors!

It's your buck. Watch it!

By and large, three factors affect a money fund's gross yield:

Maturity: "The shorter, the safer" is the watchword concerning fixed-income instruments. A fund can lengthen the maturity of its portfolio ("go long") in an attempt to capture longer-term rates that are sometimes higher—but only at the risk of fluctuation in its portfolio value and a possible reduction in yield in the interim period.

Quality: A fund can boost its yield by reaching down for some lesser quality, lower-rated money market instruments. The trade-off? Higher risk.

Instruments: The type of investment also helps determine a money fund's gross yield. These include certificates of deposit, commercial paper, bankers acceptances, and so forth. Some funds, for example, might decide to beef up their return by including Eurodollar CD's in their portfolios (CD's issued by U.S. bank branches overseas). These typically offer a higher return but may involve a potential risk common to "offshore" investing, insignificant as the risk now appears.

Gross yield in hand, the money fund deducts its operating costs and gives you the rest. This factor alone can determine your final yield without increasing your risk. Any two high-quality money funds might be expected to offer approximately the same yields, yet the one with a lower expense ratio could provide you with a substantially higher return.

A word of caution: new money funds often waive expenses for a certain period of time or until their assets reach a stated level. This common practice artificially inflates their yields, and their advertising campaigns take advantage of the fact. Here again, upon examination, an assumed superiority fades like fame at 4 A.M.

Many growth and highly volatile mutual funds such as the following are available from mutual fund "families" that also offer a money market mutual fund. AIMvestors who wish to consider investing in such fund families in order to switch back and forth between a group's money market fund and its equity funds may find this brief sampling of interest. Call any fund family for a free prospectus of the fund in which you are interested. These are all no-load funds, with the exception of Fidelity Magellan Fund and Fidelity Select Funds, which impose a 3 percent charge. American Century Investors now offers a money market fund, but its U.S. Governments Fund may be an interesting alternative to some investors. Inclusion of any fund here does not imply endorsement or recommendation.

Fund Family	Volatile Equity Funds	Toll-Free Out-of-State Phone Number
Dreyfus Funds 600 Madison Ave. New York, NY 10022	Growth Opportunity Fund Third Century Fund	(800) 782-6620
Fidelity Funds 82 Devonshire St. Boston, MA 02109	Fidelity Trend Fund Fidelity Magellan Fidelity Select Portfolios	(800) 544-8888
Invesco Funds P.O. Box 173707 Denver, CO 80217-3707	Invesco Dynamics Fund Invesco Strategic Portfolios Invesco Emerging Growth Fund	(800) 525-8085
Lexington Funds P.O. Box 1515 580 Sylvan Ave. Englewood Cliffs, NJ 07632	Lexington Growth Fund Lexington Gold Fund	(800) 526-0056
T. Rowe Price 100 E. Pratt St. Baltimore, MD 21202	Capital Appreciation New Horizons Growth Stock Small Cap Value	(800) 541-5856
The Scudder Funds P.O. Box 219669 Kansas City, Mo 64121-9669	Scudder Development Fund Scudder Capital Growth Fund	(800) 225-2470
Steinroe & Farnum 150 S. Wacker Dr. Chicago, IL 60606	Capital Opportunities Fund Steinroe Special Fund	(800) 338-2550

FUND FAMILY	VOLATILE EQUITY FUNDS	TOLL-FREE OUT-OF-STATE PHONE NUMBER
American Century Investors P.O. Box 419200 Kansas City, MO 64173	Growth Fund Ultra Fund Vista Fund	(800) 345-2021
The Vanguard Group P.O. Box 2600 Valley Forge, PA 19482	Explorer Fund Primecap Fund Vanguard Specialized Portfolios	(800) 662-7447

Although I indicated earlier that most money market mutual funds require that you write checks on your fund for amounts no smaller than $500, this restriction is of minimal consequence to you if your AIM program consists of mutual funds solely within that same fund family. When you make an exchange back and forth between your money market fund and any other mutual fund within the fund group, the $500 "floor" might not apply. Fidelity and Financial Programs require a $250 minimum, Vanguard and the Scudder Funds $100, just to name a few. American Century now permits $100 phone exchanges as well.

THIRTEEN

Questions and Answers About Automatic Investment Management

When Thomas Edison invented the first practical incandescent bulb on October 21, 1879, I suspect that there was an observer nearby who exclaimed, "Gee, that's great, Tom—but where do we screw it in?"

At the time, there were no electrical sockets and no power distribution system to supply electricity to the millions of homes that would one day be using this fabulous new development.

Nor was there any source anywhere from which Edison could purchase the parts necessary to build the generators and transmission networks that would comprise an electrical system. The parts didn't exist, any more than the system itself existed.

"It was necessary to invent everything," Edison said later. "Dynamos, regulators, meters, switches, fuses, fixtures, underground conductors with their necessary connecting boxes, and a host of other detailed parts, even down to the insulating tape."

Automatic Investment Management is not the electric light bulb (and its inventor is no Edison), but as its father, I can now sympathize with Edison's plight in having to implement what was, by and of itself, an achievement on which he could easily have rested his case as an inventor.

Thousands of my readers loved the amazing horseless

175

carriage I'd given them—but some also wanted me to design an entire interstate highway system to accommodate the new vehicle! To pursue the metaphor: "Wonderful invention, Mr. Bell, but what do I *talk* about on your telephone?"

Understandable. Human. But a bit nerve-racking for me! As the creator of AIM, I was the only person in the world, unhappily, to whom investors could turn for answers to their problems (at least so they thought); and I had my hands full trying to provide them with answers whenever possible. Some desperate souls did seek advice from their brokers, but these harried folk, in turn, had to contact me to find out what the hell their clients were talking about.

More sobering as far as I was concerned was this: The fact that I invented AIM did not and does not mean that my opinion is the last word. Neither Edison nor Bell could say that he knew everything there was to know about his invention, could spell out all the benefits or foresee all the risks. Bell, in his patent for the telephone, included copper as one of the inductive metals that could be used in the diaphragm of his telephone. You can't use copper. Copper is a conductive, not an inductive metal.* Edison insisted on the safer "direct current" to light up America with his lightbulbs—but lost the battle to proponents of "alternating current," which could be transmitted for longer distances.

My apologies all around, both to my readers and to their brokers! If I could have foreseen the many and varied questions AIM would create in the minds of my readers, I would have taken extra pains to make everything "perfectly clear." But let's be honest. There were some questions that hadn't even occurred to *me*. Too close to the trees to see the forest, and all that.

The following Question-and-Answer session includes

*There are those cynics who maintain that the reason Bell goofed in his patent is understandable: he didn't invent the telephone in the first place, but rather stole it from a poor old practical inventor named Antonio Meucci. But that's another story.

substantially all the questions that have been raised by my readers concerning my Automatic Investment Management system since the publication of this book, along with assorted comments and opinions that any new discovery is likely to elicit. I sincerely hope and believe that veteran AIM fans will find the answers they were looking for in this section, and that first-time readers of this book, who may or may not be certain they've understood everything so far, will appreciate having several points reinforced for them.

First Q & A Session

Q. Mr. Lichello, is there any reason why an AIM account entry can't be made at other times than monthly or quarterly so as to take advantage of a significant increase or decrease in stock prices?

A. Your question was whether or not you can operate your AIM program on a more frequent basis than monthly? The answer is a definite maybe. I've often compared the monthly "checkup" of your AIM program to the narrow beam of light sweeping like a searchlight around the face of the cathode-ray tube of the radar receiver. Should we speed up the revolutions of this beam, or is the object being tracked adequately monitored under the present arrangement?

Well, radar works. But could it work better? AIM works, but could it work better if we ask it to come in for a checkup twice a month instead of once a month? It is true that portfolios rarely show substantial increases or decreases in a week or two. And if they do, they are likely to maintain the increase or decrease for another couple of weeks or until your regular checkup date. It is also true that in that time span, the equity portion of the portfolio might even *intensify* its increase or decrease, permitting AIM to take more dynamic action at its regular checkup time than it would in between, so to speak.

But tests I've conducted in a sharply declining market have indicated that if an AIM investor operates his AIM program twice a month rather than monthly, he may have a greater opportunity to exhaust his CASH reserve. By so doing, he may buy more shares on the way down and chalk up higher profits when the market recovers. While I cannot draw any valid conclusion from the few tests I've done, I suspect that the AIM investor who does operate his program on a twice-a-month basis will get more action, because the figures I have do show some exciting possibilities in this area. This way, the AIM investor might have a better chance to empty his CASH reserve. With the regular AIM, this would be unlikely—even with a pretty volatile portfolio. Even in slumps, he seems to hold a lot of cash. Maybe the regular AIM is too tight with the buck for his own good. The future may prove otherwise!

So there may be a definite advantage to be gained by operating our AIM program on a twice-a-month basis, particularly for those of us who want something a wee bit spicier. Most of us probably construct a boring portfolio with sluggish movements, and therefore we hold too much cash—even during a decline. A twice-a-month checkup would probably allow AIM to buy more stock for us.

Q. Let's say that I am utilizing a once-a-month review of my hypothetically bought stock. Let's say I bought it at $6 per share. What should I do, if before the month is out, perhaps on the tenth day, the stock either drops to $3 per share, or doubles to $12 per share. My question is this: Should I take advantage of the rise or fall and at that moment either buy or sell stocks? Or do I wait it out and only buy or sell on a monthly basis? Will I lose out by not taking advantage of this change?

A. In between your checkup periods, you can sell any stock you please as long as you replace it with a roughly equal amount of some other stock so as to keep your STOCK VALUE about the same. You can sell a stock, as I said, and then use the money to buy some other stock. But you can't buy a stock and take the money out of your CASH reserve unless it's on your regular checkup date and AIM tells you to do it.

Personally, I don't want to ride herd on all my stocks every day throughout the month. You are complicating things again, and AIM is supposed to simplify. Before I would do what you suggest and check my portfolio stocks daily, I would operate my AIM program on a twice-a-month basis—as we have just discussed. That is as critical a tolerance as you'd ever want, and very few big opportunities are going to get away from you if you do that.

If you're a hyperactive "Type A" personality and chafe at AIM's restrictions, why not use AIM for the bulk of your investments and take a flier on your own? But don't be surprised when you come crawling back to AIM and say, "Here, you take care of it. I can't." I did. I owned only one stock while inventing AIM. In five years it went from $2 to $12. But how was I to know that $12 would turn out to be its peak? Nobody tells you, you know. So I held on. And what happened? The stock turned around and went down to $7, clipping thousands of dollars off my holdings. Had I included that stock in an AIM portfolio, chances are I would have been requested by AIM to sell off some shares as the price rose. And at least part of the money I lost when the stock dropped would have been safely tucked away in my CASH reserve.

You might think going it alone is fun. I don't. I can't afford it—financially or emotionally.

Q. Mr. Lichello, you wrote a book about how to make a million. My question is this: Have *you* made a million?

A. No. And the title of my book is not *How I Made a Million* but *How to Make a Million.* There's a big difference. How many people have bought those *How I Made a Million* books? Quite a number—including myself. Now, how many ever made a dime from what they learned in those books? You see, if we accept as proof the inventor's own words that his invention has performed as claimed, then we find ourselves in the same category as the gullible audience at a medicine show who place their trust in the pitch of the snake-oil salesman who assures them that his elixir has cured his own ailments. The sole validity of any inventor's claim is not that *he* has achieved the results in question but that such results may be achieved by some of those who use his invention. If it were otherwise, no legless man would be allowed to invent a bicycle.

A number of people have made a million in Wall Street—or at least have said they did. But the fact that they did it, under who-knows-what peculiar set of circumstances—luck, inside knowledge, illegal behavior, does not at all guarantee that we will make a million if we follow their instructions. Proof of that statement is the fact that people haven't made millions reading *How I Made a Million* books.

Now. Einstein didn't split the atom or build the atomic bomb. But he did come up with the formula that made it possible: $E=MC^2$. And when Enrico Fermi withdrew that last rod from the atomic furnace under the squash court at Chicago's Stagg Field on December 2, 1942, and created the first self-sustaining chain reaction on earth, which gave America the atomic bomb shortly thereafter, his debt to Einstein was obvious. Wernher von Braun designed and developed the Saturn 5 rocket that he said would take men to the moon. It did. But von Braun didn't go first to prove it. He didn't even go second. Can you blame him? Suppose he got a lemon? You never know.

I'll continue for just a moment, because this question of whether *I've* made a million is often asked of me by talk-show hosts who have interviewed me, and by listeners of radio call-in shows on which I've appeared.

Like millions of other cigarette smokers, I tried hundreds of times to quit, but without success. Finally, after more than three decades of smoking—and *needing* it to function, as any writer will testify—I managed to beat the habit. I would like nothing better than to write a book telling others how to quit smoking. I'm certain it would earn me more than a *How to Make a Million* book, since there are lots more smokers than investors. But I know perfectly well that my way of quitting would not necessarily help *you* to quit. Why? Because I do not know if my way contains any universal truth. For all I know, my way might make you want to smoke *more* cigarettes!

Further, in my book and in my various interviews, I have emphasized again and again that AIM is not a get-rich-quick scheme; it is a get-rich-certain scheme. Because any system that can get you rich in a hurry can also get you poor in a hurry. And those of us with limited resources cannot afford that much risk!

So, like starting off in low gear, AIM begins slowly, almost imperceptibly, safely, examining the terrain as it moves. This caution protects you from being whipsawed in the event a crash occurs shortly after beginning an AIM program. Anyone here would agree, after reading my book, that few investors are going to make a million with AIM. But you will also agree, I hope, that AIM is the best way, probably the only way, for a modest investor to get rich with any degree of certainty in the stock market without taking undue risks. And some modest investors may indeed make a million in time. The world does not need more rich people anyway. It needs fewer poor people.

AIM actually combines safety and performance in one technique. Until now, you couldn't have both. You had to sacrifice safety for performance or performance for safety. It was a trade-off: utility stocks with their high yields, low volatility, and relative safety, or growth stocks with their low payouts, high growth, and wide fluctuations.

What I have created, therefore, is nothing more than a mathematical formula. You can look at it and see that it works—just as two plus two equals four. It isn't necessary to ask what *I've* done with the formula. Either the formula is valid or it isn't. See for yourself.

I personally am more tinkerer than investor anyway, although I am trying to reduce this former activity and settle for the latter. And I am always conscious of the fact that any results I may obtain may have to be verified later if I should decide to publish them. Which is one reason I canceled my first AIM account with a major brokerage house when they began to reinvest my dividends in additional fractional shares of stock, no matter how often I protested. Have you any idea of the horrendous paperwork that would be involved at income tax time? If I sold $500 worth of stock, 30 shares might have been purchased at $13 a share, 1.386 shares might have been purchased through reinvested dividends at $12.25, another .446 shares purchased through reinvested dividends at $14.50 a share, ad nauseam. In an effort to simplify this task both for myself and for you, the readers of my book, I asked the Treasury Department to allow us to add up all our purchases in each stock and divide the number of shares we own into the total amount invested in this stock in order to get a Cost Per Share that would apply to every share. We are allowed to do this with purchases of mutual funds, I reminded them. Their answer: No!

Disenchanted, I started an AIM program with a whole package of mutual funds, but after several months it became clear that I was not going to get the kind of fluctuation needed for exciting results. I can't believe I was so naive as to *expect* fluctuation with that gigantic portfolio! So I closed that account and began a new AIM program with a single mutual fund. After several successful months of this, I nevertheless decided to tamper with the AIM formula in an attempt to speed up my results. This required closing the old AIM account and opening a new experimental program. After several months, I was forced to admit that the published AIM formula was better than the experimental, so I closed the account and opened a new one with a single mutual fund. Several months later—but you get the idea. There is a tinkerer, not an investor, at work here. Therefore, never ask the inventor what *he's* done with his invention. The reason he *is* an inventor is because he's never satisfied with the way things are—even if *he* helped make them that way! Which is why you were likelier to find Mr. Soichiro Honda not in the executive suite of Honda Motors in Tokyo, spiffily attired and basking in the glow of having built a motorcycle so superior that his company had become the world's leading motorcycle maker, but working in overalls alongside his engineers and producing cars so much more advanced than even Toyota's and Datsun's that Americans were lining up just to get on the months-long waiting list to buy them and pay a *premium* over list price . . . at a time when some of our own companies had to beg the government for help in order to stay alive.

One thing stands out in my mind, however, and that is the fact that virtually every AIM program I terminated was closed at a profit! So AIM even looks out for fools.

Q. Mr. Lichello, there are some questions I would like answered. First, should the portfolio be set up for each stock or for the entire total of stocks? Second, if it can be set up for either way, which is the better of the two? In other words, I want to start an AIM program with five or six stocks. Do I combine the prices of each into one figure or act independently with each?

A. Very good. This question has been asked of me more often than any other except one. AIM is a portfolio management technique. A single AIM program manages all your stocks. If you will look at any chart in my book, there is a column headed STOCK VALUE. The word "stock" is used in the plural sense. It means the total value of all the shares of all the stocks in your AIM program. I could have used STOCKS VALUE for greater clarity, but that hurts my ears. And I couldn't have used *VALUE OF STOCKS* because, as you know, the initial letter must be "S," since you need the "S" to work the formula when you do your figuring at checkup time. But because, like everybody else, I possess 20-20 hindsight, I can see that I should have used the word STOCKS or SECURITIES instead.

Ideally, a single stock might appear to be our best bet, because a single stock would be expected to fluctuate more widely than a portfolio of many stocks. And we love fluctuation.

But . . . a single stock might collapse 50 percent or more shortly after you start your AIM program. And it might stay down for years. With my luck, it would. So you would immediately lose half of your original STOCK VALUE, plus a portion of any other investments you make in this same stock on the way down. Are you prepared for this? Can you imagine all the cursing and gnashing of teeth as you sweat out this dead AIM program month after month, year after year?

Very well, you say, I'll use a separate AIM program for each one of my five or six stocks. Each stock will have its own STOCK VALUE, its own CASH reserve, etcetera. Let me just say that if I even contemplated doing any such thing, I would not only have to scream to keep from blacking out, but you would soon find me in the shipping room of the R. J. Reynolds Tobacco Company, back on the weed again in a big way! Listen, folks, I created AIM to simplify life, not to complicate it!

But you insist. All right. Let's say that a couple of your five stocks, Stocks A and B, go down and stay down. Or let's just say that they stay right where they were when you bought them, while your other three stocks behave more actively, going up and down and having a gay old time. What is happening is that 40 percent of your entire original CASH reserve is tied up in two unproductive stocks—wasted, to all intents and purposes. In the meantime, one of your frisky stocks, Stock C, might have exhausted *its* CASH reserve and be begging for more. You know in your heart that Stock C is a heck of a buy at this price. You are certain it is going to rebound soon and make you a very fine profit, especially if you can buy more at this depressed price. But you can't buy more, because Stock C's CASH is exhausted. You panic and look at Stock D. Because it has fluctuated the most, Stock D's CASH reserve is *twice* as large as its STOCK VALUE, and Stock D has been going nowhere but up lately, which is why you've been taking profits in it and transferring the profits to Stock D's CASH reserve as you're supposed to. You know that Stock D will probably never use all its huge CASH reserve . . . just as you know that you could make better use of Stock D's CASH reserve if you could steal some of it and lend it to Stock C, which really and truly needs it! But you can't. That isn't playing by your rules. You'll get so fouled up you won't know which end is up. So, to keep from blacking out, you open your mouth and scream!

You see, if you operated your AIM program the right way, with a single program covering several stocks, when AIM asks you to invest a chunk of money, *you* decide which of your several stocks deserves it most. And you simply reach into the CASH reserve, get the money, and give it to the most deserving security. And God will bless you for it, too.

I think you will create many more problems than you solve by using a separate AIM program for each stock. A single AIM program managing a portfolio of stocks is simpler and better. Though a portfolio of stocks may not fluctuate as widely as an individual stock, a *portfolio is more certain to recover from a decline.* A portfolio is the best hedge against the possibility of picking a dog of a stock that either drops like a stone or, just as bad, settles itself comfortably in a narrow trading range for the duration. A portfolio of several stocks would be likelier to *rise* if the market as a whole is rising.

There might be a middle way. What about using a single AIM program—but buying only one stock for your portfolio in the beginning? This will give you the *potential* for a wide swing, up or down. If the swing is up, no problem You take profits as AIM directs and wait to see what happens. If the swing is down, don't invest any more money in that stock, because that stock may *never* come back, but start to take positions in other stocks on the way down. This limits your risk to the actual money you invested in your first stock at the start of your AIM program. If your original STOCK VALUE is $5,000, for example, that is what you're risking. If the stock declines 50 percent, you've lost $2,500. But the stock will have performed a valuable service for you. It took down your STOCK VALUE rapidly, compelling you to make investments in other securities at low prices. And when the market does recover, your portfolio is much more certain to recover along with it than would be the case with a single security.

Q. Mr. Lichello, I can see where this idea would give us more action, if some of us wanted it. But you said if we put $5,000 in a single stock and that stock declines 50 percent, we would lose $2,500. But if it goes to zero, no matter how unlikely that may be, we would be out the whole original $5,000, right?

A. Correct. But if I take a deep breath and plunk down my whole $5,000 on a single stock at the outset of my AIM program, you better believe I'd want some quality. Because the mere fact that I own only one stock will give me the *potential* for wide fluctuation, even if that one stock is a blue chip or otherwise of very good quality. So there is no need to start off with General Drunkenness and Mayhem in the Over-the-Counter Market. Russian Roulette would be a good deal quicker and more painless, if that's what you want.

Q. But on the way down, you will be investing in other stocks, so if your first stock should go to zero, you could theoretically lose not only all of your original stock investment, but a portion of the investment you made in other stocks on the way down, because all prices are falling, presumably.

A. Yes, of course. That's the whole AIM theory. That's what we want. But I would still consider this technique if I wanted more action in my AIM program. Remember, we're presuming the worst: our original stock has gone to zero, and the others are likely to be tumbling as well. It could just as easily work out in the opposite manner. Our original stock could rocket upward and we could start taking profits.

But even if the worst happens and our original stock goes to powder, it tossed a pail of ice water in our faces. All of a sudden we get a chance to use our CASH reserve and pick up some bargain-priced shares of other companies. When the market recovers, we have a good chance of making fine profits.

Q. Yes, but what if the original stock is a dog and goes to powder in a *bull* market? Your STOCK VALUE has been yanked down and forces you to start buying other stocks maybe at their highs.

A. Interesting. Could happen. But not likely if your original stock is a quality stock, maybe one of the Dow Jones stocks. But I'll wager many impatient investors would still opt for the possibility of faster action in their AIM program by starting off with a single stock. That, however, every investor will have to decide for himself. I'm still trying to figure out why AIM works at all.

You could ameliorate your risk somewhat, couldn't you, by starting off your AIM program with two stocks? And then, if you get your sharp decline, you could accumulate two or three other stocks on the way down. At the bottom of the market, you'd be sitting pretty with a decent portfolio that is almost certain to recover when the market recovers. That should give you the extra volatility you're looking for, while at the same time affording you a fair measure of protection. This compromise seems to me most attractive. It's a little extra insurance against making a complete fool of yourself, and yet it offers the potential of catapulting us into the big time fast!

Q. Mr. Lichello, let me hazard a guess about the question I think most readers would ask of you. When AIM tells me to buy or sell, which stock in my portfolio do I buy or sell? Am I right?

A. Right as rain. That is what most readers aren't clear on. The answer is, it's none of AIM's business which stock you buy or sell. AIM does not interfere with normal portfolio management. *The one thing and the only thing AIM does do is tell you when to increase or decrease equity ownership, and how much to increase or decrease.*

In your AIM program, you may buy or sell stock anytime during the month, just as if you weren't using AIM. Let me rephrase that. You can sell a stock and buy another stock with the proceeds from the sale. If you sell $1,000 worth of stock on your own, let's say, you must replace it with $1,000 worth of another stock. That's the only thing you can do between checkup dates—exchange one stock for another. You can't take any money out of CASH reserve and go out on your own and buy a new stock just because you feel like it. AIM will place an old gypsy curse on your head if you do. And you will break out in boils.

Q. In other words, Mr. Lichello, we can act on our own at any time as long as we keep STOCK VALUE and CASH at roughly the same levels that AIM has ordered. Say AIM works on a once-a-month basis. Say it's my monthly checkup time. I personally use the first of the month. Obviously, on the first of the month I do exactly what AIM tells me to do. If it says buy $500 worth, I buy. But for the rest of the month, I can take a good look at my portfolio of stocks . . . and if I can't stand to look at my $2,000 worth of IBM any longer, I can sell it and replace it with $2,000 worth of International Harvester. Am I right?

A. Absolutely. As long as you replace the stock you sell with another stock of roughly similar value. If there are a couple of bucks left over, buy your wife a corsage with my compliments. Or deposit the excess in your CASH reserve.

So on your regular checkup date, when AIM tells you to sell some stock, the stock you select to chip away at would depend entirely on you. Ask yourself, "Which stock do I *want* to reduce?" You might decide to sell some shares of a stock in which you have a profit. That's logical. Or if you need a capital loss for your income tax return, you might decide to sell some shares of a stock in which you have a loss. Or you might decide to reduce your exposure in a stock you feel has lost its lustre and say to yourself, "Well, I'll start chipping away at this turkey because it's my least favorite. Whenever AIM tells me to sell, I'll sell some of this stock until I finally get rid of it all."

Or, if AIM says sell $1,000 worth, you might decide to sell $500 worth of *two* stocks, because you happen to have a good profit in both of them. And if AIM says buy $1,000 worth, AIM doesn't care whether you buy an additional $1,000 worth of a stock you already own, or add $1,000 worth of a new stock to your portfolio.

To simplify my records at income tax time, suppose I never increase my holdings in any stock. When AIM says buy, I'll just buy another stock. That way I'll always know my Cost Per Share price of any stock, without breaking down my holdings in any particular stock according to when I purchased each batch and how much I paid for each batch. You could make purchases in the same stock a dozen times, paying a different price per share each time. And when you sell some shares, which batch would you sell from? The first batch you bought? Fine, except that batch is worth only $600 at today's price, and AIM wants you to sell $900 worth. So you sell the first batch at $600, than sell *part* of batch #2 to make up the $900 sell order. So far so good. But now you've got a piddling amount of batch #2 left over to clutter up your records and drive you even crazier the next time AIM gives you a sell order.

These problems really don't have anything to do with AIM. Personally, I think mutual funds would be a whole lot simpler to deal with—and probably just as profitable in the long run.

Q. Could you suggest a good way to convert present holdings into an AIM program?

A. No problem. Decide how large an AIM program you want and set up your record sheet to reflect it. If you want to start a $10,000 AIM program, say, you'll naturally need $5,000 in stock and $5,000 in cash. Where you get the stock and cash is no concern of AIM's. You might have $10,000 worth of stocks right now, and no cash. You'd then have to sell $5,000 worth of stock in order to raise your $5,000 CASH reserve. If you wanted to start a $20,000 AIM program, you could use your present stock for your $10,000 STOCK VALUE section, but then you'd have to come up with $10,000 in cash.

Q. You indicated earlier that you have an antipathy toward Automatic Dividend Reinvestment.

A. Only because of income tax considerations. I find it maddening to account for all those fractional shares, because each fractional share, having been bought at various times, would have its own cost basis. And when you go to sell a batch of them, you'd need a whole page on your income tax return to list all those small purchases, and all the dates on which you purchased them.

Q. As a rule, should AIM stay out of such a program or would you treat the automatic reinvestment as a purchase and adjust SAFE and CONTROL accordingly?

A. If dividends are reinvested without cost, or for only a nominal charge, then go ahead and have them reinvested if you want. *It isn't necessary to adjust SAFE or CONTROL because when a stock goes ex-dividend, the price of that stock is reduced by exactly the amount of the dividend.* During an ordinary trading day, this may or may not be noticed, since the price of the stock depends on a number of factors, and the stock may even close higher despite having gone ex-dividend that day. Nevertheless, technically your stock is immediately marked down the exact amount of dividend paid. So if you reinvest your dividends, you are merely preserving the integrity of your STOCK VALUE, whether you know it or not. It is not, however, of critical importance in the operation of your AIM program. But if you don't mind the tax paperwork, by all means have your dividends reinvested.

A word of caution here. Some companies say they

allow you to reinvest your dividends in their stock without commission charge, but when you get the reinvestment statement from their bank, it might have a bank service charge deducted. Most people say, well, it's only 50 cents, it's nothing, really, for reinvesting my $2 dividend in additional shares. Nothing? It's 25 percent of the entire dividend, that's all it is.

Q. How do we keep the dollar amounts equally invested when we have more than one stock in the portfolio?

A. It really isn't important. Although I may have suggested somewhere in the book that such a practice might be beneficial, as have other writers, I'm not so sure this could be proved. It probably would turn out to be just a convenience. I think I may have suggested keeping half of your stock portfolio in blue chips—is that what you're referring to—and half in more volatile stocks. Other writers have suggested such a portfolio makeup for obvious reasons. It keeps us from packing our whole portfolio full of dogs and going down the drain one fine day. But don't take this literally. The 50-50 proportions aren't mandated by me. Why not 60-40 or 70-30? But I personally would feel much more confident and secure if I knew that roughly half my portfolio was made up of blue chips. They might save me some day. And I think I may have indicated in the book that it might not be a bad idea to select these blue chips from the Dow Jones Average. Some authors have suggested that many stocks or even most stocks might be rigged, and they hint darkly that the Dow Jones Average is used as a "lure" to entice people into the market or scare them out of it when it suits the plans of the stock specialists. They point out that the Dow Jones stocks are the first to move off the bottom of a market crash, so if you include some of these in your portfolio, you probably would have a better chance of participating in any rally. This is fine as wine for the AIM investor, because we buy cheap shares on the way down. And anything that gives us a leg up at the market's bottom is going to propel us into the profit column fast!

Regardless, there are some great companies here, and they do make up a cross section of American business, so I'd like to keep a couple in my portfolio for my own peace of mind.

Q. Didn't they just change some of the stocks in the Dow Jones average? The old smokestack companies were kind of going out of favor, I understand.

A. Yes. In June of 1979 they dropped Chrysler and Esmark from the Average, the first major revision of the list in a couple of decades, and replaced them with IBM and Merck. So I think we can probably look for a little more liveliness in the Dow Jones behavior now.*

Q. Mr. Lichello, why couldn't we just use all the Dow Jones stocks for our whole portfolio? I think there's a mutual fund that does that.

A. No. Too many stocks. Your results are too average. You wouldn't get the fluctuation you need for really fine performance in your AIM program. Don't worry—I've checked it out.†

Q. Should PORTFOLIO CONTROL include the broker's commissions or only the actual costs of purchasing the stock?

A. No, don't include the commissions you pay in either PORTFOLIO CONTROL or STOCK VALUE. If your broker buys you 10 shares of stock at $49 per share, which is $490, and then adds on his commission, you add exactly $490 to your STOCK VALUE, and then you

---

*Subsequently the Dow Jones Average was further amended to more adequatedly represent the modern economy, eliminating some of the old time corporations like Woolworth and Sears Roebuck and replacing them with the more swinging Microsofts and Home Depots. The 21st-century Dow bears little resemblance to the Stodgy Dow of the seventies—and may indeed prove to be a profitable vehicle for theAIMvestor of today.

†Because of sharply lower costs and improved performance, index funds like the S&P 500 Index Funds came into their own in the 1990s, as we discuss in Chapter 18.

increase your PORTFOLIO CONTROL by half of $490 . . . $245.

Q. My question is, wouldn't the commission charges on buying and selling stocks eat up the profits? I think this might be true if one invests a little money in the market. I sold a share of IBM and was charged 10 percent commission. That really hurt. I wasn't expecting terribly generous treatment, but 10 percent!

A. Yes, a number of readers feel that commissions on stock are going to dampen their results significantly. But commissions are a part of securities transactions. They existed before I created AIM, and they still exist. And I certainly don't like them any better than you do. But let me just point out something. Whether or not you use AIM, you are still going to be hit with commissions if you want to play the game. Take two investors with $10,000. Investor A is the AIM investor. Investor B is the—ugh!—ordinary investor. Investor B goes to his broker and buys $10,000 worth of stocks for his portfolio. Does he pay commissions? You bet he does! Investor A, the AIM investor, goes to his broker to start his AIM program, and guess what? He pays far less commission to his broker. Can anybody tell me why? You've got it! Because he's investing only half of his $10,000 in stock. The other half stays in cash.

So from the very beginning, the AIM investor pays far less commission to get his program started than does the ordinary investor—and those commission dollars that he saved go right into his CASH reserve and begin to earn interest immediately. Since it may be months, even years, before the AIM investor makes sufficient investments to bring his purchases up to the $10,000 level of the ordinary investor, don't you imagine that the interest he has been earning on the commissions he saved in the beginning will go a long way toward giving the AIM investor a helping hand with future commissions? Look at it this way: the AIM investor has $5,000 in a money fund. If he's only earning 10 percent-a-year interest, that's $500-a-year interest right there.

Remember, the AIM investor does not buy or sell stock every month. He may make one or two purchases this year, one sale the next, and half a dozen purchases the next. Small though his purchases and sales might be, he doesn't make them every month. Many readers forget this. They assume they are going to get clobbered by heavy commissions every month for the rest of their lives. They should be that lucky. Because if they *are* paying a commission every month, it would mean that their AIM program is being triggered constantly, and the more AIM is triggered, the more AIM loves it. Trigger it constantly and it is almost certain to become delirious and shower you with profits.

In any event, I finesse the commission problem in two ways: I deal through a discount broker, and I ignore buy-and-sell orders from AIM for less than $500. To buy or sell $500 worth of stock costs me only $24, and that's—what?—less than 5 percent. I can live with that. And a transaction of $1,000 costs me only $4 more. Total commission on a trade that size is only 2.8 percent.

A discount broker, incidentally, gives you no advice whatever and supplies you with no information about specific stocks. All he does for you is execute your trades, and that's it. There are literally dozens of discount brokers all over the United States. But even if a full service broker charges you 10 percent on a $500 transaction, a full service broker can give you lots of good ideas, so regardless of which kind of broker you use, if you ignore MARKET ORDERS under $500, commissions should be no problem.

If the truth be known, the average ordinary investor with his original $10,000 doesn't just buy $10,000 worth of stock and call it a decade. He buys and sells, buys and sells, year after year, paying hundreds, thousands of dollars in commissions—far, far more than the AIM investor. He's a trading maniac.

Some readers have criticized me for ignoring commissions in those charts of mine in the book. They forget that I also ignored commissions for the ordinary investor, with whom I was comparing the AIM investor. Ignored commissions for both of them, for the sake of clarity, in order to get a clear picture of the AIM advantage. I also ignored dividends paid on the stock owned by both investors—also for the sake of clarity. If I had factored these dividends in to my final results, the AIM investor, who often owned many more shares than the ordinary investor, would have emerged in an even more fabulous light. And since the AIM investor has, for some years now, been earning mouthwatering money market rates on his CASH balance, for months at a time, where the ordinary investor rarely has much of a cash balance, you can imagine how the AIM investor's results in my book would have been emphasized if I had credited him with those high yields instead of paltry bank interest. But why gild the lily? Many brokerage houses, incidentally, have their own money funds for your CASH reserves, which makes it most convenient. When you sell a stock, they transfer the proceeds immediately into the money fund and you start earning interest on the money right away. Good show!

Q. Mr. Lichello, your AIM is presented for investment of one's own cash only. Have you established any formulae that will likewise safeguard capital and show profits when one is investing on margin? This is a far more difficult problem, as any downturn erodes one's capital very quickly and I would be interested to hear if you have adapted the principles that apply to AIM in this situation.

A. Yes, I have given it some thought . . . about 10 seconds' worth. And that's enough. At least seven years of my life went into the development of AIM. Full-time, not part-time. So if you'd like to experiment with your margin theory for seven years or so, you have my blessing. But I don't think you will. I'm sure you have something more financially rewarding to do with your life. What do you do, sir?

Q. I'm a doctor.

A. Well, that's not as remunerative as a plumber, but

it still beats my income in those seven lean years. That
is, one month of your income would beat my entire income for seven years.

Q. Mr. Lichello, how do you factor capital gains taxes
into the formula? According to your book all sales of
stock go into the cash fund and draw interest. However,
I do not see any allowance in your charts for short- or
long-term capital gains taxes. In other words, the total
sale of stock goes into the cash fund, but at the end of
the year won't you have to pay taxes on any profits made
as well as on interest the cash fund has drawn? I am
single, 28 years old, and make roughly $15,000 per year.
Let's assume due to AIM I eventually made it to the
point where I may be showing say $40,000 to $50,000
per year capital gains after sale of stock either as short-
term or long-term after 50 percent deduction. This would
put me into the $60,000 to $70,000 tax bracket. How
could I afford to pay taxes in this bracket without dipping into AIM's cash fund? It seems that I could literally
not afford to make so much and use AIM as your
book shows.

A. That's easy. What you do is send all your profits
to me, and I will be tickled to death to pay taxes on
them. Seriously, I don't know if you're putting me on or
not. Every other stock market investor loses money and
you're worried you might *make* too much! Let's see.
Offhand, here's one thing you could do. Instead of a
money fund or a bank account for your CASH reserve,
use a tax-free municipal bond mutual fund. There are a
number of them around. I think Fidelity has one. Scudder has one. Vanguard—the same people who have the
Vanguard Money Market Fund—have one. That takes
care of your major problem right there, because in a
high tax bracket, what you don't want is high taxable
interest on your CASH balance. As for capital gains, the
long-term variety are taxable at very low rates. Even
short-term capital gains can be balanced against short-
term capital losses, as your accountant can tell you. So
any year in which you have to take big short-term capital

gains, you could also take some short-term capital losses as well to wash them out. That's normal portfolio and tax planning and has nothing to do with AIM.

Besides, if you ever do owe more tax one year on your AIM program than you can pay, you can always take the money out of your Money Machine. Simply take half of it out of CASH reserve and half of it out of STOCK VALUE by selling off some stock. Be sure to adjust your PORTFOLIO CONTROL. You do this by subtracting from PORTFOLIO CONTROL 100 percent of the amount you have taken out of STOCK VALUE. This preserves the integrity of your Money Machine.

Q. I'm sure you realize that the closer a person is to retirement age, the more volatile a portfolio he requires to accomplish his goal with AIM. I'm a stockbroker nearing that age and have been working on an idea using your formula. It entails selling the stock *short* and hopefully repurchasing it at a lower price, but I haven't been successful in establishing a PORTFOLIO CONTROL to manage the program. Have you ever attempted the procedure, or do you have any idea of how it can be accomplished?

A. No, I haven't attempted it, nor do I have any idea of how it could be accomplished. Why don't you get together with the doctor who wants to use AIM for buying on margin? The two of you could have a grand old time. My point is, AIM is what it is. I built it to serve one purpose only, and that is safety—preservation of capital—plus high performance in a single program, something that had never been done before to this extent. And the parts that make AIM work were precisely engineered for those specific functions. What you and the doctor are trying to do is insert your own diodes, transistors, and varistors into *my* Money Machine circuitry, without realizing that every action has a reaction, and that what might work over here is very likely to cause a short over there. Instead of trying to force my Money Machine to cough up trading stamps, why not start from scratch and design a machine specifically for coughing up trading stamps? I think it would be easier.

Just because you're approaching retirement age, don't ask AIM to make you rich in a hurry. As a broker, you know better than that, and I'm sure you would chastise a client who told you the same thing. AIM cannot be concerned with our age, our infirmities, our emotional needs, our pressing financial problems, our moods. It has sealed orders to perform a specific job, and it does that job in its own good time. Stocks are even more brutal than AIM. They don't have *any* job to do except perhaps to torture you.

Q. I was going to ask, will AIM work with commodity trading? The plan calls for a rather concrete investment under the MARKET ORDER column of your charts, and commodities aren't available in exact dollar amounts. Commodities certainly provide the action your Money Machine thrives on and if any way to feed them to it could be found, it could grow fat on profits in a very short time.

A. There are all kinds of ways to go broke in the world of investment. And I am content and immensely grateful that I, with only grade school mathematics, was selected by I know not what inexplicable quirk of fate, to help protect and enrich the stock market investor with my Money Machine. To prevent him from playing leap-frog with a unicorn. But from what I know about commodities, that's a whole other way of separating the investor from his hard-earned money. I know little enough about the stock market even to think about commodities. And I have no desire to wind up in Clint Eastwood Memorial Hospital with a fractured arm from too much figurework.

Q. I've compared AIM with my past lump-sum invest-ments, and the difference really is significantly in favor of AIM. My one question is: on page 64 of the paper-back, if the fifth entry in the stock price column was $3 instead of $5, you would more than exhaust your CASH supply. What do you do?

A. That's the first year of the million-dollar chart you're referring to. AIM took $10,000 and ran it into more than a million dollars in seven and a half years. But you are concerned your CASH reserve could have run out if the price had dropped a dollar at one point instead of gaining a dollar. And you ask me what I would do. I would cheer, that's what I'd do. If the price did drop to $3 and drained every cent from my CASH reserve, I'd get down on my knees in gratitude, because that's the millennium. That's exactly what we dream about: investing our very last cent at the very bottom of the market. If that happened, we'd probably have made our million dollars in this chart much sooner than seven and a half years, don't you agree?

Most ordinary investors invest their last cent at the *top* of the market. And we all know what happens to them! In 1970, 31 million people owned stocks. A decade later, only 25 million did. So they must have been doing *something* wrong.*

Here in this chart you referred to, AIM is performing its regular miracle by making its largest investments near the bottom of the market. Stock market experts and writers say that's impossible to achieve with any degree of consistency because only in hindsight can we know where the bottom was. Look at all those charts in my book and see how AIM automatically opens wide its purse at the very lows in the market! Don't you recognize a miracle when you see one?

So don't worry about exhausting your CASH. That's what you're supposed to do! And at the market lows!

Besides, that was a hypothetical single stock or stock portfolio you're looking at, and I doubt you will ever find a single stock or portfolio that volatile, as I have noted in the book. The chart was included only to subject AIM to the most vicious stresses and strains conceivable and see what it could do, and also to justify the

---

*In 2001 nearly half of all U.S. households own stock! We modestly accept some of the credit.

title of the book. In hindsight, as a few of you have pointed out to me, it is not a good title; because even though it is an honest title, it *sounds* as phony as all the rest of the how-to-make-a-million books. I'd forgotten my Aristotle.

In actual practice, your AIM program is unlikely to run out of CASH. But if it does—congratulations! Even if the market goes somewhat lower, you won't care, because when the market recovers, you will see that your major purchases were made at very near the lows!

One more thing: someday you will see that, like Lindbergh reportedly designing a slight instability into his "Spirit of St. Louis" in order to keep him alert on his historic solo trip across the Atlantic, I deliberately designed AIM not to wait for the absolute low before jettisoning cash. Because if AIM remains cash-rich and is allowed to buy too heavily at the bottom, the slightest recovery in the market at that point catapults you from the ocean depths clean up into the rainbow. Result: you get the bends. AIM's mechanism would respond too quickly to its newfound wealth and it would begin to sell off shares at a point that may be only slightly above the market bottom! For truly delicious profits, it's best to hold onto those shares until the market recovery has continued and made them even more valuable. And that's what AIM does.

Q. I made computer runs on several stocks dating back to 1969 on the AIM concept, and while there have been some moderately successful performances, most have been a disaster.* None measured up to the performance of the stock in your book, i.e., a million-dollar profit in eight years.

A. No, and none will, either. If you will reread the book, you will see that I took pains to emphasize that that was a hypothetical stock or a figure representing a hypothetical portfolio of stocks. As I've just explained,

---

*Many readers objected to this statement and deluged me with reams of computer printouts to back up their vote of confidence.

no stock or portfolio is going to behave that way, with such violence and with such mathematical regularity, for seven and a half years, doing exactly the same thing each year. Second, AIM wasn't built for a single stock; it was built for a portfolio of stocks.

The reason it was necessary to use the column heading STOCK PRICE here should be clear enough. First, it was necessary to boil down the value of the investor's stocks into a single STOCK PRICE in order to chart the ups and downs in the value of his holdings, and to show how many shares he bought and how many shares he sold at any given time. Otherwise, when AIM told him to sell $1,000 worth of stock, how could I have explained to the reader which stock he sold and why? Was it hypothetical Stock A, B, C, D, or E? If I had given this investor a hypothetical portfolio, I think the book would have been twice as long. It would take that much space to chart the ups and downs of each and every hypothetical stock in his portfolio.

Let me explain it this way. I have my own $10,000 prototype program going. And my first column is headed STOCK VALUE. That column tells me at a glance what my total stock value is at my regular checkup date. But there is a way in which I can break down my portfolio value into "per share units," just as a mutual fund breaks down their hundred-million-dollar portfolio into per share units of $10 or so. I did this in the beginning by dividing $10—because that seemed to me to be a typical price for a mutual fund share—into my total portfolio value of $10,000. That gave me a figure of 1,000— which means that my $10,000 portfolio can be broken down into 1,000 shares of a hypothetical stock at $10 a share.

So, hypothetically, I have 1,000 shares of a $10 stock.

The following month, the value of my total portfolio (which includes my CASH reserve, of course), declines to $9,000. I simply divide my 1,000 hypothetical shares into my total portfolio value of $9,000 and come up with a figure of $9.

Now the price of my hypothetical share went from $10 to $9. *But that hypothetical share exactly represents the value of my very real portfolio of stocks.*

That is what the STOCK PRICE figure stands for in my million dollar chart. It doesn't represent a single stock but a portfolio of many stocks.

Let me quickly emphasize, for heaven's sake, that you don't have to break down your own AIM portfolio into hypothetical per share units. I just do this for my own amusement and because it lets me see at a glance how much better *my* homemade mutual fund is doing than the prices of real mutual funds in the newspapers.

I'll repeat once more for the benefit of anyone who might be considering buying only a single stock rather than a portfolio of stocks: *anything* can happen to a *single* stock. Some of the finest blue chip stocks on the big board were selling for far, far less [in 1980] than they were a decade or two decades back. During 1972, for example, the huge Merck drug company sold for 45 times earnings. Doing splendidly and recently incorporated into the Dow Jones Industrial Average of 30 stocks, it is now selling at only 14 times earnings. (Note: This was in 1980. By 2001, the stock was selling at roughly 26 times earnings.)

Would you really want to place all your bets on a single stock, regardless of whether or not you were using AIM? Of course not. You are courting disaster if you select a single security for your entire investment program and hold onto it through thick and thin.

Earlier we discussed the possibility of using a single stock at the very beginning of your AIM program. If this stock plummets like a rock, at least it served a purpose: it took you down to the bargain basement fast and allowed you to do some heavy buying in other securities as the market dropped. Now suppose that original stock shows no sign of recovering as the months go by. Are you supposed to grit your teeth and hope? Do you say to that stock, *"Please* go up, *please* get up off the floor"? For one year, five years, ten years? That's what you're doing with your computer runs. If computers are so smart, why didn't *they* invent AIM?

Now, the AIM investor does it differently. He bought *other* stocks on the way down and added them to his portfolio. So even if his original stock has dropped into a senseless stupor, his other stocks are almost certain to participate in the market recovery. Besides, the AIM investor doesn't even have to hold onto that burnt-out stock. He can get rid of it, exchange it for another with better prospects, *whenever he feels like it.*

Blessed are those who do not place *all* their faith in a computer.

This bears repeating: AIM has nothing to do with normal portfolio management—with one exception. It's *your* job—with the help of your broker if you need it—to make that portfolio of stocks go up and down. It's AIM's job to adjust the ratio of your CASH to STOCK VALUE, because we feel that this is the most important and critical function in investing. And the record shows that you can't do it and neither can I. That's why you're here. That's why I'm here.

Q. In my selection of stocks, do I forget about dividends?

A. Nobody should be in the market for income. It's far too risky. If you need income, invest only in income-producing instruments such as banker's acceptances, certificates of deposits, treasury bills, and so forth, in which principal is protected against loss.

AIM has just handed me a note. It says that people who need income might take the dividends from the stocks in their AIM program in cash. It probably wouldn't bother AIM much to lose those dividends, and it might allow someone to enjoy life a little more along the way.

Q. Even if an investor isn't using AIM, that automatic dividend reinvesting idea is insane. Say you have a hundred shares of Nancy Ward Nosharamas, Inc., a chain of delicatessens, and you participate in their dividend reinvestment plan. Ten years later you decide to sell. You'll have to take 40 lines on your income tax return just to list those fractional purchases four times a year for ten years.

A. Yes, that's exactly what I tried to indicate. And if there're any stock splits, or stock dividends along the way, you'd better reserve some more lines on that tax return. And also a room at the Funny Farm.

Q. How can I be sure AIM is the best investment technique? There are a lot of investment techniques around, and a lot of books.

A. It is the glory of a free society that all of us can believe whatever we want and even write a book about it, no matter how absurd or unpopular our ideas. As consumers, we should protect ourselves. We should read up on things, compare, get other opinions, and finally, make our own decisions. That always entails a risk. Thank God for that. If there were no risk, you'd be bored to death.

A child accepts anything proffered and sticks it immediately into its mouth. But you are not children. You want to *know* what you're sticking into your mouth. When a new idea is proffered, we must examine it first and *then* decide whether to stick it into our mind.

We *should* get contrary opinions. To the man facing east, the sun never sets. To the man facing west, it never rises. They're both wrong, but if they'd only exchange viewpoints, then and only then would they see where they were wrong.

Q. Mr. Lichello, you say that you ignore advice on MARKET ORDERS under $500 because commissions are too high on small trades. How about if I bought a stock priced at $40, wouldn't it be advisable to ignore this advice under $400, $500 for a $50 stock, etc. Incidentally, the more I study and talk to myself, the more enthusiastic I become.

A. Welcome to the club. I don't know, I just think that simple things are the best things. If AIM tells me to sell $500 worth, I'm going to tell my broker to sell approximately $500 worth of the stock I want to sell. Obviously, he's not going to hit that $500 figure right on the head. Figuring in his commission, he might come only as close as $475 because he can't sell fractional shares to make it all come out even. Oh, there are some brokers who do buy fractional shares for you, but I don't think this is a real advantage.

Anyway, if I'm instructed to sell $500 worth, and I end up selling only some $475 worth, the difference isn't significant. AIM remembers. Next month, when it makes its new computation, *AIM will take that $25 differential into consideration before advising me what to do.* If it's a down market, AIM will deduct $25 from the amount of stock it wants me to buy. And if it's an up market, it will add $25 to the amount of stock I should sell. There is no escape.

Same situation if I'm asked to sell $500 worth and the closest my broker can come to it is $520, with his commission figured in. AIM knows that somebody filched a double sawbuck from my STOCK VALUE, and next month it will carry over the missing $20 and include that figure in its new computation.

Same thing when you're buying. It isn't all that important to buy the exact amount that AIM requests. Just do the best you can. AIM will keep the books open until they balance, you can be sure.

Q. If your AIM formula applies to a number of stocks rather than a single stock, wouldn't the stock movements cancel each other out working within the formula?

A. Generally speaking, they do to some extent. All portfolios, whether they be mutual funds, pension funds, endowment portfolios, whatever, can be expected to fluctuate less than the individual stocks within them. But in union there is strength. A portfolio of several stocks is more certain to go up with the market and down with the market than any single stock would be. Its performance is thus more dependable.

On the other hand, if I select only one or two stocks for my portfolio, and these turn out to be sluggards, my one or two stocks will not fluctuate as much as a larger portfolio would.

Q. In your examples in your book, your stocks go up before they go down. In my limited and totally unfortunate experience with the market, stocks drift a bit and then go down. I can visualize no clear indications to buy or sell and just collecting interest on the savings portion forever.

A. And the dividends from your stocks. Yes, that would be a real tragedy, wouldn't it? With money funds yielding nearly 14 percent on your savings portion at present, I would say, "If that's pain, hit me again!"

Seriously, if you'll check my book again you'll see that several of my charts show stocks going down before they go up. It really doesn't matter which way they go first, as long as they *go!* AIM investors love action, no matter how they get it.

But I don't think you have anything to worry about. Regardless of how many stocks you include in your portfolio, I think you are going to get buy and sell signals. I've used AIM with a mutual fund and got buy and sell signals within months, and the fund had nearly a hundred stocks in its portfolio.

Q. Mr. Lichello, what about gold coins instead of stocks? The broker I purchased through said there would be a sales tax on gold itself but not on gold stocks. What about using diamonds or other precious stones rather than a ready cash account to hold the liquid cash account? Could the AIM program be used to invest in international currencies?

A. Well, I bought a jar of instant coffee at a supermarket recently for $4.95, and then, at a second supermarket, saw the same item on sale for $3.49. So I used the AIM principle and bought two jars at that price. Result: I'd bought three jars for $3.85 each! Not a bad price at all. So I really can't tell you how AIM will function in any other situations without studying them thoroughly—and I really don't want to get started on international currencies! To quote Buckminster Fuller: "How tools are used is not the responsibility of the inventor."

As for gold coins, that's easy. They go up and down

in value, don't they? You can tell what they're worth each day in the newspaper. I'm speaking of coins containing one ounce of gold, like the Krugerrand or the Canadian maple leaf. And they're easy to buy and sell, even in small amounts. Certainly you can include them in your portfolio as just another stock. Or you could construct an entire portfolio of gold coins alone, keeping in mind that *anything* can happen to a single stock, or a single investment like gold coins, as we have already discussed.

Could you use diamonds and other stones instead of cash for your CASH reserve? No. Precious stones fluctuate in price, and the CASH balance of your AIM program must consist strictly of buying power—a fixed amount of buying power. If AIM says buy $5,000 worth of stock, and you buy it, your broker is not going to wait for his money while you run all over town trying to sell your diamonds for $5,000 to raise the money— and the most the jewelers will give you for them is $3,500. No, no, your CASH reserve is for cash only. You could possibly include precious stones in the STOCK VALUE section of your AIM program, but buying and selling those things appears to be so complicated. Besides, can you buy and sell them in reasonably small amounts?

About the sales tax on gold coins, if you live in the same state in which you buy the coins, you'd have to pay the sales tax. But there are lots of companies all over the U.S.—banks, too—outside your home state from whom you can buy gold coins without paying any sales tax. Just as you can buy any other merchandise by mail from outside your home state and not pay sales tax.

Q. Has the market situation in the past two years changed the success or formula for the use of AIM? Is there anything different one should be doing, or information no longer appropriate? Are you planning any new books? Do you feel AIM can still be successful providing the original stocks bought are adequate?

A. I don't see that anything has—or could be—

changed since the publication of my book that could
possibly interfere with its functioning. AIM is solidly
grounded in mathematics, and one and one still makes
two. On the contrary, the fabulous yields now being paid
by money funds redound to the advantage of the AIM
investor more than to any other investor I can think of.
Lord, that feels good—those bucketfuls of new dollars
being dumped into our CASH reserve every month! If
this keeps up, I don't see how any AIM investor is ever
going to run out of cash, not the way his CASH balance
is swelling.

You said something about the original stocks, "providing that they are adequate"? The original stocks don't
have to be adequate. If I don't like the way any or all
of them are behaving, I can exchange them for other
stocks any time I want to. It's my job to make my portfolio fluctuate. If I can do that with regularity, AIM will
do its job to help me reach my goal.

So nothing has substantially changed since I wrote the
book. Stocks still go up and down. Some eggs hatch,
others rot. And the ideal is still, "Buy low and sell high."
But who can do it? Nobody. Except by accident. Nobody
except AIM investors. They do it automatically. And
there will still be people who somehow will get rich in
stocks without using AIM. In the words of the old Rus-
sian proverb: "If you were born lucky, even your rooster
will lay eggs." But what do you do when your luck
runs out?

Any more questions? No more questions?

Q. Mr. Lichello, I believe I speak for everyone here
when I extend to you our deepest gratitude for your
magnificent achievement. I think what we have witnessed is one of the historic moments in all investment
history. And certainly your discovery has given us the
means by which we may hold on to our precarious future. You have given us hope, you have given us belief,
and you have given us reason to believe. Your reward?
In money, very little. In satisfaction, much, I hope.
Much. A toast to you, sir—and to AIM.

A. Ladies and gentlemen . . . thank you all. I assure you I am honored enough to have had the privilege of sharing my small knowledge with you. To all of you who wrote me letters of gratitude and praise, I will treasure them always. To those of you who write with questions about my discovery, my deepest apologies that I lacked the skill with which to express myself with absolute clarity in my book. To the very sick gentleman from abroad whose last wish was to shake my hand, and whose family saw to it that his wish was granted, and who said to me when we met, "This is the happiest day of my life," I assure you, sir, that you don't know what happiness is until someone has said to you what you said to me.

Until we meet again, ladies and gentlemen:

May you have all you need,

And all you desire,

And the wisdom to know the difference.

FOURTEEN

New Vistas for AIM

(Seminar, Twilight of the 20th Century)

I have a short statement. Since inventing AIM a decade ago, I have had the opportunity—like many thousands of the readers of my book—to sit back in relative calm and observe the smooth functioning of my Money Machine in action . . . in bull market, bear market, and blah market. Ladies and gentlemen, I am most pleased. Judging from your ecstatic letters to me over the years, so are you. Many of you told me that you were elated over the fact that for the first time in your lives, you stopped losing money in the stock market. That, to me, is as gratifying as hearing from other investors who are making a bundle, thanks to AIM.

Indeed, in the recent spectacular stock market run-up, even many non-AIM investors chalked up juicy gains on a par with ours. "What's so great about your 60 percent portfolio gain?" a New York talk-show host demanded of me on the air. "My mutual fund did that well *without* AIM." I replied, "You show me yours and I'll show you mine." He couldn't. The ensuing market slump had taken all his profit away. I still had most of mine. It had automatically been transferred to my CASH RESERVE and locked up as the market soared.

AIMvestors and non-AIMvestors alike scored large gains in the market boom of 1982–1983, but at the final gun, AIMvestors were on their way to the Super Bowl while non-AIMvestors headed for the Toilet Bowl in Sewer City. They would have done well to heed Disraeli's dictum: "Next to knowing when to seize an opportunity, the most important thing in life is to know when to forgo an advantage." It's easier to pry a terrier's teeth off your ankle than remove the average investor's hands from a stock that's risen 60 percent.

As I said at the start, I've had a chance to watch the Money Machine run for some time now, so I've taken my screwdriver and made some adjustments in the mechanism that should please present and future AIMvestors. It helps simplify the circuitry—and anything that makes life simpler is a prime candidate for my honors list.

The first adjustment is this: AIMvestors know that when they add *new* money to their AIM programs—a Christmas bonus, an inheritance, etc.—they are supposed to put half the funds into STOCK, the other half into CASH RESERVE. They are then supposed to increase their PORTFOLIO CONTROL by the amount of money just invested in STOCK.

I'll give you an example: You cash in an old war bond that's no longer paying interest and decide to put the $1,000 into your AIM program. You invest $500 in STOCK and put the other $500 into your CASH RESERVE. Now increase your PORTFOLIO CONTROL by $500. That's all. You're finished. Done. No need to make any further adjustments.

The same applies when you have to withdraw funds from your AIM program for an emergency. If you need $1,000, simply take $500 from your CASH RESERVE and sell $500 worth of STOCK. You've got your $1,000. Now *reduce* your PORTFOLIO CONTROL by $500 and you're all set. No need to reduce your PORTFOLIO CONTROL by a further 10 percent of STOCK sale— $50—as in the past.

These changes should improve your performance as well as your disposition over the long term.

I'll take your questions now.

Q. Mr. Lichello, what do you do when your mutual funds declare capital gain distributions? Do you make any adjustment in your PORTFOLIO CONTROL to reflect these? At times, they can be substantial.

A. No. No PORTFOLIO CONTROL adjustment is necessary when capital gains distributions or dividends are declared and reinvested in additional shares. Your PORTFOLIO CONTROL remains the same because the value of your STOCK remains the same. If your fund price is $10 and declares a $1 capital gain distribution, the price of your fund will drop to $9. But you reinvested your $1 and bought .111 shares with it. Presto, each share of your fund sells at $9, but you own 1.111 shares for every single share you owned before. Total value: $10. Same as before the distribution. So you do not adjust your PORTFOLIO CONTROL since there has been no change in your stock ownership.

However, if you selfishly decide to take your capital gain distribution in cash for the almost sinful reason that you want to *spend* it and not reinvest it in additional shares—and I would urge you to resist the temptation if you possibly can, because you are depleting your principal—then go, go, and don't look back. Don't talk to me. But before you go, *reduce* your PORTFOLIO CONTROL by the amount of the capital gain distribution that you have wantonly diverted from your Money Machine.

AIMvestors who have grown rich in the service and wish to start enjoying the rewards of having AIMed instead of hit-or-missed in their investment programs may in good conscience and without guilt accept their capital gains distributions in cash. Enjoy! But don't forget to reduce your PORTFOLIO CONTROL each time!

What I have just said applies, of course, only to those investors who use mutual funds in their portfolios. Investors who use individual stocks need not be concerned, since these do not declare capital gains distributions.

Q. Mr. Lichello, how do we go about selecting a mutual fund for our AIM portfolio? By that I mean, are the requirements for selecting a mutual fund the same for the AIMvestor as for the poor, average misguided investor on the street?

A. No. AIM is a special creature and requires a special diet. Unlike other investors, we aren't looking for long-term performance in a mutual fund; we're looking for volatility. Movement. Up *or* down. *That* gives us friction. *That* gives us heat. *That* gives us profits! Let us therefore go forth and seek out growth mutual funds that can offer us these wide swings in price, and let us pay special attention to those that tend to stay *fully invested* or nearly fully invested through thick and thin. Mutual funds that attempt to divine the direction of the market by going heavily into cash or bonds when they anticipate declines and becoming fully invested when they see good times ahead may be acceptable to the ordinary buy-'em-and-lock-'em-up type of investor who intends to hold onto his investment forever, but they aren't for AIM. Why? Because AIM does our timing *for* us. Automatically! We don't need anybody to *guess* for us. In AIM, we have a microchip circuit tuned into the cosmos and we don't *have* to guess. We *know.*

So we can dispense with conventional reference materials in this field to the extent that they simply give us the 5- or 10-year records of the various mutual funds. That tells us nothing. If the Pigheaven Fund has tripled in value in the past five years while the Wimp Fund has only doubled, the Wimp Fund may be far and away the best bet for AIM. Why so? During those five years, there may have been a sizable bear market somewhere. The Pigheaven Fund's management may have guessed right and gone heavily into cash or bonds just before the slump. Result? Its price suffered very little during the bear market, and as a consequence it entered the subsequent bull market in tip-top shape. The fact that Pigheaven tripled its price in five years might have less to do with management's offensive strategy in a bull market than with its defensive alignment in a bear market.

The Wimp Fund's management may have superior abilities to select stocks that perform well in a bull mar-

ket, but they may care little about going into a shell
when they smell a storm coming. For all we know, the
Wimp Fund may have tripled its net asset value per
share in the *first half* of that five-year period—and then
lost much of its gain during a slump in the second half.

So you see, the final figures don't tell us anything.
What we want to know is, one, how does the Fund perform in bull markets, and two, how does it perform in
bear markets? Two separate and distinct paradigms. The
conventional investor may also be interested in both
these categories, but where he may assign a high priority
to good *bear* market performance, the AIMvestor might
embrace a *poor* bear market record and say, "Welcome
to our bosom, fickle fund. You done good in good times,
and you done bad in bad times. Nobody loves you but
AIM."

In this connection, an annual mutual fund report like
the one published in *Forbes Magazine* each fall would be
of great help to you in selecting a mutual fund because
it measures bull market performance and bear market
performance separately. *Forbes*, along with the conventional investor, naturally considers for its honor roll a
fund that wins a high mark for each category: a "B"
for up-market performance, say, and an "A" for down-
market performance. Don't you do it! Pick a fund with a
high rating for up-markets, but a lower rating for down-
markets. That's the way you'll get the fluctuation you
need for AIM. Thomas à Kempis lighted our way more
than five hundred years ago: "The loftier the building,
the deeper must the foundation be laid." However spiri-
tual his intent, it's sound architecture and sound AIM-
vesting as well. To lay that foundation, we got to get
down, friends, get *down*. We got to get triggered. We
got to revive a fainting portfolio of stocks with a fresh,
invigorating infusion of new dollars from our CASH RE-
SERVE if we are to build our lofty edifice!

Some mutual funds derive their volatility not from a
policy of full investment at all times, like the American
Century Funds, but from concentrating their portfolios

on small, fast-moving, high-tech stocks, like Explorer Fund. Explorer might be 25 percent in cash at some times and yet move as fast in either direction as a fully invested American Century Fund.

Q. Sir, would you use two or three mutual funds in one AIM program or use a separate mutual fund for each AIM program?

A. You might get more action if you used a single mutual fund for each AIM program, with a separate PORTFOLIO CONTROL and CASH RESERVE for each program. But there might be more safety if you lumped all three funds together under a single umbrella PORTFOLIO CONTROL and CASH RESERVE. It would be hard to be dogmatic about this.

Q. Mr. Lichello, I have several AIM programs going, as well as a separate mutual fund for each program, meaning I also have three separate money market funds for my CASH RESERVE. Would there be any way of combining or consolidating my three money fund accounts into a single money fund account and giving each AIM program the interest it earns by itself? It sure would save a lot of headaches and paperwork and all those monthly statements.

A. I developed a method for my own use that you might find helpful. Use a single money market fund. When you get your monthly dividend statement from your money market fund, do this: Divide the balance— *before* the dividend—into the CASH RESERVE figure of your first AIM program. Use the result to multiply your money fund's latest dividend declaration, the total amount they gave you for the month. Finally, add the answer to your first AIM program's CASH RESERVE. That's all there is to it. Now repeat the process for each of your AIM programs. What you are doing is allotting to each AIM program the amount of interest its CASH RESERVE has earned for that month. It's a lifesaver, really, if you hate paperwork.

Q. Couldn't you just divide the money market account

balance by three and give a third to each one of your
AIM programs?

A. No, because if you have three separate AIM programs going, each CASH RESERVE will not be identical and will not have earned equal dividends. You might
start off with $1,000 in the CASH RESERVE of each
AIM program. But a year later, thanks to each AIM
program's separate and distinct buying and selling processes, #1 CASH RESERVE might stand at $ 1,050, #2
at $2,000, and #3 at $500. Each of those widely diverging
figures earns a disparate income.

Another benefit of this technique is that by consolidating all your CASH RESERVES into a single money
market fund account, you will be less likely to see your
balance fall below $500 and incur the wrath of your
money market fund. Most money market funds will close
out your account and send you a check for your balance
if it falls below $500, because it doesn't pay them to do
all the paperwork for a balance of less than that. And
when you think what a convenience and a blessing a
money fund is to us, none of us would be happy if our
money fund pulled the rug out from under us and forced
us to switch our CASH RESERVE to a bank account
paying 3 percent. With the Lichello "piggyback" Multi-
ple Cash Reserve System, such a risk is virtually eliminated.

Q. Thank you for another boon to the long-suffering
investor, Mr. Lichello. You should be declared a national
treasure. Is it possible, sir, for you to tell us which approach would be ideal, in your opinion, to use only one
growth mutual fund for each of our AIM programs—
three separate PORTFOLIO CONTROLS and three
separate growth mutual funds—and maybe get more action that way, or combine all three growth mutual funds
into a single AIM program with a single PORTFOLIO
CONTROL?

A. Thank you for the high praise. You go into my
personal pantheon, right next to the gentleman who said

I should be elevated to the sainthood. Come to think of it, maybe he really meant I should drop dead.

But I really can't answer that question for the simple reason there is no answer. If I said to you that 800 stocks are far and away too many stocks for a mutual fund to hold in its portfolio, and that you wouldn't get much action that way, the portfolio manager for Fidelity Magellan Fund might say to me, "Really? Then how do you account for the fact that Magellan's price gained nearly 400 percent in the five years ending April 1984?" And if I insisted that 44 stocks are way too *few* for a big $600 million fully invested fund to hold, Jim Stowers of American Century Growth Investors might say, "Then how come our fund gained nearly 200 percent in that period?" Which would be about twice as good as the Standard & Poor average. Both funds are volatile, and both can be expected to come back strongly after a bear market—Magellan because of its enormous diversification, American Century Growth because Jim Stowers believes some stocks are chicken eggs and some are tennis balls, and he says, "When the market goes down, we want to be rid of the chicken eggs. But the tennis balls will bounce back up like mad." And his funds do bounce back up like mad after every market slump.

So you see, for maximum convenience, you might choose to use several growth mutual funds combined into one AIM program, with a single PORTFOLIO CONTROL, and you might not have to give up as much volatility as you had thought. In addition, you'd have the added security that with three growth mutual funds rather than one in your AIM program, your portfolio would be likelier to bounce back after a bear market. As I've said on previous occasions, *anything* can happen to *one* mutual fund or *one* stock.

Q. Are you saying, then, sir, that it would be safer to include several mutual funds in a single AIM program?

A. Safety is the least impeachable component of the AIM circuitry, regardless of the number of funds you use. I cannot be doctrinaire about this and insist that you would be safer with three funds than one in your AIM program. A single mutual fund conceivably could turn out to be safer than three other funds if the three other funds come apart at the seams during a market crash and fail to recover, while the single fund does. The question should be: Whether I buy one mutual fund or 100, which is the safer way to buy them? Using Automatic Investment Management—or buying them outright, keeping no cash in reserve, and putting them in a drawer like the conventional investor? AIMvestors know the answer.

In philosophy, we have the doctrine of probabilism, which holds that certainty in knowledge is impossible and that probability is a sufficient basis for belief and action. I chart my investment course with that doctrine as my guide and AIM as my skipper because I cannot be certain of anything. I suspect that Columbus set sail with *four* ships, not three, but one fell off the edge of the world and was never heard of again. It was named the *Marrone!* At least, that's what Columbus exclaimed when he saw it disappear.

Are three funds in your AIM program safer than one? *Probably.*

Q. Sir, would ten mutual funds be too many in one AIM program?

A. Most people have too many stocks, too many possessions, too many desires, too many demands on their time clamoring for attention. In all these cases you can simplify and extend your life by dividing by 2. Keep dividing by 2 until you let out a long sigh of relief. Stop dividing at that point.

Q. I think you indicated in your book that for those of us who prefer to use stocks rather than mutual funds, a case could be made for selecting our stocks just from the stocks in the Dow Jones Average. Do you still feel that way?

A. Yes, for obvious reasons. They're big, well-capitalized companies, blue chips and all, and they're always the first to bounce back after a bear market. There's plenty of information in print about all of them. And by limiting your stock universe to the Dow, you'll save yourself all sorts of risk, time, and trouble in a fruitless search for a "new" Xerox or Polaroid, which usually turns out to be the Choong Gum Chinese Matsoh Ball Company or a Japanese firm called Kippon Trucking. And if you think you'll get only mediocre results from the Dow stocks, there's at least one investment adviser I know of who sticks exclusively to Dow stocks. And in a recent five-year period when the Dow rose only 112 percent, his model portfolio jumped 203 percent. So you see, there's a whole lot of action going on under the placid blanket called Dow Jones Average.

But now we have a way to have our cake and eat it too. Several mutual fund families now offer mutual fund portfolios that consist entirely of stocks within a single industry. For example, if you think that drugs and medical care are going to be hot in the years ahead, you would invest in their health portfolio. If you think energy stocks will be the outstanding performers of tomorrow, you'd invest in their energy portfolio. This new development can be an exotic space-age fuel for our Money Machine. The individual portfolios are exactly like mutual funds, but they confine their investments to individual industries or geographical areas: Leisure, Gold, Pacific Basin, High Tech, Service Economy, etc. Instead of prowling through dungeons and dragons to find the "right" stocks and paying high brokerage commissions, you might choose instead to select a handful of these special portfolios for your AIM program. Some of them charge no commission, others impose small charges. And because the portfolios are not diversified in the usual sense, among various industries, but rather restrict their investments to stocks within a single industry, the portfolio can be expected to provide more volatility than the conventional mutual fund. And they offer telephone switching as well. You can't get any more convenient than that.

Q. Sir, where could we get more information on those?

A. Well, Vanguard has them, as does Invesco Funds, and Fidelity—which charges 3 percent to get in and nothing to get out—and there may be others. The three companies I mentioned also offer money market funds you can switch back and forth into, so you'll find some addresses and toll-free telephone numbers in Chapter 12 of my book. Call them and they'll send you a prospectus.

Q. Mr. Lichello, I use some of the American Century funds for my AIM program, but they don't offer telephone switching. You have to write each time you buy or sell. And you have to have your signature guaranteed by a bank each time you sell, which is very inconvenient. They don't even have a money market fund, so switching is out of the question anyway. It keeps me hopping. Should I get out of these funds and get into a fund complex that does offer the telephone switching and all?

A. Many mutual funds place similar obstacles before us. American Century does have a money fund now, but it also has a high-yield U.S. Governments Fund, which invests only in longer-term securities of the U.S. Government and its agencies. So it's pretty safe, as you would imagine, although the price per share does fluctuate ever so slightly. If you can live with that—and I see no reason why you can't—you can use the U.S. Governments Fund in place of a money market fund. And you can switch by phone now between any of American Century's funds without a signature guarantee.

Q. That's really a big help. May I have a follow-up, sir?

A. Certainly.

Q. How much of a disadvantage is it for investors like myself who have to do our buying and selling by mail because our funds don't offer telephone service?

A. Less than you would imagine. But if you're concerned, use the first Friday of the month as your regular checkup day. If you operate AIM on a twice-monthly basis, use the first and third Fridays of the month. That way, you'll be using Thursday's closing price in your calculations, because that's the price in effect on your regular checkup day, Friday, the price that appears in Friday morning's newspaper. And so, by mailing your buy-or-sell request on Friday, the fund will probably get it Monday and will use Monday's closing price to execute your order. So you "missed" only two trading days—Friday and Monday.

If your fund *does* offer phone exchange, it will generally exercise your instructions at the close of business on the day you call. That way, you "miss" only one trading day, the day you phoned your order in.

Now, what "penalty" did you pay by *not* having phone exchange? One trading day. So whether you miss two trading days by doing business by mail, or one trading day by doing business by phone, the differential is insignificant.

If you have to do business by mail, all you're really giving up is convenience. But look what you're getting in return: In a falling market—when AIMvestors will be buying—stocks tend to keep on falling, and the delay caused by your having to use the mail will redound to your benefit. How? You'll buy your stocks even cheaper! The law of inertia. And in a rising market—when you will be *selling*—stocks tend to keep rising and by the time your letter arrives at the fund, your stock will probably have risen further, and you will not have to sell as many shares to realize the dollar amount AIM has called for. Just an extra little miracle engineered into the AIM circuitry.

So while mail transactions may be a trifle inconvenient, they could well earn you bonus dollars in the long run. Ten years from today, you won't remember the inconvenience, but you could have substantial rewards right in your hands as a result of it.

Incidentally, some mutual funds that insist on a signature guarantee each time you sell will not even honor an *exchange* request by mail without a guarantee. So find out beforehand what the policy is.

Q. I have a two-part question. First, why not use several AIM programs, with one stock or mutual fund to each program, with a separate PORTFOLIO CONTROL for each program, but instead of a separate CASH RESERVES for each program, why not lump all the CASH RESERVES into a single pot and just have one CASH RESERVES figure? Then, whichever fund needs the money, so to speak, just reach into that one pot and feed it the money as it goes down in price. Wouldn't that be more convenient than a separate CASH RESERVE for each AIM program?

A. I refer to that strategy as the "AIM Central Treasury." And I'm afraid of it. A single collapsing mutual fund could very well plunder your entire CASH RESERVES. Really. And who suffers? All your other mutual funds, which have lived good clean lives, worked hard, played by the rules, and now have to turn over their entire bank accounts to a no-good, long-haired wastrel fund that may *never* amount to anything in this world.

If you start off with $1,000 in a fund and it immediately slides 80 percent, it could demand *thousands* of dollars in new money along the way. But since your CASH RESERVE should be $1,000 when you started that program, that falling fund of yours doesn't *deserve* more than that; and yet it will keep whining and complaining until you feed it more. What are your other funds going to think of you when they see you pick their pockets at a time when they may be going *up* in price and earning more CASH RESERVES—and here you are spending them on a wayward fund as fast as they earn them? I wouldn't want to be in your shoes. Yes, you had a second question?

Q. What is the best way to handle all that, then—to have several AIM programs, with a separate CASH RESERVE and a separate PORTFOLIO CONTROL for each program?

A. I call that the "AIM I.C.O. Program"—Individual Cash Ownership. I think that's probably the best if you can handle the paperwork. With "I.C.O." each fund gets the CASH RESERVE it starts off with, plus whatever else it earns on the way up. Pure capitalism. On the other hand, for sheer simplicity, you could use a single AIM program—one PORTFOLIO CONTROL, one CASH RESERVE—and use several stocks or mutual funds in your portfolio for safety's sake. Each one of these "I.C.O." options offers a good balance in terms of safety and performance.

You *might* get more action in the first "I.C.O.," but it will demand a lot more action from *you* to keep tabs on all those different PORTFOLIO CONTROL and CASH RESERVE figures.

We must part now, you and I, for a little while.

May I close by saying to all of you here and in the far corners of the world who have written me your letters of gratitude, thank you. To know that I have touched so many lives, to know that even one human being breathes easier because of my work—that is my success and my treasure. Ladies and gentlemen, in life, as in investment, it is the set of the sails and not the gales that will carry you safely to your own personal El Dorado. I wish you bon voyage!

FIFTEEN

TWINVEST—World's Safest Method for the Small Investor

One of the major surprises for the author after the first publication of this book was the number of readers with very small assets who wrote to me, assets ranging from a few hundred dollars to a couple of thousand dollars. Some of these were college students. Others were individuals with low-paying jobs. The remainder appeared to be young people relatively new in the job market who, while earning fair salaries, had not yet, in their opinion, been able to accumulate a "nest egg" of sufficient size to warrant beginning an AIM program. Some of this last group seemed to believe that $10,000 was the smallest acceptable amount.

I have no idea what a minimum-size AIM program should be. It would seem that an individual with as little as $2,000 could begin a modest AIM program with $1,000 in a no-load mutual fund and $1,000 in a money market fund, provided that $2,000 doesn't represent his or her entire savings. Nobody—regardless of the size of his or her income or "nest egg"—should ever invest a dollar *if he or she cannot afford to lose it.* Certainly a savings account containing sufficient emergency money should be everyone's first consideration. Investment comes later.

And while I am convinced that AIM is the best investment technique available for those who have already accumulated a small bundle and wish to make that bundle grow, I'm not certain it's ideal for those who haven't yet put aside some meaningful dollars—even though they may have some spare cash left over at the end of every month.

Why, for example, start a small AIM program and then, once a month, feed new money into it from outside sources? At that precise moment, AIM might be flashing a "sell" signal. Why buy when AIM says sell? Obviously, when AIM wants to sell, the market has been rising and stocks are becoming riskier to buy. The fundamental philosophy of AIM is to *unload* at the highs, not take on more cargo!

When I was a child, I watched in fascination as the rubber rollers in the washing machine inexorably sucked in the soggy wet clothes and squeezed every drop of water out of them. Like a true scientist, I laid the fingers of my right hand on the bottom roller and hitchhiked a free ride. The roller carried my fingers upward, dragged them between the two rollers, and did a number on my fingers, my hand, my wrist, and my arm until my howls brought my saintly mother on the double to release me.

This is the fate awaiting all investors who allow themselves to be mesmerized by the lure of a constantly rising market and who foolishly feed their wallets between the rollers.

True, AIM *does* contain provisions for adding new money to the program *from time to time,* but not on a regular basis. And not if the new money overwhelms your portfolio. It doesn't make a whole lot of sense to dump $2,500 of new outside money into a $2,500 AIM program that has been cheerfully chugging along a couple of years. You are doubling the size of your AIM program at the expense of its memory circuits. AIM will not know whether to laugh or cry. And indeed, doubling the size of AIM in an instant is like starting a new AIM program all over again. A sudden stock somersault could cause that brand-new $2,500 to lose value fast. The loss would be bad enough. The discouragement, however, could lead to disenchantment with AIM. And that would be even worse!

It might be wiser to start a second AIM program with that $2,500 than to force it down your present AIM program's throat at an inopportune time; but the risks of investing heavily at the market highs remain the same. Besides, how many AIM programs can you handle—without a computer, that is!

So where does that leave the folks who have enough emergency money in the bank and who can now afford to start investing a small amount of money on a monthly or quarterly basis? How can they invest with *minimum risk?*

Until now, they had to be content with "Dollar Cost Averaging," a worn-out investment technique that serves the interests of mutual funds, financial advisers, and stockbrokers—*not* the interests of investors! Under certain conditions, "Dollar Cost Averaging" can be a less risky way of investing in the market than plunking down a lump sum of money at one time, but it can also result in white-knuckle losses when a long bull market turns sour and the investor is left holding large numbers of high-cost shares that are now worth a fraction of what was paid for them! It is here that most "Dollar Cost Averagers" panic and abandon their programs. That's the dark side of "Dollar Cost Averaging."

"Dollar Cost Averaging" works best in a declining market. If you buy one share of a no-load mutual fund for $10 and two shares for your $10 bill next month when its price has dropped 50 percent, you will end up owning three shares for your $20 investment. Your Cost Per Share is $6.67. When the price of your mutual fund exceeds $6.67, you'll have a profit.

But suppose you did it this way: Suppose you bought only $7.50 worth of stock in the beginning and banked the $2.50 savings. You'd have purchased .750 of a share. And when the price of the stock falls to $5, suppose you invest your full $10 and buy two more shares. You now own 2.750 shares, plus $2.50 in the bank.

Astonishingly, your Cost Per Share is only $6.36—far lower than the "Dollar Cost Averager's" $6.67—despite *the fact that you invested less money! Your loss is only $3.75. The "Dollar Cost Averager" has lost $5—a full one-third more!*

How can this be? Didn't you and the "Dollar Cost Averager" invest the identical amount when the price dropped to $5 a share? In number of dollars, yes. *In proportion to your original investment, no.* Like life itself, investing makes you pay dearly for mistakes. Success depends more on avoiding the pitfalls than on seizing the opportunities.

This, in essence, is the idea behind an exciting new continuous investment plan I call TWINVEST. TWINVEST makes fewer mistakes than the "Dollar Cost Averager" and recovers from them far more rapidly. It is the simplest, safest, most efficient investment system ever invented for the small investor.

TWINVEST achieves its superiority over "Dollar Cost Averaging" by recognizing that "good shopping" should apply to investing as well as to household management: *When prices rise, cut back on purchases; when prices fall, stock up!* Today, especially, the TWINVEST philosophy of "Make every dollar count" is needed as never before.

TWINVEST features the TWINVEST CODE, a code number into which is packed an incredible amount of information and investment analysis.

Each investor's TWINVEST CODE will be different and will depend on the initial price of the mutual fund the investor wishes to use and the amount of the monthly or quarterly investment he or she can afford.

It will take you only one minute to calculate your own TWINVEST CODE, and from that moment on, your personal CODE will achieve for you investment results that have never before been possible!

Once a month, or once every three months if you prefer, you use your TWINVEST CODE. *Instantly,* your CODE signals to you the exact amount of money you should invest in your mutual fund.

Miraculously, this amount increases or decreases, depending upon the action of the mutual fund you're investing in. Yet your out-of-pocket investment remains the same—never more or less than you had planned in the beginning!

The goal of TWINVEST is to match the performance of "Dollar Cost Averaging" with substantially less risk. I believe you will find, however, that TWINVEST *more* than achieves its goal!

I suspect that TWINVEST will appeal not only to investors with limited resources who *must* have that extra margin of safety that TWINVEST offers, but to well-heeled residents of the "Gelt Belt" as well, who are more interested in *accumulating* stock than buying and selling it as our AIM does. TWINVEST takes less time and trouble at income-tax time, too, because you don't have to report any sales. There *are* no sales. And no income taxes to pay on your gains!* That last factor alone should endear TWINVEST to the upper-brackets folk. Besides which, TWINVEST is wonderfully simple and blissfully free of paperwork. *That* should endear it to everyone.

We emphasized simplicity, and here's the proof:

What's your *Available Monthly Investment*—the amount of money you'll be able to invest every month (or quarter) with no trouble whatever, through thick and thin? Most investors make a critical error here. They *think* they'll have no trouble coming up with $200 a month, say, and for a while, they're right. But let the market head for Sewer City as it did in 1970 and 1974, and your average investor makes a mad dash for the exit. "Don't send good money after bad," he mutters, mopping his brow.

It is much better to scale down your *Available Monthly Investment* to a sum that may seem insignificant, and be absolutely sure that you won't miss that money in good times and bad, than to begin your investment program with an unreasonably high figure and abort the

---

*You must, of course, pay taxes on capital gains distributions if your fund declares them. Even TWINVEST can't help you there!

program at the very time when continued investments will do you the most good: at the bottom of the market! I cannot emphasize this point strongly enough. It is the single most critical error "Dollar Cost Averagers" make. And if you make it, you're almost certain to lose!

Very well, then. In view of the above, say you've decided on an *Available Monthly Investment* of $100. Write it down like this:

$$\underline{\$100}$$

Next, divide by 4 and write the result directly below the line, like this:

$$\frac{\$100}{\$25}$$

Now multiply the bottom figure, $25, by 3. That gives you your *Coding Multiplier*—in this case, 75.

Finally, pick out a mutual fund you wish to invest in and multiply the price it's selling at by your *Coding Multipier*. If the price is currently $10 a share, multiply $10 by your *Coding Multiplier,* which in this hypothetical case is 75. 75 × $10 = 750. That is your TWINVEST CODE. If your CODE contains a fraction at the end, round it off to the nearest full dollar.

That's all the information you need to operate your TWINVEST program. It belongs at the top of your record sheet as follows:

$$\frac{100}{25} \quad \text{CODE:} \quad 750$$

Once a month—or once a quarter, if you like—check the price of your mutual fund in the newspaper. Let's assume it's still $10 a share. Divide that price into your TWINVEST CODE, and the answer pops up like magic: $75. TWINVEST is directing you to invest $75 in your mutual fund. And since you have $25 left over from your *Available Monthly Investment,* put it in a bank account.

(When Twinvest asks you to invest fractional amounts, simply round them off. Thus, $75.49 becomes $75; and $75.50 becomes $76.)

Next month, the price of your mutual fund may be $11 a share. Divide $11 into your TWINVEST CODE. The answer is $68. TWINVEST has scaled down your investment because the churning market is trying to lure you into putting your hand between the rubber rollers. This month you have $32 left over from your *Available Monthly Investment.* Put that in the bank as well—or money market fund if you prefer.

Those other two figures to the left of your TWIN-VEST CODE tell you two things: The top figure, $100 in this case, is your *Available Monthly Investment.* No matter what, you know you never have to come up with more than $100 *out of your own pocket* on your regular investment day. At times, TWINVEST may direct you to invest more than that. Don't do it unless you have the extra money in your special TWINVEST bank account.

The bottom figure, $25 in this example, is your *minimum* investment. You may not invest less than that— ever. Years from now, when TWINVEST asks you to invest a sum that is *less* than that bottom figure, it is a signal to you that the mutual fund has tripled in price and that your TWINVEST program is over. You have ridden this particular horse as far as it will take you. Time now to start another TWINVEST program.

To keep things straight, I use a plus sign after my *Available Monthly Investment* figure:

$$\underset{25}{\underline{100+}} \quad \text{CODE:} \quad 750$$

Although I know instantly that my *Available Monthly Investment* is $100 and that TWINVEST will never demand more of me than that *out of my own pocket,* the plus sign reminds me that if TWINVEST ever calls for *more* than $100, I may take the balance over $100 from my TWINVEST bank account—if it will accommodate me. If TWINVEST asks me to invest $125 and there is $25 in my TWINVEST bank account (or in a money market fund earning even higher interest), I can obey TWINVEST and invest $125. Even if there were only $10 in my TWINVEST bank account, I would invest $110—my *Available Monthly Investment* of $100 plus the $10 from my bank account.

A TWINVEST program will probably last for many, many years before it "matures" and signals a halt. It may surprise the average investor to learn that *very* few mutual funds triple their net asset value per share in fewer than 10 years—even if you *begin* in a bear market year when prices are lowest. The reason is not that mutual funds can't cut the mustard; a large number of them *have* tripled their stockholders' money over the past decade. But mutual funds periodically declare dividends and capital gains distributions. When this happens, the fund price drops by the exact amount of the distribution. So while the value of a single mutual fund share with all dividends and distributions reinvested may have quadrupled over the past decade, the fund *price*—the net asset value per share—that appears in your daily newspaper may not even have doubled in that same period! And the fund *price* is what you hook your TWINVEST rocket to at the very beginning.

Take a good growth stock fund like the Morgan Fund, for example. Morgan started business in 1968 at the price of $6.67 a share. At the close of 1984, 16 years later, its price per share was approximataly $11 a share. So if you had chosen Morgan for your TWINVEST program back in 1968, you could still be using it because the price per share has not even doubled, let alone tripled. The *real* performance of the Morgan Fund (as with any other mutual fund) is reflected not in its asset per share, but in its value per share with all dividends and capital gains distributions reinvested. Using that yardstick, the Morgan Fund started out at $6.67 a share in 1968 and rose to approximately $27 at the end of 1984,

TWINVEST VERSUS DOLLAR COST AVERAGER

$100
$25

CODE: 750

Price	Invest	TWINVEST				DOLLAR COST AVERAGER		
		Shares Bought	Shares Owned	CASH	Total Value	Shares Bought	Shares Owned	Total Value
$10	$75	7.5	7.5	$25		10	10	
$11	$68	6.2	13.7	$57		9.1	19.1	
$12	$63	5.3	19.0	$94		8.3	27.4	
$13	$58	4.5	23.5	$136		7.7	35.1	
$14	$54	3.9	27.4	$182		7.1	42.2	
$15	$50	3.3	30.7	$232		6.7	48.9	
$14	$54	3.9	34.6	$278		7.1	56.0	
$13	$58	4.5	39.1	$320		7.7	63.7	
$12	$63	5.3	44.4	$357		8.3	72.0	
$11	$68	6.2	50.6	$389		9.1	81.1	
$10	$75	7.5	58.1	$414	$995	10	91.1	$911

$100 Monthly Investment

TWINVEST VERSUS DOLLAR COST AVERAGER

		TWINVEST				DOLLAR COST AVERAGER		
Price	Invest	Shares Bought	Shares Owned	CASH	Total Value	Shares Bought	Shares Owned	Total Value
$9	$83	9.2	67.3	$431		11.1	102.2	
$8	$94	11.8	79.1	$437		12.5	114.7	
$7	$107	15.3	94.4	$430		14.3	129	
$6	$125	20.8	115.2	$405		16.7	145.7	
$5	$150	30.0	145.2	$355	$1,081	20	165.7	$829
$6	$125	20.8	166.0	$330		16.7	182.4	
$7	$107	15.3	181.3	$323		14.3	196.7	
$8	$94	11.8	193.1	$329		12.5	209.2	
$9	$83	9.2	202.3	$346		11.1	220.3	
$10	$75	7.5	209.8	$371	$2,469	10	230.3	$2,303

	TWINVEST	DOLLAR COST AVERAGER
Total Investment:	$2,100	$2,100
Closing Value:	$2,469	$2,303
	(stocks plus cash)	

While the DOLLAR COST AVERAGER invested the *full* $100 a month in stock, the "careful shopper" TWINVESTOR invested only a *portion* of the $100 during periods of high prices and banked the savings! These savings allowed the TWINVESTOR to invest *more* than $100 in those months when the stock was selling at a bargain!

233

quadrupling your investment. Our hypothetical TWIN-
VESTor would be enjoying a huge profit today in a program that is still a long way from being mature.

If you select a poorer-performing growth fund or a
less-risky "balanced" mutual fund (a fund that combines
stocks and bonds), a typical TWINVEST program should
take at least a generation to mature, and perhaps much
longer. Regardless of your TWINVEST's life span, the
important thing is the amazing safety of your investment
throughout. TWINVEST cuts back on purchases as the
price of your mutual fund rises, and steps up its buying
as the price declines into "bargain basement" territory.

As you can see from the chart, TWINVEST treats
each price level in a particular way regardless of whether
the fund is increasing or decreasing in value. At the first
$11 a share price, for example, TWINVEST shelled out
$68—because that's all that TWINVEST feels this price
level is worth. The price subsequently rose to $15, then
retreated. And when it touched the $11 price level again,
TWINVEST carefully counted out exactly $68. It is that
measure of safety and dependability that gives TWIN-
VEST the edge in any kind of market.

At the conclusion of the chart, TWINVEST emerges
victorious with a portfolio valued at $2,469 versus $2,303
for the "Dollar Cost Averager." But the *real* margin of
victory is this: TWINVEST's Cost Per Share is only
$8.24, compared with the "Dollar Cost Averager's"
$9.12!

The most graphic proof of TWINVEST's magic security blanket occurs in the chart at that point where most
Monthly Investment Plan investors fly the coop: at the
very bottom of the market. Here, the "Dollar Cost Averager's" portfolio is worth only $829. The TWINVES-
TOR's portfolio—stock and cash—is worth $1,081.

To appreciate this enormous advantage, multiply these
figures by 20 to simulate a longer investment program.
TWINVEST emerges with $21,620, the "Dollar Cost Av-
erager" with $16,580!

At other times, of course, the TWINVESTor might

not boast such a walloping superiority; or, by the same token, it might chalk up a margin of victory so breathtaking as to be beyond belief. Certainly after years of rising prices, the "Dollar Cost Averager," who has been investing the same amount of money each month all along, is terribly vulnerable and can suffer enormous losses when the market turns down—losses far in excess of those risked by the much more careful shopper, TWINVEST. In any case, the stated goal of TWINVEST is to match the performance of the "Dollar Cost Averager" with substantially less risk. Anything more than that is just plain gravy!

During the course of your TWINVEST life span, you may, for one reason or another, become disenchanted with the mutual fund you are riding and decide to switch horses. This can be accomplished as follows:

Divide the present price of your fund into the price of the fund you desire. Multiply the answer by your TWINVEST CODE. The answer is your *new* TWINVEST CODE. The switch is thus accomplished without missing a hoof beat, and your TWINVEST program is not disturbed in the least.

Please realize that TWINVEST has nothing whatever to do with AIM: they are two separate and distinct investment techniques.

Enjoy my Money Machine, AIM, and now my TWINVEST. May they enrich you beyond your grandest expectations. But please be patient. Remember the wise words of Sophocles: "One must wait until the evening to see how splendid the day has been."

SIXTEEN

AIM-HI—2001: The Investment Odyssey Continues!

In the Stock Market zap of 1973–1974, a certain investor assessed his gloomy financial situation.

His portfolio had been cleanly halved by the guillotine smash of 1970. And now his few remaining pesos had been chipped, chopped, and chiseled by a Wall Street demon gone berserk before the investor had emerged from his shock long enough to dump all his stocks.

He had $2,000 left—mere shreds of a once cozy security blanket.

Well, back then, with $2,000 he could buy a snazzy new Japanese small car. Or a VW Bug for that matter. It would be the first car he'd ever bought in his life! Why not? Why not enjoy what little loot he had left?

How about it, investors? Did he buy the car?

He did not. He decided, instead, to buy 1,000 shares of the "Barmecide Insurance Company."

His broker returned his check with a note suggesting that the investor had obviously made a mistake and had intended to buy some other security with perhaps a similar name?

"No mistake," the investor told his broker on the phone. "I want to buy Barmecide Insurance."

"Perhaps you've been out of the country," the broker said patiently. "There have been lawsuits against the president, the chairman, and others within the company. In this morning's *Journal*, now the SEC has filed a civil suit against the company and five of its officials charging

236

them with fraud. At last report, the company was losing money. Well, the stock is selling for little more than a dollar a share. That should tell us something, I think." He paused. "Two years ago it was selling for thirty a share. So it *is* down somewhat. That is, it is down to almost nothing, isn't it? I really wouldn't recommend that you buy it. I would stay far away from something like this."

"I appreciate your advice," the investor said. "But I've read all the books on the stock market. I've followed all their advice. I bought good, sound stocks in good growing companies. The result? I've lost nearly everything."

"Well," said the broker, "that would apply to just about all of us these days—professional and amateur alike. It has been a pretty bad time."

"I've given up on the orthodox approach," said the investor. "This is an out-and-out gamble. It's my last shot, and I'm shooting from the hip. Buy me Barmecide Insurance. It's the one company I could find with no prospects whatever."

Five years later, the investor's 1,000 shares of Barmecide Insurance had mushroomed in value to $12,000!

"Mirror, mirror on the wall, who is the shrewdest stock market wizard of them all?" whooped the investor. "It's an eight-letter name," he prompted, "and it begins with L."

"Lady Luck," said the mirror.

"No, no. Lichello! He ran one thousand into twelve thousand in five years!"

"Show me the twelve thousand, please," said the mirror. "What you have there is one thousand shares of Barmecide Insurance."

"Which I can sell for twelve thousand!"

"Ah, but you won't," said the mirror. "As any farmer will tell you, it's a lot easier to sow than to reap. In twenty years of investing, you have never maintained a position in a stock that tripled, let alone sextupled. Let go of *that* catch? I doubt it. Besides, you never sell into strength. Like every other losing investor, you panic and sell a *falling* stock."

"Oh, yeah?

"Yeah."

Down went Barmecide Insurance.

"How much is your stock worth *now*?" said the mirror.

"After commissions and income taxes on the capital gain, maybe five thousand."

The mirror cracked a smile. "Well, congratulations anyway. Very few investors equaled your record in the past five years. And just think, you might have thrown away that two thousand on a new car instead of investing it in stock. So what are your plans?"

"I don't know—buy a new small car, I guess. I can afford it now."

"Really? Your five thousand *might* buy you a new small car. But your original two thousand definitely would have bought you one five years ago. So for all your sweat and strain, for all your luck, for all your self-proclaimed stock market wizardry, you've only been running in place. Any boob could have bought a new small car in 1974 for two thousand, sealed it in a baggie, and opened it today. You're both even. And the fact that your dumb investment just happened to come up roses does not alter the fact that it *was* a dumb and desperate move. As Mr. Thoreau phrased it, 'It is a characteristic of wisdom not to do desperate things.' But think of it: Just to *break even* in this debilitating decadigit inflationary climate, you had to achieve *extraordinary* results with your investment. Your experience reminds me of the college professor who decided to stay overnight in a sorority house to prove that rumors of wild parties there were unfounded. He was right. Bored, he went to bed at midnight. An hour later a coed entered his bedroom and woke him up. 'Did you want me?' the professor asked. The coed said, 'Not especially. I just drew you.' The Wheel of Fate just happened to stop on your number this time."

"Maybe it was just cars that doubled in price in the past five years," the investor said hopefully.

"Yes," clucked the mirror, "and maybe just a hot dog from a sidewalk vendor. Maybe just Broadway orchestra seats. Leave out oil and gasoline, which way more than doubled. Maybe just hospital rooms. Maybe just houses and apartments. Maybe just fish. Maybe just magazines, newspapers, books, shoes—"

"And in the next five years . . . ?" the investor quaked.

"Probably worse," the mirror reflected. "To avoid tar and feathering, prophets tend to err on the side of rationality. Back in the mid-sixties, they were warning that college costs could soar to four thousand a year by 1980! Can you imagine? Why, you can't even send a kid for a year to the State College for the Terminally Unlettered for · four thousand dollars. It's a souped-up treadmill upon which the investor must run faster and faster just to remain in place. *So any investment that merely doubles in five years is no investment; it's a box lunch.* You're simply freezing your buying power. Thaw it out five years later and it'll perform pretty much as it did fresh. You hope."

"To double your money every five years," the investor moaned, "you'd need to earn . . ."

"About fourteen and a half percent a year," said the mirror.

"Where can you get *that* kind of return? The highest a bank has paid for savings on a thirty-month account was twelve percent a while back. At that rate your money wouldn't double for . . ."

"Six years. You see, the magic number is seventy-two. Divide twelve percent into seventy-two and you get six. Your money doubles in six years. Ostensibly."

"Ostensibly?"

"Even if you're only paying thirty percent in state and Federal income taxes, that cuts your actual return down to eight-point-four percent. And with inflation at, say, only twelve percent a year, you're *losing* almost four percent a year. How many portable radios from Hong

Kong would the bank have to give you as a gift to make
up for *that*? By the way, that magic number seventy-two
works another way too. Divide the rate of inflation into
seventy-two and it will tell you how many years it will
take for your dollar to lose half its value."

The investor shuddered. "Then this is the end of investing. And probably of everything else as well. Because if you have to achieve *exceptional* results year after
year—an absolute impossibility—just to stay even, nobody will save or invest. It's like making an omelet. Is
it really worth all that trouble?"

"Pessimism, dear boy? A few years ago you invented
a new continuous investment system for the small investor called Synchrovest. Why?"

"To give him at least a shot at survival in the investment arena. To wean him away from that deceptive and
deadly Dollar Cost Averaging and hit-or-miss investing
that did us all in."

"Commendable. And then you invented AIM—Automatic Investment Management. Why?"

"To give the investor at least a chance to make a good
deal of money over a period of years without exposing
him to undue risk."

"Over a period of years. How many?"

"Who can tell? Ten, fifteen, twenty."

"But with money losing half its value every five years,
the investor has to quadruple his money every decade
just to stay even. Think of it! Your ten thousand dollars
today must grow to forty thousand within ten years if
you are to maintain your purchasing power!"

"What are you talking about, Mirror? The government says inflation is running only three or four percent
a year."

"Negatory, good buddy. A lot of pension plans and
Social Security are *indexed* to inflation. Therefore, the
official inflation rate is way understated. Saves money!
The true inflation rate is still in double digits. Along
with thousands of your readers, I implore you to go back
to the drawing board and improve your AIM system to

give the investor a better chance to *get rich fast* without undue risk. Not for the sake of his greed. For the sake of his *survival*. Because the way things are going, only the very rich and the very poor in some cases are going to make it! I believe you can turn your AIM into the World's Greatest Investment System."

"Simply that, huh? Listen, I swore I'd never do any more work on investment systems!"

"I swear you'd better. Time's running out on a whole way of life, my friend. We're all going to be working on the plantation for coolie wages. New World Order, you know."

"Why can't it be done with real estate? We've all heard the expression, 'Get a lot while you're young.' "

"Too specialized. Too illiquid. And the value of a single family home has increased little more than six percent a year on average in the past fifteen years. Besides, in a bust, real estate will collapse just like stocks. And who's got the kind of financial reserves to 'average down'—to buy more and more houses as their prices are marked down? Because that's your immutable philosophy, isn't it—buy straw hats in winter?"

"You're not asking much. Mutual funds, pension plans, bank investment trusts—if they could even double your money in *ten* years, they'd shout it from the housetops. And you want me to invent a high voltage system that will double your money every *five* years!"

"More often than that if you can."

"Thanks. Just take a look at this Mutual Fund prospectus in my hand."

"I'll have to take a little time here because I'm a mirror and read things backward, you know. Oh, yes, I know the fund. Very big. Very well known income fund. Turn the page and let's see the record. Oh, I see. From 1967 to 1978, virtually no gain at all. The price went from twelve dollars a share to about twelve dollars a share if you add up the capital gains distributions they paid. What's so unusual about that? I know lots of investment companies that did even worse!"

"Look at their management fee for 1978: two-point-five million dollars!"

"So what? Percentage-wise, their fee isn't out of line. It just happens to be a big fund. Ergo, their fee looks big."

"Yes, and since their total assets were roughly the same in 1978 as they were in 1967, that means they pocketed two-and-a-half million a year just over that eleven-year period—a total of twenty-seven-and-a-half million dollars—for their accomplishment in boosting their per share value from twelve dollars all the way up to twelve dollars! Dat'sa some spicy box lunch!"

"Meaning?"

"Meaning why butt my head against the wall of the establishment? Why not open the door and try to get in on the game? Remember de Tocqueville: 'It must, I think, be rare in a democracy for a man to suddenly conceive a system of ideas far different from those accepted by his contemporaries; and I suppose that, even should such an innovator arise, he would have great difficulty in making himself heard to begin with, and even more in convincing people.' "

"It's true that the financial community may resist you. After all, they have a vested interest in the status quo. But John and Jane Public are having their heads kicked in by inflation. They desperately need you. They told you so in those countless letters of gratitude they sent you after you published, *How to Make $1,000,000 in the Stock Market—Automatically!*"

"But now you want me to develop my system even more?"

"You have to. The times demand it. We both know that the future belongs to stocks. As did the past. It's the one thing historically that offers us hope for economic survival. Both the small investor and the large investor can buy them and sell them, instantly, in any amount and at any time. Stocks pay dividends and require no upkeep. On land and buildings you have to pay real estate taxes and hire people to watch out for your interests and so on. Precious metals pay no dividends; you even have to pay somebody to store them in a safe place for you. When everybody was touting gold back in the seventies, remember, one voice cried aloud in the wilderness: yours. You devoted a chapter—chapter nine—advising against gold. You were right, and you saved many people from losing their life savings. And as we saw recently in the Persian Gulf war, the price of gold huffed and puffed and rose a paltry thirty five dollars an ounce for about ten days and then settled back to its original price. So much for gold as a hedge against war and uncertainty. I repeat: stocks and Mutual Funds are our only hope. But the old ways of investing in them are no longer valid in today's world. Too risky, too uncertain, too hit-or-miss. To a large extent, your AIM discovery removed most of the risk. Too much so, some say."

" 'Caution is the eldest child of wisdom.' "

"Caution is for Savings Bonds, and even they can't save us. Listen, my friend, we're bleeding all over the place and you're afraid of hurting us! The seeds have already been planted for tragedies that will make 1974 and 1987 pale by comparison. Take just one area: hundreds of thousands of ordinary working people are contributing to their own personal retirement plans—the IRA's and the Keogh Plan, the 401(k)s and all the rest. Many of these benighted souls are, like most of us, financial illiterates. Many of them are investing their annual pension contributions in stocks and mutual funds, as is permitted by law. Now, as you pointed out in one of your books, stocks and mutual funds are good tools; but the tool cannot be expected to do the whole job by itself. The tool needs a hand and a mind behind it—a template, if you will."

"Exactly. And that's what I was striving for during those long and lonely years inventing the AIM system."

"Yes. Now what is going to happen to those people I just mentioned if, as they approach their golden retirement years, the market suffers a horrendous reversal of the magnitude of 1974 or 1987 or even worse? Tell me, what is going to happen to those poor souls, expecting a blissful retirement, if they are all of a sudden jolted with a rip-roaring loss of fifty, seventy, even eighty percent of their hard-earned, irreplaceable, and painfully saved retirement dollars? It is easily possible that, after thirty or forty years of participation in such plans, an individual could have hundreds of thousands of dollars invested. *And he could easily lose most of that money in a single year: the year he retires.* Can you imagine the consequences and the anguish of a loss on that kind of scale and at that particular time? Can you imagine if the market takes several years to recover—or *decades* as it did back in the thirties? Boy, build my people an ark to carry them safely over troubled and perilous waters to the golden shores of financial security!"

"You ask much of me for so little reward."

"We have the promise of Emerson that you will ultimately prevail: 'If the single man plant himself indomitably upon his instincts, and there abide, the huge world will come round to him.' I repeat: Equity investment will save us. Equity investment is the future. But not just Equity. Something more than Equity. Equity with an extra dimension. 'AIM' with the kind of pizzazz and explosiveness all of us *must* have now not only to survive, but to prosper!"

"I'm sick of stocks. I'm sick of stock investment formulas. I want to write my novel. Leave me alone!"

"Come, step into the mirror a moment. Visit the ghosts of victims past. Look, a seventy-six-year-old widow living alone in a damp garage in a high-crime neighborhood in Florida. It is 1974. See that old second-hand refrigerator on the open porch? It contains what little food she can afford. That's her 'kitchen' there—a rusty hot plate and an old, old laundry sink. No bathroom. No heat. One bare unshaded bulb. Sometimes she bumps into things. She is going blind. For the elderly in 1974, my friend, inflation doesn't mean substituting hamburger for steak or skipping a weekly movie. It often means going without any food at all for a day or two.

Or skipping a badly needed visit to the doctor. We are in Chicago now. A seventy-eight-year-old woman lies unconscious on the floor of her plain room in a hotel for the elderly. For three months she has been living on oatmeal moistened with a dab of milk. It is all she can afford. And back to Florida, that paradise for the elderly. The old man mowing yards to make extra money. He is almost blind, but his wife walks beside him, directing him so he won't miss any grass. And everywhere, my friend, in the big cities, the elderly picking through garbage cans. Then, in the eighties, inflation worsens, savings evaporate, and mental health experts see the awful frustration and the physical and psychic damage in its wake: an increase in broken marriages, suicides, heart attacks, deaths, alcoholism, violence, rape (the need to control at least *something* in a world in which the individual feels he has lost control of his own destiny). Revulsion on a grander scale—the elderly in their sunny 'paradise' buying canned dog food to eat, losing their homes when their cash-strapped state doubles and triples their real-estate tax and sometimes generously offers to employ them at minimum wage to work off their debt to the state—"

"Stop the tape! That's me: That's me sitting in the kitchen of that tumbledown house on a lonely country road in upstate New York. That's Rosie—that little old widow with the biggest heart in the world is Rosie. She's serving me coffee there."

"Who is Rosie?"

"I lived a few miles down the road from her when I was working on my Automatic Investment Management system. She really was my best friend. When I didn't have a car, she drove me to the supermarket. She was always there to help me as she helped others, driving the elderly to the markets and to the doctors. She lives on a small Social Security pension. Nothing else. She's in her eighties. And her real-estate tax has just gone up to something like fifteen hundred dollars . . ."

"You once said it yourself: 'The world has enough

rich people. What it needs are fewer poor people.' I'm
waiting for your answer."

"Not even a sink in her bathroom. Not even an electric outlet. God, Rosie, what have they done to you?"

"There are many Rosies, and there will be many
more."

"Are you telling me that any investment formula
could make a difference?"

"You think not? Saving pennies in a bank will not
rescue them from that fate. You yourself have seen your
own modest investments in AIM grow far beyond what
would have been available to you in banks and such. I
am telling you that there is a formula for bread, and
there are formulas to make money to *buy* bread. Either
can change a destiny. Either can save lives. Can you
make bread, my son?"

"No."

"Make a money formula then."

In the nearly 25 years that have elapsed since I first
introduced AIM to the public, I have received literally
thousands of letters from both here and abroad. Of particular interest to me were those from brokerage houses
and investment authorities who sent me reams of computer printouts along with a note that generally read:
"We tried to beat your figures with our own computer
programs and couldn't! Congratulations!" After all,
when you've spent several years developing an investment formula using nothing more exotic than a ball-
point pen (and a cheap pocket calculator in the last year
or so when I decided to go "high tech"), a little chuckle
of satisfaction should be permitted.

I have also over the years received a number of querulous
letters, accompanied by mind-numbing charts, demanding
to know why their own results were so disappointing. In-
variably, their error lay in assuming that AIM could perform the entire job for them all alone and that the fuel
itself—the choice of a stock or mutual fund—was of
minor consequence. Nothing could be further from the

truth. Throughout the book and in my various TV and radio discussions I have emphasized that a stock or mutual fund is only a tool, and you cannot expect a tool to do the job by itself. This flies in the face of conventional thinking, of course, which holds the view that you buy a security and hold it and eventually, if you've bought the right security at the right time and you sell it at the right time, you should come out all right. I and millions of other disenchanted investors suspect that this philosophy originated with a famous Indian named "Sitting Duck." And I for one want better odds than that.

You cannot expect AIM to roll up its sleeves and hew the wood day after day on a diet of Twinkies and diet soda. You've got to gas it up at the high-test pump.

A typical example that comes to mind was the chart that one disgruntled reader sent me whose results were so pallid that I could only stare at them in disbelief. Normally, this would have been an exercise in futility; and normally, I could not have been expected to devote my time to doing an analysis of the many charts readers have directed to me. But an AIM program that achieves only a 10 percent profit in the span of two years cries out for critical examination. Hey, it's my baby he's throwing out with the bath water!

What on earth could have accounted for such a dismal performance? Were his figures correct? They were. Had he obeyed the proper signals and bought and sold when he should have? He had. Then why? I looked closer. The mutual fund he had chosen for his AIM program had started out at something like $10 a share and had concluded the two-year span at approximately $10.50 per share—a really big increment of 5 percent. Comatose but not terminal: AIM couldn't care less about the performance of a mutual fund so long as the price fluctuates. The million dollar chart in this book shows very clearly that a stock or mutual fund need not rise a cent above its original price for AIM to achieve truly extraordinary results. While we have emphasized again and again that the million dollar chart is strictly hypothetical and that such extreme volatility cannot be expected in the real world, the chart does show what AIM can accomplish if the stock doesn't go up when you buy it (the typical investor's experience) but rather fluctuates at various price levels *below* your original price. Obviously, in actual practice, stocks and mutual funds display a much more moderate volatility than that shown in the million dollar chart; and yet, as has been shown elsewhere in this book and in the actual experience of thousands of AIMvestors over the years, even moderate volatility is sufficient to trigger AIM from time to time and by so doing achieve often incredible results.

I reminded this AIMvestor that he must judge the results of his program *relative to the performance of the fund itself*. True, AIM had presented him with a very modest profit of only 10 percent. But had he purchased that same torpid fund *without* using the AIM system, his profit would have proved even more minuscule: 5 percent!

So here was an AIMvestor complaining that AIM had only *doubled* his profit: Picky, picky, picky.

In the following chapter I will discuss how funds of very moderate volatility such as this one *can* be used by AIMvestors with special requirements, investors who are not so much concerned with a high-voltage performance of their AIM program as they are with current income coupled with the proven safety factors built into the AIM system. AIM will *always* offer the opportunity for growth regardless of what you feed it, but its acceleration will depend largely on the octane in its tank. And that's something only you, the AIMvestor, can give it. I designed the vehicle, but you have to drive it. That's not too much to ask, is it?

So far in this book we have addressed the majority of investors, those whose primary aim is to achieve peak performance from their investment programs. Most of us have tried to accomplish the same goals without AIM's assistance—AIM having arrived only in 1977—and have failed miserably at the task. With our new ally, it has been shown, our goals are now within our grasp. AIMvestor after AIMvestor has boasted not that they have made a million dollars (if they had, they'd probably keep it quiet anyway) or even $10,000, but rather that they are now logging only profits on their Schedule D Income Tax Forms, whereas in previous years, it was a laundry list of losses. And that is no small feat!

Obviously, AIMvestors will show *no* losses on their tax form because AIMvestors don't *take* losses during the normal operation of their AIM programs. When AIM says, "Sell!" we always sell at a profit, as far as I can gather, never at a loss. And as many AIMvestors have learned to their delight, they don't really incur the tax liability on each sale that they might have expected. Because when AIM directs us to sell $500 worth of stock, for example, *not all that $500 is profit*. The actual amount of the capital gain involved depends on what you *paid* for that $500 worth of stock, and that's purely a function of your own personal record-keeping, not AIM's decision-making. As you may already have discovered, only a gleefully small portion of that $500 might be subject to capital gains tax.

AIM cannot be concerned with tax consequences. Its sole function is to adjust your cash and stock ratio periodically in order to reduce your exposure to risk and prepare you for the banquet to follow. If it has to take capital gains from time to time to do that, fine; and although it has never happened to me over the years, I cannot rule out the possibility that an occasion could arise in which AIM could flash a "sell" signal that could translate into a tax loss. I can envision this happening, for instance, if an investor decides to begin an AIM program with stocks or mutual funds he has owned for some time. AIM has no way of knowing how much the investor paid for the securities: its mission is to take the ball and run with it. Ask not how the touchdown was made; just look at the scoreboard.

An investor might begin an AIM program with securities in which he already has a loss. Then, during the course of the AIM program, the stocks might rise to such an extent that AIM will flash a "sell" signal.

As far as AIM knows, you have a profit and attention must be paid. But since your stocks or mutual funds are still valued at far less than you paid for them, even though they've moved up in price a bit, that sale you just made might really be a loss. You might even enjoy the loss to wipe out a previous gain on your Schedule D. AIM doesn't care. The things that are Caesar's, you yourself must render unto Caesar on April 15.

There is a circumstance in which an AIMvestor could if he wished deliberately take a loss on his Schedule D, and that would occur if he or she decided to dump a losing stock or mutual fund and replace it with another. But an AIMvestor should have very sound reasons for doing so, since the theme song of AIM is "Somebody down there likes me." Vigorous buying during a stock plunge is our very bread and butter. Like Dracula, we gloat at chaos and chortle: "Go ahead, make my night!" Contrarians we are, and tumbling stock prices we love. Nevertheless, if we conclude that a particular fund or stock in our program is taking a dive from which it might not recover (and we should have very strong and valid reasons for so believing) it might be in our best interest to jettison the turkey and latch onto a likelier candidate.

To repeat: For maximum performance in our AIM programs, we must use high-octane fuel. We don't use "growth and income" mutual funds, we don't use "equity income" funds, we don't use "balanced" mutual funds. What we do use are the "aggressive growth" funds and the "long-term growth" funds (there are several hundred in each category to choose from). Periodically, magazines like *Kiplinger's Personal Finance Magazine, Business Week*, *Forbes, Money*, and even *U.S. News and World Report* chart the performance of various funds in their respective categories. It couldn't be simpler to locate the kind of fund you're looking for.

Once you've narrowed down your possibilities, call or write for a prospectus. Toll-free numbers are generally given in the financial magazines just mentioned. I know that earlier in the book I had a little fun with prospectuses and advised you to make an airplane out of them and sail them out of the nearest window. I was only half-joking. Read the prospectus, but don't base your final decision on what you find there. You may want to seek corroboration elsewhere, perhaps in one of the financial magazines listed. I'm referring specifically to the performance figures of the fund. If you think I'm erecting straw men, take a look at this letter I wrote in May 1991 to a large Mutual Fund:

Dear Folks:

There seem to be some serious errors in your latest prospectus.

On page 6, where you are comparing the "Life of the Fund" performance with that of the S&P 500 during the same period, S&P emerges with a huge advantage over your fund: 268.14 percent vs. 130.78 percent. This places your fund in a poor and unfair light. Apparently, you are using the *ten-year* performance figures of the S&P and comparing those with the *six-year* figures for your Fund.

Further, the Life of the Fund comparison stuns the readers with the assertion that, even though your fund was soundly outclassed by the S&P 500, its average annual return of 14.63 percent bested the S&P 500's 13.92 percent. I simply cannot understand how this is possible.

In your previous prospectus, your fund was shown to compare quite favorably with the S&P 500. And in the ensuing year, nothing in the performance of either vehicle could account for the nosedive of your fund in the comparison figures.

I would be interested in knowing if I am correct in my observations, because as a shareholder, this worries me sick.

In its reply, the Fund admitted that I was correct and that they had erred in their prospectus. They had, in effect, "cut their own throat." A prospective investor, reading this prospectus for the first time and noting the dismal performance figures, might easily have tossed it into the wastebasket and resumed his search for a more competitive fund even though this one might have satisfied his needs perfectly. So it only makes good sense to crosscheck the performance figures!

Next to the performance of the fund you are considering, the most important figure to examine in the prospectus is the "Operating Expense." Every fund has an Operating Expense, whether it is a *load* fund or a *no-load* fund. A load fund, of course, is a mutual fund that charges a commission to buy it—generally 8½ percent. Don't even *think* about those! A no-load fund charges no commission and performs, on average, just as well. *Do* think about those. They simply don't have any salesmen to push their wares (and to pay). *You've* got to seek them out and find them, and information about them abounds today.

The line you're looking for in the prospectus usually appears in the first few pages under a heading reading something like "Financial Information," "Per-Share Income and Capital Changes Table," "Selected Per-Share Data and Ratios," or something similar. Find the column headed by the most recent year and run your eye down to the line reading: "Ratio of expenses to average net assets." This is the total percentage of the fund's assets that the Fund charges annually to manage your money and includes everything from their management fee to printing costs to legal fees. The more the management takes out of your fund, the less is left over for you. You don't see it being winnowed from your fund, but it's always reflected in the price per share that appears in your newspaper. It may appear in the prospectus as .53 percent or .78 percent or .88 percent or .95 percent, and I can live with that. But personally I get nervous when the Operating Expense exceeds 1 percent and I'll rarely consider a Fund that levies much more than that. I will even think long and hard if the Operating Expense is given as 1.25 percent. It has been my experience that once you exceed 1 percent by any substantial amount, you don't get what you pay for.

Finally, check to see if the fund has a 12b-1 Plan in effect, which allows the fund to boost its expenses to make *you* pay for publicity and advertising. The 12b-1 fees were authorized by the Securities and Exchange Commission in 1980. Thankfully, not all mutual funds have seized the privilege. Try to select one that hasn't. That extra largess, which legally can escalate to 1¼ percent with shareholder approval, belongs in *your* pocket, not theirs.

And never buy a fund that imposes a redemption fee, something called a "back-end load." Many of these Funds masquerade as no-load funds, and it's true they charge nothing to buy them. But when you *sell*, down comes the guillotine blade. Look at the not-so-funny mathematics: Buy $5,000 worth of such a fund and pay no "load." In a few years, you hope, you double your money and decide to sell. They charge you a 5 percent exit fee of your $10,000 or $500. Now $500 may be only 5 percent of your $10,000, but it is *10 percent* of your original investment!

I couldn't live like that.

Once the preliminaries are over and done with, the only decision you'll have to make is how many AIM programs you care to manage at one time. As simple as AIM is to operate, it still requires *some* record-keeping and *some* attention—at the very least a few minutes once a month if you operate AIM on a monthly basis, or a few minutes twice a month if you prefer the biweekly option.

The simplest way to go for busy folks is a single AIM program. It may contain one or more stocks or mutual funds. If you are using only one security, your Stock Value column will reflect the current dollar value of that one stock or mutual fund. If you are using two or more securities, your Stock Value column will contain the dollar value of all of them. In the latter event, should AIM flash a market order to buy or sell, say, $500 worth, you yourself must decide which of your stocks or funds to buy or sell. It's easy. I *sell* shares of my least favorite mutual fund in my portfolio and I *buy* shares in my favorite fund. That way my portfolio is continuously being energized. You might even decide to buy or sell $250 worth of *two* funds in order to comply with AIM's Market Order of $500.

Obviously, no such decision is necessary if your AIM program contains only one security. You would simply buy or sell $500 worth. Even I know that.

Nevertheless, there are AIMvestors with and without computers who prefer to operate several AIM programs, each of which contains a single security. That would be the way to go for maximum volatility and action. The choice, however, is an individual one.

No matter which AIM option you choose, the two most perplexing questions in the investment universe have already been answered for you: when to buy and when to sell. And perhaps a third question as well, which some may consider the most baffling of all: Is now the proper time to get into the market? AIM always answers yes, because it knows you are not rushing full bore into equities with 100 percent of your capital. AIM keeps a goodly chunk of your cash safely on the sidelines until the desperate merchant marks his prices down and the bargains are plentiful!

Two signal events occurred in the year 1977 that directly impact our discussion here today: the first publication of this book and the launching of the space probe Voyager 2. Both vehicles, astonishingly, are still viable, still traveling on course and transmitting valuable data to the world. Voyager 2 has logged many billions of miles, while our more modest craft continues to be refined and streamlined as it orbits our globe.

With the publication of this Fourth Revised Edition,

and the introduction of our latest improvements in the Automatic Investment Management system that I first unveiled nearly 25 years ago, I am convinced that our AIM probe now has the power to continue its mission for many years to come, performing each function exactly as planned and transmitting messages of hope to the world below.

These latest advances, I'm sure you'll agree in the pages to follow, top all the previous ones because they answer—in spades!—probably the only valid complaint leveled against AIM: that it's *too* conservative, *too* safe, *too* downright stingy with its cash! Longtime AIM fans know why: I designed the AIM formula on the heels of the worst stock market debacles in my lifetime, 1970 and 1974, in which I and millions of other investors suffered a bombing and strafing that left us shell-shocked for years afterward. The very reason I invented AIM in the first place was to protect us all against a recurrence of that horror. And if I skewed it toward the pink lemonade pitcher and away from the martinis, you better believe I knew *exactly* what I was doing!

What I didn't know was how *far* I was tilting toward the lemonade, and it didn't really bother me as my own AIM programs continued to chug out lovely profits with no perceptible risk and happy AIM fans continued to shower me with thanks. I had no reason to regard my swollen cash balances with anything other than smug satisfaction. Certainly it was a novel experience for me (and my readers) to have a nice fat cash hoard burgeoning in our portfolios, along with stocks and mutual funds that rarely stopped rising. And I for one never suspected that although AIM was the star, a vigorous bull market was surely the "prompter" whispering my lines from stage left. How could I? *Before* AIM, I hardly knew what a profit looked like. Man, keep on hittin' that plus key— I'm startin' to *like* it!

But soon it became apparent that our heavy cash balances were acting as a drag on our profits, and several years ago I began to experiment with a new kind of

AIM program using an opening Cash Reserve of *less*
than 50 percent. This meant that I could reduce the
"drag" on our future profits by allowing us to buy more
stock up front with our money. An AIMvestor with
$10,000 can buy only $5,000 worth of stock at the outset,
with the remaining $5,000 to be kept temporarily in cash.
That "temporary" sometimes threatened to become permanent. Even more frustrating, the cash hoard often
continued to grow to herculean proportions, with no end
in sight, as AIM flashed "sell" signal after "sell" signal
and exchanged more and more stock for cash in a soaring market.

Not that AIM wasn't performing wonders for us. It
was. But could we stop grinding it out on the ground
and take to the air, kick that fat backup quarterback in
the seat of the pants and tell him, "Get in there and
do something"?

The task required several years of hands-on testing. I
no longer possessed the physical and emotional stamina
to fill a room with pages and pages of failed formulas
as I did during the invention of AIM (a man is mature
when he has more brains than guts), so I took the alter-
nate route: I opened several actual AIM accounts, each
using an initial Cash Reserve of *less* than the 50 percent
we've all come to know and love.

My "failures" brought more of a smile to my lips than
did my eventual success. They showed quite clearly that
even though I had the percentage of cash wrong for
optimum performance, AIM had been so well designed
and engineered in the first place that I came out smelling
like a rose—even though I'd hoped for orchids. Case in
point: One AIM program was riding the most volatile
vehicle I could find at the time, Twentieth Century Ultra
Fund, a fund that remains fully invested through thick and
thin in small, thinly capitalized stocks. I began the program
with an incredibly small 20 percent Cash Reserve. This
freed up a huge 80 percent of my funds for direct investment in stock. I theorized that the humongous equity
side of my portfolio would, in a rising market, throw off

tons of cash as it sold stock. It began to do just that, but before it had a chance to build up large reserves, 1987 struck. Ultra plunged something like 40 percent in price and the AIM siren wailed constantly for more capital. But since there was so little fuel in the tank, AIM sucked it dry within a single month (the program was being operated on a biweekly basis).

At the very moment when massive reserves should have been moving from the cash to the equity side, AIM ran out of gas and drifted helplessly watching the bargains at the bottom of the market go begging!

Mirabile dictu, AIM held my loss to 3 percent—no small consolation. And the buying AIM did do when the stock fell proved quite profitable (in the context of my small investment in this AIM program) when the price recovered. AIMless investors, let me remind you, weren't buying at all during the decline, as usual.

Granted, I had selected the most volatile fund possible; granted, I had begun my program with an almost insignificant amount of cash—20 percent; and granted I had run smack dab into a barnburner of a crash, a triad of horrors that would have elicited sympathy from Job himself. Nevertheless, when you subject a new technique to all the stresses and strains imaginable (as I had subjected AIM itself to such, earlier in this book), it either lies there dissolving in a plume of smoke like the Wicked Witch of the West or it emerges limping but proud from the swirl of combat, head held high and saluting smartly, as AIM had, ready for debriefing, sir.

I did not realize at the time, however, that I *had* finetuned my program to the exact point I had always sought: an optimism balance between risk and reward. I understood it only when I saw that using a twice a month checkup could become a "bear trap." Thereafter I returned to my old tried-and-true *monthly* protocol—and AIM-HI, Aim High Intensity, was born!

Come closer, I want to show you something. Instead of beginning your $10,000 AIM program (just to keep it simple) with half in cash and half in stock, do this:

Multiply the $10,000 by .80—80 percent. That goes directly into stocks. The remaining $2,000 becomes your Cash Reserve!

What you have now is power plus. If the market declines, you have enough Cash Reserve to accommodate you in all but the most severe circumstances. And if the market rises, which it does much more often, that hefty stock portfolio will start spinning off cash like a cotton candy machine; and as I have seen again and again, your Cash Reserve can equal and exceed the stock portion of your portfolio! And *then* should the market collapse, it's Katy, bar the door! Katy will say, "Is that a roll of bills in your pocket or are you just happy to see me?" You could end up owning the store.

Because our new AIM-HI purchases, at the start, 60 percent more stock than before and reduces its cash by 60 percent, its results could prove to be at least 60 percent greater. In practice, that figure could multiply like compound interest, because we have much more stock working for us at the starting gate. *Moreover, the advantage continues throughout the life of the program because the base—aided and abetted by any optional 80-20 subsequent additions to the program—is more heavily weighted toward the equity side.* The unconscionably large cash balance required by the old AIM program, which acted as a drag on percentage profit *forever*, has been pared to a leaner and meaner reserve cache.

Any additions to the investor's AIM-HI program, we repeat, share in this explosive advantage because *only 20 percent of his additional investment is deposited in the relatively unproductive cash balance of the program.*

If you wished to add new money to your AIM-HI program, simply multiply it by 80 percent. If it's $1,000, you'd put $200 into your Cash Reserves and invest the remaining $800 in stock.

Here's something to think about on a rainy night: Since the *New* AIMvestor starts out with 60 percent more stock than did the old AIMvestor, isn't he placing himself more at risk? On the contrary, he might be *less* at risk! The old AIMvestor with $10,000 put $5,000 into stock and $5,000 into Cash Reserve. But the *New* AIMvestor needs only $6,250 to start off with the same amount of stock: $5,000 in stock and $1,250 in cash! Stranger still, when the market dives, the old AIMvestor may have to place at risk $5,000 of his Cash Reserve, investing in stock on the way down! The New AIMvestor, owning the same amount of stock, may have to place at risk only $2,000 in cash!

To put it another way, the old AIMvestor from day one is risking a total of $10,000. The New AIMvestor, starting his program with the same amount of stock, remember, is risking a total of only $6,250!

The New AIMvestor not only commands more bang for the buck, he also requires fewer Band-Aids for his wounds!

Go figure.

We speak of relative risk and all that, but AIMvestors know very well that the great triumph of AIM in the first place was its astonishing safety. Though I've beaten it and flayed it, though I've probed it and poked it, AIM's stubborn fist held my investment above water while I tinkered!

Now I want to show you firsthand the amazing potential of our AIM-HI. Here is an actual monthly AIM-HI account I began at the end of 1990.

Please note that you are also looking at a redesigned AIM chart. I find that this one is simpler to read because all the important information appears on a single line. *On my regular checkup day, I open my record book and read the last line on my chart. That line tells me (1) the date, (2) the previous Portfolio Control, (3) the amount of cash in my Cash Reserves, and (4) the number of shares I own in my fund.* All I have to do now is fill in the current price of my mutual fund, my current Stock Value, and, if I wish, the Total Value of my portfolio (cash and stock combined) and my percentage profit. Those last two are my favorites!

I do believe you're looking at an historic chart. *In the*

AIM-HI Chart A

SECURITY: VANGUARD PRIMECAP FUND

Date	Portfolio Control	Stock Value	Cash*	Action	Shares	Price	Total Value
1/2000	8,000	$8,000	$2,000	Start	128.9	$62.07	$10,000
2/2000	8,000	7,918	2,000	P: 0	128.9	61.43	9,918
3/2000	8,000	9,136	2,000	S: 0	128.9	70.88	11,136
4/2000	8,000	9,565	2,000	S: 0	130.6*	73.24	11,565
5/2000	8,000	9,402	2,000	S: 0	130.6	71.99	11,402
6/2000	8,000	8,953	2,000	S: 0	130.6	68.55	10,953
7/2000	8,000	9,308	2,000	S: 0	130.6	71.27	11,308
8/2000	8,000	9,158	2,000	S: 0	130.6	70.12	11,158
9/2000	8,000	9,837	2,000	S: 0	130.6	75.32	11,837

*Capital gains distribution reinvested.

short space of eight months, AIM-HI has racked up an impressive 18.4 percent gain—an annualized rate of some 25 percent! Meanwhile, gasping alongside us, our old original AIM could manage a much slimmer purse of only 11.5 percent—little more than 15 percent annualized! We didn't add Money Market dividends on our Cash Reserve. Didn't need to. The point was made for us when AIM-HI handed us a profit for those eight months in the amount of $1,837—a staggering 60 percent more than old AIM's $1,146! *And this despite the fact that both investors committed the same amount— $10,000—to their programs:*

	1/2000–9/2000	
	AIM-HI	*ORIGINAL AIM*
Stock:	$9,837 (130.6 shs.)	$6,147 (81.609 shs.)
Cash:	$2,000	$5,000
Total Value:	$11,837	$11,147
Profit:	18.4%	11.5%

Aim-Hi Advantage: 60%!

Studying our AIM-HI Chart A, veteran AIMvestors will suspect that AIM-HI appears to be on the verge of increasing its Cash by an extra thousand or so. Correct. When the Fund price rises by another $1.25 or so, it will trigger a stock sale of more than $1,000, which conforms to our Minimum Transaction of 10 percent. And AIM-HI, with $3,000 in Cash, will have another "bird in hand" when the market turns down!

During the nineties I observed how old AIM's more cumbersome Cash Reserve acts as a lead weight on its leg forever. It's like being born with two noses—do you ever really outgrow your self-consciousness?

Or like the "child-resistant" cap on a medicine bottle. It may save some young lives, but I can't help suspecting that it costs more adult lives when they can't open the bottle in an emergency!

Note that the old Market Order column has been replaced by the Action column. The Buy(Sell) Advice column has been eliminated altogether: you can do that figurework on a scratch pad, and if you're given a Market Order, simply enter it into the Action column. Why clutter up your permanent records with needless and possibly confusing figures?

For the sake of simplicity, the Safe column has also been expunged. Safe is nothing more than 10 percent of your Stock Value anyway, and to get 10 percent of any figure, all you need do is drop the last digit: 10 percent of $2,000 is $200. Even I can do that in my mind. With a $5 calculator in my hand, I have no problem entering these figures as I go along.

It's possible that some of you may prefer, for whatever reason, the old AIM chart. You have my blessing to continue to use it.

The AIM-HI chart also introduces another major advance in AIM technology. Heretofore, there was one piece of unfinished business in the AIM formula as far as I was concerned: the minimum amount of stock we should buy or sell. Earlier, I advised AIMvestors to ignore Market Orders under $100 as too small to fool with. Now that makes sense for small investors using no-load mutual funds, first, because there's no commission charge, and second, because $100 transactions can be a significant chunk of a stockholding worth $1,000 or so. But $100 ain't worth three dead flies to an investor with a substantial stockholding of $5,000 and up—nor to an investor buying individual stocks: The commission would clobber him.

For a while I experimented with a minimum Market Order of 5 percent of my Stock Value—an amount, in other words, half of the Safe figure. My AIM machine, faced with a record bull market, went into overdrive, spitting out cash like a punch-drunk ATM machine. Each of my programs, using only Mutual Funds, was "selling" almost monthly! Having begun my AIM-HI programs with what I feared to be a puny 20 percent Cash Reserve, I was soon inundated by a flood of new money that raised my Cash Reserve to levels nearly equal to my Stock Value—and this in such prosaic investments as diversified Mutual Funds! No wonder AIM-HI cried out for Valium!

The cure took another year to develop, and it's simply this: Make your minimum purchase or sale 10 percent of your Stock Value. Another way to look at it is this: The amount you insert in your AIM-HI Action column must be at least equal to your Safe figure. Thus, if your Stock Value is $2,000, your Safe figure would be $200. And the *minimum* figure in your Action column must be at least that much: $200. Otherwise, just insert a zero in the Action column.

The 10 percent minimum transaction works so well because it accommodates Humble Bob as well as Snooty Sal. A 10 percent minimum transaction for Humble Bob's modest $2,000 stockholding would be $200. I can live with that. The $200 may make only a small contribution to my Cash Reserve, but as I say, it does grease the mechanism. And a 10 percent minimum transaction for Snooty Sal's $20,000 stockholding would be $2,000. Do you see the relationship, the very real and meaningful impact on both investors? The minimum purchase is equally valuable to rich and poor alike. And because it *is* a percentage, it *understands* the difference between a small and a large portfolio.

In sum, it's damned democratic if you ask me!

SEVENTEEN

Retirement AIM—
A New Dimension for Retirees!

Banker: "We recommend a thirty-month C.D."

Retiree: "At my age I won't even buy green bananas!"

Nonsense. With today's retirees living longer than ever, the rewards *and* the risks still gallop alongside us all on the happy trail. Old age does have its rewards. After all, what's the alternative? The risks are a bit more difficult to quantify, but most of them come dressed in dollar signs. True, we're all living longer; but without sufficient green stuff you may find yourself questioning whether it's worth the effort.

I began to ponder this problem seriously a few years after the first publication of this book when more and more senior citizens (Oldies but Goodies) wrote me fan mail. They applauded the concept of AIM, they thanked me for inventing it, and they related their fascination with its mechanism. Curiously, however, they had not yet begun their AIM programs; they "planned to do so" sometime in the future. Again and again their letters revealed a reluctance and a trepidation to commit their hard-earned capital to a new and apparently high-powered investment formula. Many times their letters told of their having bought the book several years earlier, read it with excitement, and then laid it aside while they ruminated over its implications. Had anything changed over the years, they asked me? Did I still feel the same about AIM? Now that they were in their seventies and even eighties, was it too late to begin their AIM program?

Well, certainly AIM has changed over the years; this edition of the book will testify to that. And certainly I still feel the same about AIM: It has occupied my attention for nearly 25 years now and has cost me dearly in lost income through neglect of the economic necessities of life while I pursued my own "impossible dream." I have taught the hungry how to fish.

In this special chapter I will try to teach the aged, as well as those who for whatever reasons do not have access to the job markets and must make do with fixed or reduced incomes, and those who have only a "nest egg" to see them through their remaining years.

Does AIM-HI exist for these? It surely does.

And here's why: Even though I invented AIM-HI and have observed it more closely than anybody else for some two decades, and even though, intellectually, I know that AIM is a magnificently safe investment concept (you take profits at the highs and reinvest them at the lows—and you almost always have a Cash Reserve for extra ballast), I sometimes have trouble believing what I see before my very eyes. AIM-HI works so well and makes it look so easy that I find myself from time to time casting a wistful glance backward in time to the more sexy and alluring Miss Lumpsummer, forgetting for the moment what she did to me and my fellow investors way back when. Then I catch myself, damn my roving eye, and return to my loyal and dependable Mrs. AIM-HI.

Over the years the AIM programs I have initiated have performed very well indeed. The only surprise has been in AIM's conservatism (like father, like son). It proved to be safer by far than I had anticipated. I had erred on the side of the angels! And because of this finding, I would have no hesitation now in recommending that the new AIM-HI program can be used by retirees looking for income, safety, and growth in the "investment" portion of their retirement funds.

Obviously, they should not commit *all* their resources to this or any other investment arena; but as a repository for a portion of their assets, AIM-HI should prove to be a valuable adjunct to a complete retirement program.

So because I have had my own problems believing what I see, I can understand the hesitation of those older readers who were reluctant to start an AIM program.

At first blush, AIM-HI might appear more intimidating to seniors than the original AIM, which required a 50-50 division of assets to start: half cash, half stock. We are, after all, dealing here with folks whose primary requirements are (1) safety of capital and (2) generous income. The third leg, (3) potential growth, is the special kick that only AIM-HI can provide!

Look closer: *While AIM-HI starts with 80 percent in stock and only 20 percent in cash, that Cash Reserve is actually 25 percent of your Stock Value!*

There are two important modifications in our so-called "Retirement AIM" to consider, and they both involve not the formula itself but rather the special fuels it must be fed. For the equity side, our Retirement AIM must be fed a diet consisting exclusively of no-load growth and income funds—not aggressive growth funds or long-term growth funds!*

Growth and income funds are a specific category of mutual funds. Many of them have splendid long-term performances, even in comparison with their more rambunctious brethren. Because their managers buy stocks as well as bonds and other income-producing instruments, growth and income funds tend to be safer on the downside than the aforementioned aggressive growth funds and long-term growth funds. Dividends have a way of softening a fall. So our Retirement AIM will not and should not offer the volatility of our other AIM programs. It will, however, be triggered from time to time and sell off stocks as the fund price rises. It may do this

*Some so-called Equity Income Funds and Balanced Funds may qualify so long as their portfolios contain bonds as well as stock.

even more frequently than you had suspected, because while more aggressive funds are spurting up and down within an imaginary box, your growth and income fund, like the tortoise, is likelier to pursue a steadier course upward and trigger your sell mechanism!

We now have the equity portion of our Retirement AIM yielding *substantially* more income than before, since aggressive funds pay little or no dividends. What remains is the Cash Reserve portion which, heretofore, has been kept in money market mutual funds. They're safe, convenient to work with (they maintain a fixed per-share asset value of $1), and impose no penalties on withdrawals, as do some bank accounts. And there have been those heady years in the past in which Money Market Funds have provided our Cash Reserve with fabulous yields of 16 percent and more—sometimes even outperforming our equity side! Alas, as Mr. Housman lamented, "Golden lads and lasses must/as chimney sweeps turn to dust."

Money market mutual funds at this writing are yielding little more than the formerly scorned passbook savings account—something in the neighborhood of 5½ percent! If interest rates turn up again in the future, of course, our money market funds will participate. But "life is what happens when you're planning something else." You can't buy today's medicine with tomorrow's yields. Therefore, to complete our Retirement AIM program, we are going to dispense with money market mutual funds and substitute something spicier: a short-term bond fund.

A short-term bond fund is essentially the same as a money market fund with one significant difference: it buys short-term bonds instead of short-term commercial paper. And a bond is simply a longer-term version of commercial paper. While the maturity of the commercial paper held by a money market fund is measured in months, the maturity of the bonds held by short-term bond funds generally runs between two and five years. What this means to you is that you will receive often more return for a slightly higher risk than the virtually risk-free money market funds. In 2000, many short-term bond funds yield about 7.15 percent, versus 5½ percent for money market funds. That's 30 percent more interest on your money.

Short-term bond funds are much safer than long-term bond funds because of the shorter maturity dates of their underlying securities. In addition, the price of your short-term bond fund will tend to fluctuate ever so slightly, as compared with the much wider price swings of a longer-term bond fund. But the price does fluctuate, if only insignificantly as a rule, and that is the main reason I have not recommended the use of a short-term bond fund as a repository for our AIM-HI Cash Reserve, even though the higher yields would improve our results. Not because the fluctuation is terribly important in and of itself—it isn't—but because when you buy *any* security at various prices, the IRS insists that you keep records so that when you sell shares, you must report it on Schedule D of your Income Tax return as a loss or as a gain. Now who needs all this extra record-keeping and paperwork? I certainly don't. And heretofore our AIM-HI couldn't care less about a couple of lousy percentage points in extra interest. It did just fine on plain old vanilla money market funds, thank you.

Many short-term bond funds offer free checking privileges, exactly like money market mutual funds; and I suspect that some investors use them like money market funds without suspecting that every time they write a check against their short-term bond fund, the IRS considers it a sale and it would like to know, please, if a capital gain tax is due as a result.

The typical AIMvestor working for a living probably doesn't have the time or the energy to keep tax records on all his stock purchases and sales, as well as the few extra records required to operate the AIM-HI system—and then in addition be advised to keep his cash reserves in a short-term bond fund that *also* would require him to keep tax records on every sale and purchase! In the words of that famous Chinese pessimist, No Wei, "An extra penny earned may not be worth the trouble."

But for retirees, who often have a good deal more time on their hands, a short-term bond fund may very well be worth the trouble—particularly since the extra 2½ percent or more in yield can give their Retirement AIM an even greater margin of safety and peace of mind. On a Cash Reserve of $10,000, that 2½ percent will slip an extra $250 into their pocket every year.

Where do you get a short-term bond fund? Probably from the same fund family from which you got your other mutual funds. Most big fund families have a short-term bond fund. Some also have a short-term government bond fund for even greater security, though slightly less yield. And the same financial magazines we've referred to within these pages often rate bond funds at the same time they rate diversified stock funds, so there is plenty of information available.

So now our older AIMvestors have a comfortable, easy-to-live-with program in which both the equity and cash sides throw off very decent income. The income can be spent if desired or reinvested if not currently needed. And the big plus: the potential for significant growth in the years ahead. To those of you who still hold back through fear of the unknown, please remember that when the first escalator was installed in Harrod's Department Store in London, brandy was served to passengers who felt faint!

You don't have to commit wholeheartedly. Start out small, if you like; and then as you gain confidence in AIM-HI's ability to handle your investments, you can add more money to your program.

Either way, it's a good feeling. As the man said, "Whether you're rich or poor, it's always nice to have money!"*

And the older we get, the nicer it is!

---

*With a knowing nod to the late Will Rogers, who said: "I am more concerned with the return *of* my money than the return *on* my money!"

EIGHTEEN

The AIM-HI Ark and the Coming Storm

"Why the big grin?" my Magic (bathroom) Mirror said to me one frosty evening in December of 1999. "Are you getting ready to celebrate the millennium next month?"

"The millenium doesn't start until January of *2001*," I replied.

"I know that," said the Mirror. "I was merely referring to the conventional wisdom."

"In any case, I feel like celebrating everything! Take a look at this."

"What is it?"

"My experimental AIM-HI chart—AIM High Intensity."

"AIM-HI? You weren't satisfied with AIM?"

"Not totally. Not completely. I kept accumulating these humongous cash reserve balances. I didn't think I'd *ever* get to make use of them in the market, although the interest they were earning in my Money Market Fund did warm my heart!"

"Well," said the Mirror, "you *were* using Mutual Funds in your AIM programs, and they pretty much track the market. Individual stocks or a small portfolio of well-chosen individual securities would have given you more volatility and you would have been more likely to get a buy signal along the way than with Funds. But that was *your* choice: convenience over high tech. Catch the tides and leave wave surfing to the bronze young beach boys with their computers. However, even with those hefty cash reserves of AIM's acting as a kind of ballast, what was wrong with your results and the *safe* way you achieved them?"

"What's not to like about a money machine that keeps spitting out profits month after month? Nothing was really wrong. Like every other AIMvestor I cheered the 'up' Dow and hoped for a 'down' Dow. But I kept wanting to 'oomphasize' my performance. After all, it was you in the first place who played 'pity party' with me over the desperate *need* for a better and better investment system."

"Guilty as charged, my son. What have you done now?"

"To reduce the likelihood that my cash reserve would grow too fast and put a drag on my performance, I reduced the ratio of stock to cash to 80-20. Meaning you start your program with 80 percent stock and 20 percent cash."

"I like it already. Even numbers. Easy to calculate. Sounds good. And if you don't like multiplication, couldn't you simply divide your original pot by 5 and put the result in your Cash Reserve? What's left over goes directly into stock. It comes out the same."

"Right. And you do the same if you ever want to add new money to your program. When you do that, of course, you would simply increase your Portfolio Control by the amount of money you have just added to the *stock* portion of your portfolio. Every AIMvestor knows that protocol already."

"So because you start off with a much lighter ball and chain around your ankle from day one," mused the Mirror, "you can travel faster."

"Yes. But then a decade or so ago when the stock market started heading toward the sky, just about all my programs began to trigger sell signals nearly every month, it seemed. You can imagine how many tax computations that required and how many lines it took to document those sales on my income tax form! Don't get me wrong, I certainly enjoyed regularly skimming off the cream of those lovely profits, but it sure kept me hopping. But to my dismay, my Cash Reserve kept increasing to levels I felt were too high. To slow down the number of sell signals I was getting, I changed the Minimum Transaction of my programs from 5 percent of my Stock Value to 10 percent. That did put the brakes on a bit, but during the nineties I still did get quite a few sell signals and my Cash Reserve still kept swelling, but at a slower rate, I think."

"But this was during the nineties, son. The stock market, as measured by the Wilshire 5000 Index, generated an incredible average return of 17.6 percent for the decade. Do you realize what an anomaly that was? Since 1925—even before you were born—the average annual return from the stock market has been only 11 percent! So when the market presented your AIM-HI Money Machine with a return that was more than 1½ times the average, it functioned exactly as designed: It triggered sell orders that you at first thought were excessive. They *were* excessive—but so were the stock market averages during that amazing decade that saw the Standard & Poor 500 stock average soar 18.2 percent per year! In 1999 alone, it leaped by 21.1 percent!"

"Meaning?"

"Meaning that during normal times, when the market 'reverts to its mean'—returns to its accustomed less manic behavior—your AIM-HI will become far less frantic at snatching profits. Your Internal Revenue Service Schedule D will thank you, AIMvestors everywhere will thank you, and *I* thank you for AIM-HI!"

"And thank *you*, Magic Mirror, for your continued support—and harassment! Well, I've finished brushing my teeth. Should I turn off the light?"

"Suit yourself."

I switched off the light. "Well, good night."

"Good night. Oh, Bob?"

"Yes?"

"One more thing. About AIMless investors who might wish to convert to your new religion. They own stock right now . . . but how much Cash Reserve would they need to start an AIM-HI program with that stock they already own?"

"Divide the stock value by 4. Or they can multiply it by 25 percent—.25. Either way it will tell them the exact amount of Cash Reserve they need to start an AIM-HI program with the stock they already own. Their portfolio will then commence operations with the exact 80 percent stock and 20 percent cash required by AIM-HI, which I believe to be the optimum allocation of assets at the start. Be aware, though, that if they do begin an AIM-HI program with stock they already own, AIM-HI will treat that stock as though it had been acquired on the very day the program starts, and will henceforth flash buy and sell signals purely on a mathematical basis, that is, without regard for the tax consequences of its action. I believe, however, that the very real benefits of the AIM-HI system will vastly outweigh any possible adverse tax consequences, which would be minor in any case, since AIM-HI is quite gentle in this area anyway."

"God bless AIM-HI and all it stands for."

"Thank you. But you know, Mirror, some AIMvestors may be concerned that a Cash Reserve of 20 percent could prove too lean to start off with, fearing that a sudden steep stock slide at the very beginning of their AIM-HI program might quickly deplete their reserves. But the engineering here is sound: First, AIM-HI is designed to operate on a monthly basis, and your seemingly small Cash Reserve could well last for several months and accommodate several delightful buying opportunities before running on empty. Second, with AIM-HI, Cash Reserve dollars are *worth* more—in *buying* power—than any other kind of dollar because they buy only at bargain prices: marked-down merchandise. So a little bit goes a long way! Third, AIM-HI longs for a complete bowel movement, a total evacuation to rid itself of all that filthy lucre it has been piling up in a long-running bull market such as we have seen in the nineties.

And to put the results to good use as a fertilizer in order to grow even more bountiful crops in the future."

"I knew that," said the Mirror.

While AIMvestors (using the old AIM system before the publication of this Fourth Revised Edition) blithely and profitably operated their Money Machine during the unprecedented bull market of the nineties, many AIM-less investors found a fascinating new way to lose money fast: the Internet. Investors of previous generations (myself included) had to rely on lunchtime, martini-soaked visits to our broker around the corner and up our street, or more often frantic phone calls in between bites of our lunch. The more foolhardy or pseudo-sophisticated among us opted to buy put and call options from time to time, 90 percent of which—even to this day—expire worthless. All of mine did!

The temptation to control, say $10,000 worth of stock for 90 days or so at a cost of a few hundred dollars was irresistible. If the stock was selling at $80 a share or so, the "strike" price—the price at which you could begin to make a profit by exercising your call option to buy the stock—might be listed in your option document as $84. So this hot stock would have to go up only a teeny $4 for us to start making a profit on the 100 shares reserved for us at the price of $80. A lead pipe cinch! In the end, of course, the lead pipe was rapped across our knuckles as our option expired worthless, as usual, and we were relieved of our few hundred dollars fast with nothing to show for it except bruised pride and knuckles. And did I and my fellow losers blame the system, the broker, the puppeteer manipulating the strings above the stage who, during those tense 90 days, maneuvered the stock price so skillfully and so tantalizingly upward that it almost, almost, *almost* kissed its strike price before our option expired? Naturally not. We blamed our luck, our lack of knowledge, our bad choices. *Next* time we would choose the *right* option! (If ifs and buts were nickels, we'd all be millionaires.)

Road rage on the Investment Highway! But nowhere near as ferocious as what the computer introduced in the nineties: day trading. Anyone with a room temperature IQ and a computer could buy and sell stocks in a frenzy of greed, buy a stock and sell it a few minutes later, buy it again and sell it again as the stock gained a point or lost a point. The investor was encouraged to do this by the mouthwatering low commission rates offered by innumerable financial firms in this hotly competitive and extremely profitable field. It was not a new merchandising technique. Supermarkets for some time had been advertising specials from time to time on various items: these were identified as BOGO—Buy One Get One Free. The careful and experienced shopper might discern that you weren't really getting much "free" because the price of the merchandise had been marked up before the sale, and with that extra profit in hand the store could well afford to throw in an "extra" without suffering much diminution in income—especially considering that the items may have been gathering dust on the shelves or spoiling in the freezer anyway. It was also an excellent advertising technique to lure customers into their stores to buy lots of overpriced merchandise that was *not* BOGO!

By the same token, many investors flocked to day trading because financial firms seemed to be vying with one another to offer lower and lower commissions, blanketing the nation with mail solicitations and stuffing the financial magazines with expensive, glossy full page ads. The financial publications, for the most part, were only too happy to run heartwarming articles about just plain ordinary folks who had made a bundle day trading. Investor response was predictable. They looked at the tempting commission rates that were dangled before them and said: "Gee, at *those* rates, I could afford *two* or even *three* times as many trades as now! And the stock wouldn't even have to move up much, maybe a couple points or so, for me to make a profit!"

The second villain, of course, was the machine itself—

always there, always ready, promising unimaginable excitement and riches with a few clicks of the computer mouse. Alas! If the mouse were as lithe and agile as the cat, what would the cat do for food? Day traders—the mouse—slowly and painfully discovered that the cat—the financial firms catering to this hyperactivity—had not the slightest intention of missing any meals. The cats pounced on the hapless mice, toyed with them by offering rock-bottom commissions, then swatted them with the information that *those* rates applied only to certain *kinds* of orders. Or: "Oh, *that* fee on your trade confirmation. We call that an add-on fee. Don't worry about it." Or: "That other fee over there on the right? That's just what we call a maintenance fee." Or: "That fee over there on the left? That's an inactivity fee. Keep trading, Bubba, keep trading."

And Bubba, just in case you beat the odds and accumulate a pile of chips in front of you, don't reach for it just yet. Keep your bony hands off the table until Uncle Sam's greedy fingers peel as much as 40 percent off the top because profits from stock held less than a year are *short-term* and are taxed at the highest rate. Long-term profits escape with a maximum bite of 20 percent. All the while, of course, keep one eye on your state tax collector; those folks will take a nip of what's left over. Adding insult to injury, some online brokerages gouge your Money Market sweep account, in which the cash proceeds from stock sales are deposited, with an expense ratio that can exceed 1.2: $1,000 less 1.2 percent means they take $12 a year off the top before giving you the interest your Money Market Fund has earned. $5,000 less 1.2 percent adds up to a pilfering of $60 a year from your Money Market sweep account. For purposes of comparison, the average Money Market Fund has an annual expense ratio little more than half that, and the gigantic and conservatively managed $45 billion Vanguard Prime Money Market Fund earns a satisfactory profit from a minuscule fee of .33 percent—$3.30 per $1,000! As of December 31, 2000.

On sizable Money Market balances, of course, the pre-occupied online investor could lose hundreds of dollars a year in interest from those cash-gobbling sweep accounts. In the threadbare Depression days of the thirties, some restaurants posted a sign reading, "Please Watch Your Hat and Coat." Of which a wag once remarked, "While I was watching my hat and coat, someone stole my hamburger!" Day traders take notice: Pay attention to your stocks but don't ignore your Cash Balance!

In any event, day traders have been running into their own Depression: studies show that 70 percent of them are wiped out! And more and more evidence continues to surface that modern technology—the computer—does not match the investor results of old technology: the telephone. No doubt the 19th-century back-to-nature guru Henry David Thoreau would have characterized the computer as "improved means toward unimproved ends." The University of California at Davis recently conducted a study of online trading. The professors focused on an elite group of investors who did their buying and selling by phone while outsmarting the market by two percentage points a year—no mean achievement, particularly during the nineties when most Mutual Funds proved unable to match the performance of plain vanilla index funds like the Standard & Poor 500, this despite the fact that the funds were professionally managed while the S&P Index, on automatic pilot, virtually ran itself.

The two professors, Brad Barber and Terrance Odean, studied the trading results of 1,607 "phone investors" between 1991 and 1996 who decided to switch to online trading to improve their already spectacular performance. This particular elevator did not whisk them to the penthouse, as they had hoped, but straight down to the cellar! After switching to the E-trade route, these savvy investors began to *under*perform the market *by more than three percentage points*! After analyzing this startling turnaround, the professors discovered that online investors trade more frequently: their rate of turnover increased from 70 percent on the phone to 90 percent on the computer! Perhaps even worse, these formerly careful, restrained, and thoughtful investors began to catch gambling fever: their speculative trades, held to a respectable 16 percent on the telephone, jumped to 30 percent online—very nearly double! Why? Overconfidence, concluded the professors, together with easy access to a huge amount of data that created the "illusion of knowledge."

If that's what happens in *good* times such as the booming nineties, imagine the disaster that awaits day traders when the bear comes knocking, as he inevitably will! A hint of what's to come arose a few months into 2000 when the Nasdaq, the favorite haunting ground of the "fast crowd," hiccupped and barfed high-flying high tech stocks all over the place, wiping out a good portion of the online population.

Good time for more studies. One recent one revealed that men trade 45 percent more than women and earn an annual adjusted net return that is 1.4 percent less than that earned by women. Single men perform even more poorly: They trade 67 percent more than single women and earn an annual adjusted rate of return that is a whopping 2.3 percent less! Is it so far-fetched to suggest that *activity* generates plenty of heat but little light? This study as well as several others also provides an additional insight into this landmine area of fast-on-the-trigger investing: When people sell stock A and buy stock B, stock B on average *underperforms* the stock they got rid of—stock A! Better I should have "stood in bed," said a wag.

It remained for the big Vanguard Fund family to hone in on the growing problem. Ever true to its conservative tradition, Vanguard asked in one of their recent reports to shareholders this burning question: "Have the Principles of Investing Changed?" Noting the rapid and often bewildering changes occurring in business, technology, and financial markets, Vanguard expressed the belief that the *principles* of investing remain the same: understand the risk and stick with a long-term investment program.

Vanguard ticked off the challenges confronting investors in the 2000s: Market indexes at or near their historic highs; the power and length of the bull market inflating expectations of future returns and decreasing the recognition of growing risk; the astonishing divergence of stock prices—some tech stocks doubling and then some in 1999 while prices *declined* for more than half all stocks!

"And then there is the Internet," Vanguard continued. "Undeniably, it is a powerful medium for communications and transacting business. For investors, the Internet is a vast source of information about investments, and online trading has made it inexpensive and convenient to trade stocks and invest in mutual funds.

"*However, new tools do not guarantee good workmanship.* (Emphasis supplied.) Information is not the same as wisdom. Indeed, much of the information, opinion, and rumor that swirl about financial markets each day amounts to 'noise' of no lasting significance."

The "noise," of course, can often be downright dangerous to unsuspecting investors. In the fall of 2000 the feds arrested a young college student and accused him of generating a phony press release on the Internet that caused the stock of a company to lose more than $2 billion of its value in minutes as nervous shareholders dumped their holdings. The student took advantage of the opportunity, played the swings in the stock, and pocketed a quick $186,000, say the feds. In a similar ruse, a 15-year-old boy was fined a record $285,000 by the Securities and Exchange Commission which accused him of using an E-trade account on the Internet to manipulate values by falsely touting the value of certain stocks and duping dopey investors into buying them, thereby driving up the price. One sadder but wiser investor who followed his advice and lost a bundle said later: "We all thought he was 40 years old, he talked such a good game." The SEC allowed the youth to keep $500,000

he'd made from 16 other trades on the Internet because
they couldn't prove fraud.

Even in the absence of scam artists, day traders face
daunting odds. As the Vanguard Group cautioned in the
aforementioned recent report to its shareholders: "Frequent trading is almost always counterproductive because costs—even at low commission rates—and taxes
detract from the returns that the markets provide."

How to swing the odds back in your favor? Reduce
the frequency of trading, as the studies have suggested.
Tune out the "noise." And don't believe the propaganda
that "everybody else but you is getting rich, so why not
hop aboard?" In August, 2000, a U.S. Senate subcom-
mittee went on record to warn of the risks of day trading: Investors are not being advised of the true risks,
they said. Ditto Arthur Levitt, Chairman of the Securities and Exchange commission, who in that same month
warned of the dangers of day trading. "People might just
as well go to the track and bet on horses; it's not investing," he said. Ralph Bloch, stock analyst for Ray-
mond James & Co., observed the frenzy of younger
stock speculators and commented, "All these baby
boomers and Generation X-ers have been functioning
like Pavlov's dogs."

As the 20th century waned, stocks had become a national mania. Almost half of U.S. households owned
stock, directly or indirectly in Mutual Funds; in 1983 the
figure stood at a mere 20 percent. The speculative mood
became inflamed almost to the point of hysteria when
the tech-heavy Nasdaq Composite index smashed
through the 5000 barrier on March 9, 2000, only to collapse to a new low for the year a scant seven months
later—virtually guaranteeing new attendance records at
Gamblers Anonymous meetings.

Even more ominous in many respects is the burgeoning growth of private pension plans—IRA's and the
401(k) plans. In an earlier chapter, we warned of a potential catastrophe of unprecedented proportions should
the market collapse near your retirement date when you

press the "Commence Distributions" button and hear a sucking sound instead. Bad enough when your day trading turns into a nightmare and you are wiped out at a relatively young age (you might even feel you deserved it for being so foolhardy)—but to lose your slowly and painfully acquired assets in your private pension plan at the age of 55, 60, 65? Willy Loman took the gas pipe for less.

In 2000, assets in the nation's 401(k) plans—most of which are invested in stock—stand at a record $1.5 *trillion,* nearly four times what they were just ten years earlier. Worse, market *risk* has risen correspondingly with the major indexes floating at record highs! Today, in October of 2000, the stock market is on track for its worst year since 1994. The indexes have backed off— and *then* some—from their highs, and a major "correction" could be waiting in the wings. We believe, more strongly than ever, that our precious and irreplaceable IRA and 401(k) assets should be safely tucked under the wing of our AIM-HI . . . one less thing to worry about in feverish, work-till-you-drop 21st-century America!

In the year ended September 30, 2000, more than 175 Mutual Funds had thrown in the towel, nearly breaking a record that had stood for years. And Mutual Funds, of course, are managed by high-paid *professionals*: investing is their full-time job! And if so many of *them* find the going too rough—in a fairly ordinary period— what do you think *your* chances are? Particularly in a Noah-sized gullywasher the likes of which today's money managers have never experienced. Not to mention the stockbrokers themselves who caught the online fever and lost their savings as well as their jobs. *You* can do better?

AIMvestors can and do. Blaise Pascal, the 17th-century French philosopher, wrote: "All the troubles of man come from his not knowing how to sit still." One of my favorite quotes, for it perfectly describes the veteran AIMvestor, who has seen through all the sham and the hoopla, the famous stock analysts on TV who in reality serve their own master, certainly not us, and the glitzy, million-dollar TV commercials inviting us to make our fortunes with a keystroke. In your hat!

The anonymity of the Internet has brought stock fraud schemes within the reach of children, as we have already seen, which compounds the risks that have always been associated with the stock market. But the scariest thing isn't the age of the scammer, a stock fraud expert commented after the New Jersey teenager was fined by the SEC, it's "all the stupid people out there willing to throw money at stuff like this."

The Vanguard Group was right on target with their brilliant observation that new tools do not guarantee good workmanship. And that's all the computer is: a tool. Like all tools, it can hurt you or help you, enable you or disable you. It just does it quicker.

And I believe that I was pretty close to the truth from the very beginning of my development of Automatic Investment Management when I opined that the search for the "right" stock or the "right" Mutual Fund leads straight to the poorhouse, for there really is no such thing.* I said then and I say now that a stock or Mutual Fund is simply a tool: do not expect a tool to do the whole job by itself. It wasn't really all that radical of a philosophy—still isn't—but it lacks the "sexiness" and the marketability of hot stock tips or a sizzling new Mutual Fund that doubled in price last year (which, of course, was not even *available* to the public last year and which, of course, lost the portfolio manager who achieved those results to a rival firm)!

A 1986 study of pension fund portfolios by First Chicago Investment Advisors and SEI, the pension consultant, found that a portfolio's *asset mix* explained roughly 93 percent of its performance! Think of it: *neither stock selection nor bond selection played a major role in the*

---

*Some of my younger readers might look up from their computers and ask, "What's a poorhouse?" You'll know when you see it!

success of a portfolio! What *did* matter was the proper
shift between stocks and bonds (cash equivalents) at the
proper time—like, dare we say it, *decreasing* equity exposure as the bull market persists and *increasing* it as
the bear lumbers in. Veteran AIMvestors may nod
knowingly.

More recent research, such as that published in *Financial Analysts Journal,* May–June 1991, by Brinson et al.,
provided almost identical results: 90 percent of pension
fund investment returns are determined by the asset mix.

Well, easy for *you* to say! That would be the prevail-
ing opinion when such studies were announced, because
superior asset allocation is the most difficult goal to
achieve in the entire investment arena. Just as very few
portfolio managers predict stock movements with any
degree of reliability, fewer still know when to "hold 'em
or fold 'em," as the old saw goes —or how *much* to hold
and how *much* to fold. And this is precisely where our
AIM-HI shines: we've removed the luck, the guesswork,
and the timing; it's all blissfully automatic!

"The test of a sound investment strategy isn't just how
much money you make; it's whether the strategy lets
you sleep at night," wrote *U.S. News and World Report*
on September 14, 1998, following the market plunge of
512 points in a single day. "And over the past weekend,
many small investors were no doubt still tossing and
turning, taking a mental inventory of their portfolios and
tallying the losses sustained in last Monday's market
madness."

Could we rely on the professionals for a consensus on
what action we should take in the midst of such turmoil?
One portfolio manager called the market gloom "the
buying opportunity of a generation." A chief economist
and investment strategist warned, "Things could get a
lot uglier."

AIMvestors hoped *both* of them were right!

AIMvestors make money the *new*-fashioned way: They
AIM it!

In the years to come, many other investment plans,

schemes, formulas, and techniques will bloom and fade. At the dawn of our new century, day trading remains at center stage even though securities officials warn that too many financially unsophisticated people are being lured into a trap. "The day-trading firms are welcoming every Tom, Dick, and Harry—and Sally—that walks into the door," said Denise Voigt Crawford, Texas's securities commissioner in May of 1999. "We have instances in Texas where people have lost their homes and their entire retirement."

Heavyweight boxing champion Mike Tyson made the most astute observation of "the plan." Said Iron Mike: "Everybody has a plan until they get hit." And that, it seems to me, should be held up as the final test of whether the "plan"—*any* plan—proves valid: can it take a hit and keep on plodding forward? What do you prove by strutting in the sunshine?

Some plans strut for a year or two, some hang on in jubilant times a little longer until the wind changes and they are torn from their branch like a withered leaf and are flung onto the ash-heap of investment history. For nearly a quarter of a century our bold new Money Machine—Automatic investment Management—has taken all the punches that the market (and the critics) have thrown at it and has thrived.

If the past is prologue, the next quarter century belongs to AIM-HI!

YOU'VE GOT MAIL!

Q. In one of the editions of your book you said you used a single money market fund to hold the cash reserves of all your own AIM programs, and you came up with a formula that would give each one of your programs the exact amount of interest its cash reserve earned each month. AIM is so simple to operate, this other thing with our cash reserves takes a good bit of figuring each and every month. Do you still use this formula, or have you improved on it? Maybe I'm running too many AIM programs at one time.

A. I guess you could call that cash reserve formula of mine a Model T: It served its purpose at the time, but it would prove to be a little cumbersome to operate if you are operating a large number of AIM programs. I no longer use that technique. For awhile I used a single money market fund to hold the cash reserves of all my AIM programs, but I simply ignored the dividends earned by my money market fund. I felt then and I feel now that my money market interest dollars aren't critical to the success of my money machine. Why gild the lily and all that? Of course, if you have a single AIM program consisting of stocks or a mutual fund, one money market fund is all you need to keep perfect track of the interest earned: It all belongs to your mutual fund or stocks. As the lawyers say: *"Res ipsa loquitur"*—"the thing speaks for itself." But in the year 2000 I've decided that I don't even need a special money market fund to hold my cash reserves in—I can "piggyback" my cash reserves in a money market fund I already use for my personal affairs! My AIM (now AIM-HI) records alone tell me how much cash reserve each one of my programs is entitled to. A simple 3 × 5 index card tucked into my personal money market checkbook shows me at a glance the amount of cash that is earmarked for my AIM-HI programs. Anything I can do to cut down on the volume of statements, reports, and prospectuses that pile up in my mailbox means a great deal to me. Maybe it will to you too.

I must emphasize once again that even if your cash reserves earned no interest whatever, they are constantly growing stronger by virtue of what I call "internal dividends." Spend a dollar today and you get a dollar's worth of stock; spending that same dollar at a later date when the sock is selling at half price means that your dollar will buy $1.50 worth of stock! Without earning a single penny in *taxable interest,* your dollar has gained 50 percent in value!

See the AIM-HI chart (page 260) that ignores dividends altogether. It's no longer important—even for bragging rights!

Q. When you redesigned your AIM chart, why did you put the Portfolio Control column and the Stock Value column right next to each other? Couldn't we sometimes make a mistake and confuse one with the other when we are doing our calculations?

A. Not if you put a dollar sign on the figures in your Stock Value column. It makes sense that your Stock Value *is* a dollar amount (depending on what your definition of *is* is), while your Portfolio Control is *not* a dollar amount but a traffic cop who directs you to the right or to the left.

This was a streamlining effort on my part to make the AIM formula even simpler to operate! Now, at a glance, we can look at those two contiguous columns and *instantly* determine the higher figure. If it's Portfolio Control, we can *immediately* enter the letter P in our Action column. Right away we know—even without any mathematical calculation at all—that AIM-HI is in a "Purchase" bias mode. No matter what the outcome of your calculations, you know beyond the shadow of a doubt that the outcome will be BUY, not SELL! And by entering that letter P instantly, you have eliminated any possibility of error later on when you have completed your calculation.

Particularly if you are doing your charts on paper, such as a sheet in a loose-leaf notebook as some of us do, and are operating several programs, this lightning-fast, fool-proof "Direct Entry Express" goes a long way toward making our Money Machine truly automatic!

I continue to cut paperwork to a minimum, even to the point of eliminating the CASH column altogether:

DATE	PORTFOLIO CONTROL	STOCK VALUE	ACTION	SHARES OWNED	PRICE	PORT. VALUE
1/2001	8,000	$8,000	0	800	$10.00	$10,000
	CASH:	$2,000				

On two spare lines of my compact 8½ × 5½ inch loose-leaf binder, I've packed all the information necessary to operate my AIM-HI program with peak efficiency using a single Mutual Fund. If AIM-HI directs me to make a $500 purchase, say, I enter $500 in the ACTION column. If this order results in the purchase of 50 shares, I enter 50 just below the $500—directly to the right of that $2,000 CASH figure. If it's a SELL order for $500, I write ($500) in the ACTION column and record the sale of 50 shares like this in the ACTION column (50) just below the ($500). (Any figure in parentheses indicates a subtraction, of course.)

These shortcuts help me manage my investments with minimal time and effort. They may indeed do the same for you.

"Make it easy on yourself," a weekly news magazine advised a decade ago. "The simpler your investment plan, the more likely it will work."

Believe me, if I could make AIM-HI any simpler than it already is here in the year 2000, I certainly would!

Q. What would be wrong with using an index fund for one of my programs, like the Standard & Poor 500 Index Fund? My finance magazine says they wouldn't be safe in a market crash because they don't have anybody managing it like other Mutual Funds because they are 100 percent in stock at all times. In other words, they are on "autopilot." If the market goes down, so do they.

A. You have given me several good reasons to *include* an S&P 500 Index Fund in our AIM-HI universe. Because they are, as you say, on "autopilot," they will go down with the market as a whole and they are likelier to suffer a steeper decline than the average fully managed Mutual Fund, which is exactly what AIM-HIpers dream about! But your word "safe" doesn't compute: a bank CD is not really safe because when you adjust for taxes and inflation, you are likely to have *lost* value. One writer has dubbed them "certificates of guaranteed confiscation." But you might be close to the truth if you consider S&P 500 Index Funds to be riskier than the average fully managed Fund which is not 100 percent into stocks at all times, and at least theoretically can ease up on stocks if they see a slippery road ahead. But you forget that an S&P 500 Index Fund, being composed of the largest and most successful corporations in America and being fully invested at all times, is also likelier to rebound after a market mauling.

In my opinion, an S&P 500 Index Fund is a "no brainer" for one of our programs—perhaps a major portion. We could legitimately describe it as a "tennis ball Fund," not an "egg fund": you can depend on it to go down with the market, and you can also depend on it to bounce back up with the market. When contrarians like us are asked to feed money into a falling market, while all around us other investors are are *dumping* stock, what a comfort it is to remind ourselves that we are not throwing good money after bad, but investing good money in America's premier corporations temporarily selling at a discount!

No, you won't be able to ride the waves in an Index Fund, but you'll be certain to catch the less exciting but more dependable tides!

One caution: If you want an Index 500 Fund, buy one; but avoid imitations. Some Fund families offer what may appear to be an S&P 500 Index Fund but which, in reality, is an Index Fund that has been "manipulated" a bit to heavy up on certain stocks of the S&P 500 and lighten up on others, thus hopefully to improve results, both on the upside and the downside. On October 12, 2000, for example, the Standard & Poor 500 Index lost a jolting 35 points. A true S&P 500 Index Fund like Vanguard's dropped a delightful (to AIMvestors) 2.5 percent, while a "technically enhanced" S&P 500 Index Fund like Scudder's slid nearly a full percentage point less: 1.6 percent!

On Columbus Day, you would expect truer navigation than that!

Over the past decade or so, very few fully managed

Mutual Funds have been able to beat the S&P 500 Index with any degree of consistency, which may explain why investors have made Vanguard's S&P 500 Index Fund—the first one available to the general public—the nation's largest Mutual Fund. But a rising tide floats all boats, as we have seen in this historically long bull market; and when stocks experience their inevitable collapse, investors may flee to less volatile venues, such as balanced Mutual Funds or bank CDs. That is, AIMless investors will!

But there is one other factor that should endear an S&P 500 Fund to *every* investor—not just the AIMvestor: At year-end, they don't dump a daunting pile of capital gains distributions into your account—*taxable* capital gains! In their normal course of business, Mutual Funds sell some of their stocks in which they have achieved their profit targets, as well as some losing stocks that are no longer deemed desirable; the excess of profits over losses is then passed on to their shareholders as capital gains. These distributions are "neutral" as far as you are concerned: they neither increase nor decrease the profitability of your account, but they *do* add to your tax burden at year-end! In a profitable year, you might consider those a necessary evil; in a year dripping with red ink, when *your* account shows a horrendous loss, you will be sorely tempted to roll up that capital gains distribution statement into a ball and return it to your Fund with this advisory: *"Stick it where the sun don't shine!"*

Of course, *my* readers would never use such bad grammar.

But S&P 500 Index Funds do very little selling. Their job is to track the S&P Index of 500 stocks as closely as possible and to match the percentage of each stock in the Index, not to heavy up on a more promising security at the expense of a laggard. Hence, very little capital gains at year-end.

Those investors who might scoff at an Index as being too tame should consider this: in the year ended December 31, 1999, the S&P 500 Index gained 21 percent. What a wonderful year for the stock market! Not. More than

60 percent of all the stocks listed on the New York Stock Exchange, home of the "blue chips," actually *declined* in price in 1999; ditto 48 percent of the Nasdaq stocks! (And let's not talk about the Nasdaq in the year 2000.) What are *your* chances of picking the "right" stock?

By the way, if you *really* want to put your AIM-HI program on "automatic pilot," use an index fund but operate your program on a quarterly, rather than on a monthly, basis. In normal times—definitely *not* the nineties—the S&P 500 does not offer the kind of volatility that AIM-HIpers desire. By using the end of each quarter as your "checkup" date, you compress three months of price activity into one day. One month in the price pattern of the S&P may not result in as much change as would a full quarter.

Q. Is AIM a "timing" program or long term? Some companies say they can time the market and tell you when to get out and when to get back in, which would give you bigger profits than just investing for the long term where you have to ride the market up and down.

A. AIM (now AIM-HI) is definitely not a timing program! I knew from the get-go that this was not a direction I wanted to take, because if such a system were possible with any degree of consistency it would probably destroy the stock market as it existed as an efficient auction mechanism. If everybody knew when the market was going down, every investor would rush for the exits at the same time yelling, "Sell! Sell!" And the brokers would repeat the age-old joke, "Sell? To whom?"

An oft-quoted study by Dr. H. Nejat Seyhun at the University of Michigan highlights the folly of market timing. He discovered that $1 invested in the S&P 500 Index in 1963 would have mushroomed to $23.30 over the next 30 years. But if you were a market timer and missed the best 90 days during that period (a little over 1 percent of the trading days) that dollar would have grown to $1.10! Don't spend it all in one place!

And then there's human nature: investors who flee the stock market in bad years and seek the sanctuary of CDs and money markets almost never go back to stocks in time and therefore miss the Bull Market Express!

Our AIM-HI gently takes a little off the table every once in awhile. We're long term, yes, but we know if we walk into your kitchen and steal your five-pound salami, you'd be mighty upset. You might even call the cops. But if we crept in and stole a couple of slices today, and a couple of slices tomorrow, you might not even notice. We might eventually steal your entire five-pound salami; that way, piece by piece, with complete impunity. For that matter, we could knock on your door and *ask* you for a couple of slices of salami; you'd probably cooperate. But suppose we knocked on your door and asked you for your entire five-pound salami, would you hand it over? I don't think so. We're restating, of course, the old cautionary tale about how to boil a frog to death: Toss him into a pot of boiling water and he'll jump out. Place him in room-temperature water and *then* slowly bring the water to a boil, and he's likely to sit there watching mindless sitcoms or playing vicious video games while he insensibly cooks to death.

And in my dreams, as the new year 2001 crept toward me, I found myself on the slope of a mist-shrouded mountain. "How do I get to the summit?" I asked a hooded figure sitting cross-legged nearby.

"It is written," he said. "Put one foot in front of the other and repeat as necessary."

"You mean walk?" I said.

"You got it."

Many hours, perhaps days, elapsed before I reached the snow-whipped aerie of the legendary Kaputa Deitreda. Exhausted, I could barely lift the red telephone off its hook. "For the meaning of life," said a pleasant female voice, "press 1. For AIMvestors who think they have too much cash reserve, press 2." I pressed 2. "Your call is important to us," said the voice. "Kaputa Deitreda will see you in approximately 12 minutes. Meanwhile, settle back, relax, and enjoy the "Va Pensiero" chorus from Verdi's opera *Nabucco*. Notice near the climax of this famous chorus how unison vanishes and is replaced briefly by harmony singing and just as abruptly returns to unison. Thus, unison is made even more dynamic than if it were used throughout. That's why AIMvestors enjoy skimming a little cream off the top every so often when AIM tells them to. It 'oomphasizes' their pleasure!"

Eventually, Kaputa Deitreda emerged from his Shangri-la.

"You have reduced the quantity of cash reserves in your new formula?" he asked.

"Yes, master."

"You have altered the AIM minimum transaction to allow more time for new profits to accumulate before energizing the selling process?"

"Yes, master."

"And to allow sharper losses to occur before triggering the purchase process?"

"Yes, master."

"Good balance. Good balance. Yin and yang. I like it already! And for the 21st century, you call this magical formula. . . ?

"AIM-HI, master. AIM High Intensity."

"But you are still concerned that some investors will not understand that their cash reserve may appear too large, but that even if sparingly employed, acts as a ballast to their entire program, and serves to insure peace of the soul and confidence and security, oh what blessed security! *Listen* . . . did you hear that?"

"What? I didn't hear anything."

"Yonder in the distance! A wind is rising now . . . can you hear it?"

"Yes. Sounds like . . . sounds like a bugle."

A strange smile lit up the old man's face. "It is! It's the army of AIMless investors fleeing a plunging stock market! They're sounding retreat because they have no reserves! And they're retreating toward us! It's what we've been waiting for all these years! We're ready for them! AIMvestors, man the barricades! Lock and load! AIM-HI AND KEEP YOUR POWDER DRY!"

BUSINESS SUCCESS FROM SIGNET

THE RICHEST MAN IN BABYLON
George S. Clason
0-451-20536-7

Hailed as the greatest of all inspirational works on the subject of thrift, financial planning and personal wealth, this classic volume has helped over 2 million readers since its original publication in 1926, remaining one of the bestselling books of its kind.

QUALITY IS FREE
Philip B. Crosby
0-451-62585-4

This book details easy-to-implement programs designed to benefit any management team. It clearly and concisely explains how to manage quality so that it becomes a profit source.

"THE EXECUTIVE WHO SPENDS HALF A DAY DIGESTING THIS BOOK MAY FIND IT ONE OF THE MOST VALUABLE INVESTMENTS OF TIME HE OR SHE HAS EVER MADE."
—BUSINESS WEEK

Available wherever books are sold or at
penguin.com

Penguin Group (USA) Online

What will you be reading tomorrow?

Tom Clancy, Patricia Cornwell, W.E.B. Griffin,
Nora Roberts, William Gibson, Robin Cook,
Brian Jacques, Catherine Coulter, Stephen King,
Dean Koontz, Ken Follett, Clive Cussler,
Eric Jerome Dickey, John Sandford,
Terry McMillan, Sue Monk Kidd, Amy Tan,
John Berendt…

You'll find them all at
penguin.com

*Read excerpts and newsletters,
find tour schedules and reading group guides,
and enter contests.*

Subscribe to Penguin Group (USA) newsletters
and get an exclusive inside look
at exciting new titles and the authors you love
long before everyone else does.

PENGUIN GROUP (USA)
us.penguingroup.com